PAULINE THEOLOGY

Pauline Theology

Ministry and Society

by

E. Earle Ellis

WILLIAM B. EERDMANS PUBLISHING COMPANY
GRAND RAPIDS, MICHIGAN

THE PATERNOSTER PRESS
EXETER, UK

First published by Wm. B. Eerdmans Publishing Co.
255 Jefferson Ave. S.E., Grand Rapids, Mich. 49503

Reprinted, June 1990

Printed in the United States of America
for
Wm. B. Eerdmans Publishing Co.,
255 Jefferson Ave. S.E., Grand Rapids, Mich. 49503
and
The Paternoster Press Ltd
3 Mount Radford Crescent, Exeter UK EX2 4JW

Library of Congress Cataloging-in-Publication Data

Ellis, E. Earle (Edward Earle)
Pauline theology: ministry and society / by E. Earle Ellis.
p.   cm.
A revision and expansion of lectures delivered in the United States,
England, South Africa, and Ciskei.
ISBN 0-8028-0451-9
1. Bible. N.T. Epistles of Paul—Theology. 2. Clergy—Biblical teaching.
3. Church—Biblical teaching.   4. Holy Spirit—Biblical teaching.
5. Gifts, Spiritual—Biblical teaching.   6. Woman (Christian theology)—Biblical
teaching.   7. Sociology, Biblical.
I. Title.
BS2651.E53   1989
262'.1'09015—dc20   89-39186
                                                    CIP

Paternoster ISBN 0 85364 503 5

*To the
faculty and trustees of Wheaton College
in expression of appreciation
for the conferring of the degree of
Doctor of Divinity*

About the Author

E. Earle Ellis is research professor of theology at Southwestern Baptist Theological Seminary, Fort Worth, Texas. He is the author of six books, including a *New Century Bible Commentary* volume on the gospel of Luke. A collection of essays entitled *Tradition and Interpretation in the New Testament* (edited by Gerald F. Hawthorne with Otto Betz) was published in Ellis's honor in 1987.

Contents

Preface

The present volume is a revision and expansion of lectures delivered in the United States and, on tour, in England, South Africa, and Ciskei. It treats five aspects of ministry in the Pauline church—specifically, (1) ministry as a concept in Paul's theology, (2) its source in gifts from the ascended Christ, (3) its bearing on the role of women and (4) on official or ordered status in the congregation, and (5) its place in the social order of the Greco-Roman world. The lecture format has been retained in a way that, I hope, will be helpful to the student and the general reader and at the same time not without interest for the New Testament specialist. The translation of biblical texts is my own.

In at least two respects the volume may strike some readers as unusual in its approach. First, while it is an essay in historical criticism, it also gives attention to the implications of Paul's thought for the church today. Biblical theology, particularly in this area, cannot, I think, be content with historical analysis alone but should also show its relationship to contemporary Christian concerns. Whether the present work has done this successfully must be left for the reader to judge.

Second, the book includes all thirteen canonical letters of Paul in its assessment of his thought and practice. The nineteenth-century theory—still widely followed—that rejected the authenticity of a number of the letters and dated them to a generation or more after the Apostle's death was based on misconceptions, common to the period, about the nature of authorship and the method of the letters' composition. In my judgment it has been shown to be without historical basis and does not provide a reliable framework to understand Paul's mission and teaching. Reasons for this view of the matter will be noted at appropriate points in the volume. However, even if the theory is assumed to be true, many of the observations made in these pages will not be greatly affected since they are supported from Pauline letters undisputed by a large majority of contemporary students.

Different portions of the book were given as the Nils W. Lund Memorial Lectures (North Park Seminary), the Trinity Lectures (Trinity Episcopal School for Ministry), the Conference Lectures (Church of God School of Theology), the Kershner Memorial Lectures (Emmanuel School of Religion), the Christian Study Center Lectures (Yale Divinity School), the Day-Higginbotham Lectures (Southwestern Baptist Seminary), and the Deere Lectures (Golden Gate Baptist Seminary). They were also delivered as guest lectures in England at the University of Durham and in South Africa at the Universities of Stellenbosch and Pretoria.

Parts of the volume were also presented as the Divinity School Lecture (Cambridge University), the Faculty Forum Lecture (Concordia Seminary), the Anselm Society Lecture (University of Kent at Canterbury), and the Origen Society Lecture (Oxford University). They also formed the substance of individual papers at Princeton Seminary, Trinity Evangelical Divinity School, and Wheaton Graduate School; in England at the Universities of Birmingham and Manchester, at Ridley Hall, St. John's College (Nottingham), and Tyndale House; in Ciskei at the University of Fort Hare, and in South Africa at the Cape Town Baptist Theological College and at the Universities of the Orange Free State and of Witwatersrand. I am very grateful to those at each of these institutions who, with helpful criticisms, sharpened my presentation and increased my understanding.

I am also greatly indebted to Juniata College and to the trustees of their J. Omar Good Visiting Distinguished Professorship, who during my delightful year there graciously provided the leisure for me first to put to paper a number of the ideas in this book.

I also wish to thank my colleague, Dr. Bruce Corley, for reading the manuscript and for making most helpful suggestions; my assistants, Sherry Livengood, David Sapp, and David Edwards, who prepared the indices, and a number of secretaries for their indispensable assistance, including Miss Deborah Savage, Mrs. Edgar Kemp, Mrs. Donna Collins, and Mrs. Nancy Owen.

Southwestern Baptist   E. EARLE ELLIS
Theological Seminary, Fort Worth
Pentecost 1988

List of Abbreviations

BOOKS OF THE BIBLE

Old Testament

Gen	1 Sam	Esth	Lam	Mic
Exod	2 Sam	Job	Ezek	Nah
Lev	1 Kings	Ps	Dan	Hab
Num	2 Kings	Prov	Hos	Zeph
Deut	1 Chron	Eccl	Joel	Hag
Josh	2 Chron	Song Sol	Amos	Zech
Judg	Ezra	Isa	Obad	Mal
Ruth	Neh	Jer	Jon	

New Testament

Mt	1 Cor	1 Thess	Heb	3 Jn
Mk	2 Cor	2 Thess	Jas	Jude
Lk	Gal	1 Tim	1 Pet	Rev
Jn	Eph	2 Tim	2 Pet	
Acts	Phil	Tit	1 Jn	
Rom	Col	Phlm	2 Jn	

Apocrypha

1 Esdr	2 Esdr	(= 4 Ezra)	Tob	Jdt

Ad Esth	Bar	Sus	1 Macc
Wis	Ep Jer	Bel	2 Macc
Sir	Song 3 Chil	Man	

Dead Sea Scrolls

1QIs^a	First Isaiah Scroll
1QIs^b	Second Isaiah Scroll
1QLevi	Second Testament of Levi
1QpHab	Habakkuk Commentary
1QS	Rule of the Community (Manual of Discipline)
1QSa (= 1Q28a)	Rule of the Community (Appendix)
1QSb (= 1Q28b)	Collection of Benedictions
1QM	War of the Sons of Light against the Sons of Darkness
1QH	Hymns of Thanksgiving
4QFlor	Florilegium, Cave 4
4Qtest	Messianic Testimonia, Cave 4
4Qpatr	Patriarchal Blessing, Cave 4
4QSi	Songs of the Sabbath Sacrifices, Cave 4
CD	Fragments of a Zadokite work (Damascus Document)

OTHER ABBREVIATIONS

ABR	*Australian Biblical Review*
ANRW	*Aufstieg und Niedergang der römischen Welt,* edd. H. Temporini and W. Haase (Berlin, 1972–)
BJRL	*Bulletin of the John Rylands Library*
BK	*Bibel und Kirche*
BTB	*Biblical Theology Bulletin*
c.	*circa* = about
CBQ	*Catholic Biblical Quarterly*
CIG	*Corpus Inscriptionum Graecarum,* 4 vols., ed. A. Boeckhius (Berlin, 1828-1877)
CIJ	*Corpus Inscriptionum Judaicarum,* 2 vols., ed. J. B. Frey (Rome, 1936, 1952) (I; New York, ^{2}1975)
CIL	*Corpus Inscriptionum Latinarum,* 16 vols., ed. T. Mommsen (Berlin, 1863-1936)
Compendia	*Compendia Rerum Judaicarum ad Novum Testamen-*

	tum, 6 vols., ed. S. Safrai et al. (Assen and Philadelphia, 1974–)
DACL	*Dictionnaire d'archéologie chrétienne et de liturgie,* 15 vols. in 30, ed. F. Cabrol (Paris, 1907-1953)
Digest.	*Digesta Juris Romani* in *Corpus Juris Civilis,* 3 vols., edd. T. Mommsen and P. Kruger (Zurich, 1970)
EQ	*Evangelical Quarterly*
ET ´	*Expository Times*
ET	English Text, Translation
FT	French Text, Translation
GT	German Text, Translation
HE	*Ecclesiastical History* (Eusebius)
HJ	*Heythrop Journal*
HRel	*History of Religions*
HTR	*Harvard Theological Review*
HUCA	*Hebrew Union College Annual*
IDBS	*Interpreter's Dictionary of the Bible: Supplement,* ed. K. Crim (Nashville, 1976)
ILS	*Inscriptiones Latinae Selectae,* 3 vols. in 5, ed. H. Dessau (Berlin, 1962 [1892-1916])
Int	*Interpretation*
JAC	*Jahrbuch für Antike und Christentum*
JBL	*Journal of Biblical Literature*
JETS	*Journal of the Evangelical Theological Society*
JRH	*Journal of Religious History*
JRS	*Journal of Roman Studies*
JSNT	*Journal for the Study of the New Testament*
JSOT	*Journal for the Study of the Old Testament*
jTaan	Tractate Ta'anith, Jerusalem Talmud
JTS	*Journal of Theological Studies*
JTSA	*Journal of Theology for Southern Africa*
LCL	Loeb Classical Library
MT	Masoretic (Hebrew) Text
NAS	*New American Standard Version*
ND	*New Documents Illustrating Early Christianity,* ed. G. H. R. Horsley (Sidney, 1981–)
NT	*Novum Testamentum*
NTS	*New Testament Studies*
OCD	*Oxford Classical Dictionary*[2]
OGIS	*Orientis Graeci Inscriptiones Selectae,* 2 vols., ed. W. Dittenberger (Hildesheim, 1970 [1903-1905])

RAC	*Reallexikon für Antike und Christentum*, edd. F. J. Dolger et al. (Stuttgart, 1950–) .
RSV	*Revised Standard Version*
RTR	*Reformed Theological Review*
SJT	*Scottish Journal of Theology*
ST	*Studia Theologica*
SWJT	*Southwestern Journal of Theology*
TB	*Tyndale Bulletin*
TDNT	*Theological Dictionary of the New Testament*, 10 vols., ed. G. Kittel; tr. G. W. Bromiley (Grand Rapids, 1964-1976)
TJ	*Trinity Journal*
TLZ	*Theologische Literaturzeitung*
TR	*Theologische Revue*
TRE	*Theologische Realenzyklopädie*, ed. G. Krause (Berlin, 1977–)
TS	*Theological Studies*
TSF	*Theological Students Fellowship*
TU	*Texte und Untersuchungen*
TZ	*Theologische Zeitschrift*
ZNTW	*Zeitschrift für die neutestamentliche Wissenschaft*
ZWT	*Zeitschrift für wissenschaftliche Theologie*
†	date of death

– I –

Ministry for the Coming Age

The activities of the Apostle Paul are usually summed up under the umbrella term "ministry." But what do we mean when we speak of "the ministry of Paul"? The term itself may be understood as an ordinary act of aid or service to another[1] or as service rendered to God and to others in God's name. It is used by Paul almost exclusively in the latter sense,[2] and is probably best understood in the light of (1) the Apostle's Jewish background and (2) his interpretation of ministry exclusively in terms of Jesus the Messiah.

    1. In the highly developed conceptions of ministry in first-century Judaism at least three types may be distinguished, the priestly act of mediation between God and man, prophetic gifts of the Holy Spirit, and various kinds of teachers and administrators. (1) The *priestly ministry* at the Jerusalem temple had a flourishing and central role for Jewish piety. (2) While those extraordinary "men of the Spirit" (Hos 9:7), *the prophets,* were no longer a dominant factor in first-century Judaism, the nation still anticipated a renewal of the prophetic word and, even more, the coming of a messianic "prophet like Moses" (Deut 18:15). Many Jews identified John the Baptist and Jesus as prophets (Mt 16:14;

---

1. E.g., Lk 10:40, διακονία, διακονεῖν.
2. However, in Rom 13:1-6 even the secular authority, in his duties, is regarded as God's minister (διάκονος, λειτουργός).

1

21:26). (3) Among the several kinds of recognized teaching ministries the *wise teachers* at Qumran, the strict religious community near the Dead Sea, manifested a number of prophetic qualities.[3] In other Jewish groups teachers of scripture, with the title *rabbi* or *scribe,* exercised considerable authority in the life of the nation generally, some being employed even to teach the priests.[4] The title *elders,* used politically for the heads of leading families,[5] could also designate religious teachers. These were local synagogue leaders and others with teaching and "service" functions.[6] Somewhat less prominent was the *shaliaḥ,* probably to be translated "apostle," which was a designation in Judaism for one who fulfilled an occasional role as a commissioned representative, that is, a deputy or proxy, in a number of legal and religious activities.[7]

3. 1QS 9:12-19; 1QH 2:13f.; 12:11f.; 1QpHab 7:4f. In the Qumran Temple Scroll (e.g., 45:10-14) the author, like the Old Testament prophets, uses the first person for God's speech. Cf. J. Maier, *The Temple Scroll* (Sheffield, UK, 1985), 3. On similarities between the wise teachers *(maskilim)* at Qumran and the pneumatics of the Pauline community cf. E. E. Ellis, *Prophecy and Hermeneutic* (Tübingen and Grand Rapids, 1978), 30-36. On the similarities between the "supervisor" or overseer *(mebaqqer* and *paqid)* at Qumran and the bishop in early Christianity cf. 1QS 6:12, 14, 20; CD 9:13-15; 13:6-9; 14:9-12; J. Jeremias, *Jerusalem in the Time of Jesus* (London, 1969), 260ff.; B. E. Thiering, *"Mebaqqer* and *Episkopos,"* *JBL* 100 (1981), 59-74.

4. Mt 23:2, 7; cf. 13:52. Cf. Josephus, *Antiquities* 11.128; 12.142 = 11.5.1; 12.3.3.

5. Cf. Jeremias (note 3), 222-32; Num 11:12-25; Ezra 5:9; 6:7f. (*zeqenim* = πρεσβύτεροι); Lk 19:47 with 20:1.

6. Cf. Lk 7:3ff. The Letter of Aristeas (? c. 100 B.C.) 32; 39 mentions elders skilled in the biblical law and able to interpret it. In the rabbinical Mishnah (c. A.D. 200) ordained teachers are called elders (Erubim 3:4; 8:7; Sanhedrin 11:2; cf. Kiddushin 32b). Cf. also Josephus, *Antiquities* 10.51; 10.91; 12.39 = 10.4.1; 10.6.2; 12.2.4.

7. In 1 Kings 14:6 LXX-A ἀπόστολος is the Greek rendering of *shaluaḥ.* The latter term, in cognate forms, is an established usage for the commissioned representative in rabbinical writings from the second century A.D. and was probably used in the same way at the time of Jesus' ministry. Cf. Berakoth 5:5; Rosh Hashanah 4:9; Gittin 4:1; Mekilta on Exod 12:3. Cf. F. H. Agnew, "The Origin of the NT Apostle-Concept," *JBL* 105 (1986), 93f.; C. K. Barrett, "Shaliah and Apostle," *Donum Gentilicium,* ed. E. Bammel (Oxford, 1978), 88-102; K. H. Rengstorf, "ἀπόστολος," *TDNT* 1 (1964/1933), 413-45.

2. In this milieu early Christian ministry, including that of the Pauline churches, had its primary background and in some measure received its titles and functions. In one respect, however, it differed radically from ministry in other segments of Judaism, that is, in being perceived and experienced totally in terms of the mission, death, and resurrection of Jesus the Messiah. Since it was viewed in this way, the ministry of the early Christians was, in important respects, patterned on Jesus' ministry and took it as a model and archetype. This is indicated in a general way by the claim of the disciples to have Christ's Spirit and to proclaim his teachings and, more specifically, by the striking words of Paul: "Be imitators of me, as I am of Christ" (1 Cor 11:1f.). The correspondence of Jesus' ministry with that of his followers is reflected as well in certain titles for Christian ministers that are also occasionally ascribed to Jesus, for example, apostle, prophet, bishop, shepherd, and teacher.[8] In other imagery Jesus was termed the "high priest" of the new covenant whose priesthood his followers were to share[9] and the "servant of Yahweh" whose suffering and humility they in their ministry were to exhibit.[10]

Paul also understood his service to God in this christological frame of reference, especially in two respects. First, he regarded his own ministry as a fellowship in Christ's sufferings and a conformation by spiritual and physical afflictions to Christ's death (Phil 3:10). More broadly, he defined the whole of Christian ministry as gifts from the exalted Lord. His perception is perhaps best set forth in Eph 4:8-12, which is a part of a (preformed) commentary on Ps 68:18:

8. Heb 3:1; Acts 3:22; 1 Pet 2:25. Cf. Mt 28:20; Jn 16:13ff.; Acts 3:22f.; Rom 8:9; 1 Cor 2:12; 11:23ff.; Gal 4:6; Phil 1:19; Col 2:8; 1 Thess 1:6; 1 Pet 1:11f.; E. E. Ellis, "Traditions in 1 Corinthians," *NTS* 32 (1986), 481-502.

9. Cf. Heb 5:6; 1 Pet 2:5, 9; Rev 1:6. Paul does not use the term "priest," but he does refer to Christ's priestly, that is, sacrificial role (cf. 1 Cor 5:7; 10:16) and uses cultic metaphors and analogies to describe the Christian life and ministry (Rom 12:2; 15:16; 1 Cor 9:13f.; Phil 2:17; 3:3; cf. Col 1:24).

10. 1 Cor 4:9-13; 2 Cor 4:7-12; 6:4-10; Phil 3:10; 2 Tim 1:8, 11f.; 3:10-14; Heb 13:12f.; 1 Pet 2:21.

"When Christ ascended on high . . .
He gave gifts to men." . . .
He gave some to be apostles, some prophets, some evangelists,
    some teaching-shepherds,
For the equipment of the saints,
For the work of ministry,
For building up Messiah's body.[11]

In this passage Christian ministry manifests three principal characteristics. First, it is a gift. It may result in achievements, but it is itself not an achievement. Since the gifts may elsewhere be called "charisms" (χαρίσματα), ministry may be described under that idiom as "charismatic."[12] Second, ministry is diverse and in the Pauline churches is manifested in a variety of charisms and of gifted individuals or "charismatics." At present we will defer consideration of these two aspects of ministry and will confine our attention to a third. It is a unique and perhaps the most important characteristic of Christian ministry, and it largely determines one's interpretation of Paul's teaching on the subject. It concerns the source of ministry in the ascended Christ, that is, its eschatological dimension. This dimension may be approached in terms of the relationship of ministry to three specific themes: the kingdom of God, the body of Christ, and the secular world. To understand it one must turn again to Paul's Jewish background.

11. Cf. also Rom 12:4-8; 1 Cor 12:4-11, 28-31. Eph 4:7-16 is a midrash, that is, a commentary on Ps 68:18, apparently a preexisting piece that Paul has incorporated here and drawn on in Colossians (1:28; 2:19). On the Pauline authorship of Ephesians cf. M. Barth, *Ephesians,* 2 vols. (Garden City, NY, 1974), I, 36-50; A. Van Roon, *The Authenticity of Ephesians* (Leiden, 1974); E. E. Ellis, "Dating the New Testament," *NTS* 26 (1980), 495-500. Some commentators do not place a comma after saints (Eph 4:12) and regard the gifted individuals to be those who "equip" the saints, that is, the believers generally; it is the saints, then, who do the "work of ministry" and the "building up." However, in the context the gifted ones, the pneumatics, are most likely the subject of all three tasks. On the activity of ministry as a "work" cf. 1 Cor 3:6-10; 9:1; 1 Tim 3:1; 2 Tim 4:5. Such "work" must, however, be distinguished from obligations and philanthropic activities in the world to which believers also are exhorted, activities that they share with the noble pagans. See below, 18-24, 152-59.

12. Cf. 1 Cor 12:4: gifts = χαρίσματα. In Eph 4:8 the word used for gift is δόμα.

4

MINISTRY AS A MANIFESTATION
OF THE KINGDOM OF GOD

The Old Testament prophets predicted the "last" (ἔσχατος)[13] days or latter days in which God would accomplish the final redemption of his people and the destruction of their enemies. Later "apocalyptic" writings emphasized that this last or "eschatological" redemption would be "revealed" (ἀποκαλύπτειν) by God at his sovereign pleasure and would encompass not only the nation but the whole created order. They interpreted the redemption in terms of both a continuity and a catastrophic discontinuity between the present age and the new cosmic creation, that is, the coming age of the kingdom of God. These writings, in particular the book of Daniel and the Qumran literature, provide the most significant background for understanding the teaching of our Lord and of his apostles about the kingdom of God.[14]

Standing in this tradition, John the Baptist proclaimed the imminent arrival of God's kingdom, stating that one coming after him, that is, Jesus, would accomplish the final redemption and judgment:[15]

He will baptize you with the Holy Spirit and fire.
His winnowing fork is in his hand,
And he will clear his threshing floor
And gather his wheat into the granary,
But the chaff he will burn with unquenchable fire.   Mt 3:11f.

This final consummation of blessing and judgment, proclaimed by the Baptist, was affirmed by Jesus with certain qualifications. In the teaching of Jesus the arrival of the kingdom of God is said to take place in two stages. The first had already

13. 'aharith is the Hebrew equivalent to the Greek ἔσχατος. Cf. Num 24:14; Isa 2:2; Dan 10:14; Hos 3:5; Mic 4:1.
14. Cf. Mt 24:15, 30; 26:64; Rev 1:7, 14; H. Ringgren, The Faith of Qumran (Philadelphia, 1963), 152-98. Note Rev 1:1: "The revelation (ἀποκάλυψις) of Jesus Christ. . . ." On the apocalyptic character of Paul's theology cf. J. C. Beker, Paul the Apostle (Philadelphia, 1980), 135-81.
15. Mt. 3:2, 10ff.

appeared in his ministry and was shortly to be revealed in an even greater degree in the midst of the present age.[16] The second stage, the arrival of the kingdom in universal judgment and final redemption, was reserved for Jesus' future second coming, his parousia as the glorious Son of man.[17] These two stages are alluded to in Luke's (11:2f.) version of the Lord's Prayer:

> . . . Your kingdom come.
> Our morrow's [kingdom] bread continue giving us each day.

The presence of the first stage of the kingdom is identified in the Gospels with the actions of the Holy Spirit in Jesus' ministry[18]— his healings, his forgiveness of sin, and his exorcisms. In one saying Jesus puts it thus:

> If I by the Spirit of God cast out demons,
> Then the kingdom of God has come upon you.   Mt 12:28

Yet, as his parables illustrate, this action of the Spirit, whether

16. The presence of the kingdom is (with Kümmel) to be understood christologically and eschatologically and not to be interpreted (with Chilton) within a transcendence/immanence paradigm which, it seems, falls back into philosophical categories quite alien to the New Testament and to biblical perspectives generally (Cullmann). But it is mistaken (*pace* Cullmann and Kümmel) to interpret Mk 9:1 of the parousia and, consequently, to conclude that Jesus expected the consummation of the kingdom of God in his generation (cf. Ellis). Cf. B. Chilton, ed., *The Kingdom of God in the Teaching of Jesus* (Philadelphia, 1984), 26 (Chilton), 39-42, 45 (Kümmel); O. Cullmann, *Salvation in History* (Philadelphia, 1967), 166-85, 186-291; E. E. Ellis, *The Gospel of Luke* (Grand Rapids, [5]1987), 141; idem, *Eschatology in Luke* (Philadelphia, 1972), 5-20.

17. Mt 24:33-36; Lk 21:31. For the juxtaposition in the Gospels of future and present aspects of the kingdom of God cf. Mk 8:38 with 9:1; Lk 11:2 with 11:3; 11:2 with 11:20; 17:28ff. with 17:20f.; 23:42 with 23:43; Jn 5:28f. with 5:25; 6:54; 11:24 with 11:25; 14:2f. with 14:18; perhaps, Mt 5:8f. with 5:10. Further, R. Maddox, *The Purpose of Luke-Acts* (Edinburgh, [2]1985), 100-105; E. E. Ellis, *Eschatology* (note 16), 16-20; idem, "Present and Future Eschatology in Luke," *NTS* 12 (1964-65), 27-41; idem, *The World of St. John* (Grand Rapids, [2]1984), 37-42; idem (note 3), 163ff. Cf. J. Jeremias, *The Lord's Prayer* (Philadelphia, 1964), 23-47.

18. Mt 12:28 = Lk 11:20; Mt 11:2-6 = Lk 7:18-23; Mt 13:16f. = Lk 10:23f.; Mt 10:20; Lk 4:14-21; 10:9; 16:16; cf. W. G. Kümmel, *Promise and Fulfillment* (London, 1957), 105-40.

in his work or his word, was a hidden manifestation of the kingdom that was recognized to be such only by disciples who were "given to know the mysteries of the kingdom of God" (Lk 8:10). To others the meaning of Christ's ministry remained an enigma.

The same presence of the kingdom is represented in the Pauline epistles as the continuing activity of the Spirit among Christ's followers after his exaltation to heaven. It is manifested not just in talk but in power (1 Cor 4:20), not as material benefits but as life in the Spirit. In Paul's words,

> The kingdom of God is not food and drink
> But . . . peace and joy in the Holy Spirit.   Rom 14:17

Elsewhere this peace and joy are called "the fruit of the Spirit."[19]

In the Apostle's writings Christian ministry is also viewed as part of this first stage of the new work of the Spirit, being described as "gifts" of the Spirit.[20] More specifically, it is regarded as a means by which the Holy Spirit mediates the blessing and power of the age to come into the present age of sin and death. In a word, for Paul ministry is a present manifestation of the coming kingdom of God.

MINISTRY AS AN ACTIVITY
IN THE BODY OF CHRIST

If ministry is understood as part of the new activity of the Spirit, it is also by that fact limited to the persons and the community where that activity takes place. For Paul that community is the church, the body of believers, who have received the Spirit and whose ministry is a means to mediate the Spirit and his gifts and

---

19. Gal 5:22, 25; cf. Col 1:13. The view that for Paul any participation in the kingdom of God or in Christ's resurrection life awaits the parousia is not supported by the texts. See below, note 32.

20. 1 Cor 12:4-11. In 2 Cor 3:7ff. the present ministry (διακονία) of the Spirit is contrasted to the law of God, which is a ministry "of death" and "of condemnation." Cf. Rom 1:18–3:20. However, the gospel message can also be "an odor from death to death" (2 Cor 2:14ff.).

benefits to others.[21] In at least two respects Paul's understanding of the church is bound up with his understanding of ministry: (1) The nature of the church's own existence determines the nature of its ministry. (2) The nature of the church's ministry illuminates its relationship to the present world or, in a modern phrase, to secular society.

The Corporate Dimension of Human Existence

What is the nature of the church's existence that is so significant for understanding its ministry? In a word, it is its existence as the corporate "body" of the resurrected Christ, made up of individual believers who have become part of that new resurrection reality. The Apostle believed that Christians were participating in a reality that was so different, so radically divorced from all that went before, that it could be called "a new creation." And he would not have disagreed with a second-century writer who described the Christian community as "a new race."[22] To express the corporate dimension of the new creation Paul spoke of the believer's existence as being "in the Spirit" or "in Christ," and he designated the church as "the body of Christ."[23]

This corporate dimension of the man Jesus Christ is best explained from a context in which man as such is recognized to be a corporate as well as an individual being. Within this perspective the leader, for example, of the family or the nation is understood to incorporate in his own person those who belong to him. The idea has its primary background in the Old Testament. It is presupposed, for example, in the Psalms, where the "I" may represent not (only) an individual but the nation.[24] It also appears in Isaiah,

21. Rom 8:9; 1 Cor 12:13; Gal 3:2; 1 Tim 4:13f.; 2 Tim 1:6f.; Tit 3:3-8.

22. 2 Cor 5:17; Gal 6:15; Epistle to Diognetus 1:1 (καινύν γένος). Cf. Clement of Alexandria, *Stromata* 6.5, citing the *Kerygma of Peter;* Tertullian, *To the Heathen* 1.8.1.

23. E.g., Rom 12:5; 1 Cor 4:15; 12:27; Gal 3:27f.; 5:25; Eph 1:22f.; 2:5f.; cf. Rom 6:8-11; 2 Cor 13:4f.

24. E.g., Ps 44:4-8; 81:1-10; 129:1-3. Cf. S. Mowinckel, *The Psalms in Israel's Worship,* 2 vols. (Nashville, 1962), I, 42-46; A. R. Johnson, *The Cultic*

where "the suffering servant" has both an individual and a corporate dimension,[25] and in Daniel, where an individual, one like
"a son of man," is apparently identified with the collective people
of God, "the saints."[26] Furthermore, this concept seems to provide
the implicit ethical rationale for a number of biblical passages in
which the sin of the leader is punished[27] or the righteousness of
the leader rewarded[28] in the persons of those who belong to him.
David provides two examples of this conception. In a striking instance in 2 Sam 24 he sinned in taking a military census and was
punished by God through a pestilence that destroyed many of his
people. As the context makes clear, it is David who was at fault
and who received the penalty, but he was punished not in his individual body but in the nation, his corporate body. On the other
hand, in later times when the nation was unfaithful and subject to
judgment, God remembered David's faithfulness and for his sake
withheld the punishment.

The Old Testament conception of corporate solidarity includes the idea of "corporate personality" in which the group is
understood to exist in certain respects as the extension of the "person" of the leader. It has affinities with "realism" in medieval
philosophy and with certain modern anthropological theories
about primitive attitudes toward the "extension of personality."
But it is not to be identified with either of these views and, unlike
them, it reflects a more balanced appreciation of both an individual

---

Prophet and Israel's Psalmnody (Cardiff, 1979), 6-12. The conception also underlies many Old Testament passages in which there is an oscillation between
the singular and the plural. Cf. A. R. Johnson, *The One and the Many in the
Israelite Conception of God* (Cardiff, 1961), 1-13.

25. Cf. Isa 50:4-9 with 48:20. See H. W. Robinson, *The Cross in the Old
Testament* (London, 1955), 67-80. G. von Rad (*Old Testament Theology*, 2 vols.,
[London, 1975 (1960)], II, 259ff.) recognizes a "collective" aspect of the Ser-
vant, but the "corporate personality" conception escapes him.

26. Dan 7:13f., 27. S. Kim, *Origin of Paul's Gospel* (Tübingen, ²1984), 247.

27. E.g., that of Korah, Achan, and David. Cf. Num 16:31ff.; Josh 7:24f.;
2 Sam 12:7-15; 24:10-15. The idea of communal responsibility is somewhat different; cf. D. Daube, *Studies in Biblical Law* (Cambridge, 1947), 154-89.

28. E.g., that of Noah, Lot, David, and Josiah. Cf. Gen 6:9; 19:12-29;
1 Kings 15:1-5; 2 Kings 8:19; 22:16-22.

and a corporate existence of man.[29] Nevertheless, for most of us it is a very strange idea indeed. In our modern Western mentality the perception of a corporate dimension of human existence has been largely lost, although something of it may still come through to us in the words of John Donne:

> But who can remove [his eye] from that [funeral] bell,
> Which is passing a piece of himself out of this world?
> No man is an island entire of itself;
> Every man is a piece of the continent, a part of the main; . . .
> Any man's death diminishes me,
> And therefore never send to know
> For whom the bell tolls;
> It tolls for thee.[30]

Human Existence in Adam and in Christ

Paul makes a similar assessment to that of John Donne in 1 Cor 15:22: "All in Adam die." However, he then names Jesus Christ the "eschatological Adam" and declares that "all in Christ shall be made alive." That is, the Apostle expresses the most comprehensive human solidarity as one that embraces in two groups the whole of humanity, man-in-Adam and man-in-Christ. In designating two "Adams," he identifies two worlds or societies made up of those who belong to the one or to the other and regards Jesus as the resurrected leader, the new "Adam," of the coming eschatological age in whom believers are incorporated as the body of Christ. His resurrection was the first manifestation of the coming age, an act of God that foreshadowed and determined the in-

29. Cf. H. W. Robinson, *Corporate Personality in Ancient Israel* (Philadelphia, 1980 [1936]); A. R. Johnson, *Psalmnody* (note 24), 10f. On the issue in medieval philosophy cf. F. Copelston, *A History of Philosophy,* 8 vols. (Westminster, MD, 1960-66), II, 136-55. Modern studies of primitive mentality may have sparked further investigation and influenced the description of this aspect of Old Testament thought, but they were hardly as decisive as has been supposed by J. W. Rogerson, *Anthropology and the Old Testament* (Atlanta, 1979), 53-65. Cf. Ellis (note 3), 170n.

30. J. Donne, "Devotions upon Emergent Occasions XVII," *Works,* 6 vols. (London, 1839), III, 575.

dividual future destiny of Christ's followers.[31] It was also an event in which his followers even now corporately share. The Apostle presents this teaching in Romans and 2 Corinthians and then in summary form in Eph 2:5f.:[32]

> Even when we were dead in trespasses,
> [God] made us alive together with Christ . . .
> And raised us up with him,
> And made us sit with him in the heavenly places
> In Christ Jesus.

In contrast to the Christian community that is incorporated "in Christ," the society of this world, the world "in Adam," constitutes not a community of the resurrection but a community under the sentence of death. In Paul's usage, the "world," which is represented primarily by the words κόσμος and αἰών or age, has two quite distinct meanings, as it does elsewhere in the New Testament. Understood as "natural creation" or as "lost humanity," the world is the object of God's redeeming mercy.[33] Understood as "world order" or "society," however, it is destined for divine destruction. Paul's pessimistic verdict on the present world order becomes evident (1) in his predictions of a coming judgment, which we shall look at later, (2) in the terms that he uses for Adamic society, and (3) in the sharp division that he makes between it and the community of Christ.

Society incorporated in Adam is represented, for example, as "the old man," "the body of sin," "the body of (mortal) flesh," and "the body of death." These expressions of Paul refer not primarily to the individual body but to the corporate "body of Adam," that is, the society of this age, even though the Apostle

31. 1 Cor 12:27; 15:23, 45; cf. Acts 26:23; E. E. Ellis, *Paul and His Recent Interpreters* (Grand Rapids, [5]1979 [1961]), 36-40 (= *NTS* 6 [1959-60], 212-16); C. F. D. Moule, "The Corporate Christ," *The Origin of Christology* (Cambridge, 1978), 47-96.

32. The believer's present (corporate) resurrection life with Christ or in Christ is not limited to Ephesians, as some have supposed, but appears also in Rom 6:10-13; 8:30; 2 Cor 5:1; 13:4; Gal 2:19f.; Col 1:13; 3:1-3; 1 Thess 5:10. Cf. Ellis (note 31).

33. Rom 11:23, 15; 2 Cor 5:19; cf. Rom 8:21ff.; Heb 1:10ff.; 2 Pet 3:12f.

does not use those precise phrases.[34] They denote a sphere of existence "in Adam,"[35] in which, of course, individual existence is implicated, a sphere that is in alienation from God and consequently under impending death. Man-in-Adam and, indeed, the whole present creation is a cut flower in "bondage to decay"[36] and inexorably bound up in a process of death.

This sphere or world is set in contrast to the new existence "in Christ," an existence that is reconciled to God and thus is bound up in the bundle of life with the Lord.[37] These discrete spheres of existence are expressed by Paul in a variety of contrasting idioms that designate the one or the other sphere. This may be observed in the following lists in which some phrases point directly to the corporate sphere, some to the individual existence comprehended within it.[38]

in Adam	in Christ (1 Cor 15:22)
the first man	the second man (1 Cor 15:45ff.)
the man from earth	the man from heaven (1 Cor 15:47)
the old man	the new man (Eph 4:22ff.; Col 3:9f.; cf. Rom 6:6; Eph 2:15)
the outer man	the inner man (2 Cor 4:16; cf. Rom 7:22; Eph 3:16)
the natural man	the spiritual man (1 Cor 2:14f.)
in sin	in righteousness (Rom 6:1, 11f.; cf. Eph 4:24)
in the world	with Christ in God (Col 2:20; 3:3f.; Eph 2:6)

34. Rom 6:6; 7:24; Col 2:11. For a possible allusion to the "body" of Adam cf. the analogy between an unfaithful church and Eve in 2 Cor 11:3.

35. 1 Cor 15:22.

36. Rom 8:21.

37. Cf. 1 Sam 25:29; E. E. Ellis, "Life," *New Bible Dictionary,* ed. J. D. Douglas (Wheaton, IL, [2]1988), 697-701. The revised volume has appeared also under the title *The Illustrated Bible Dictionary,* 3 vols., ed. N. Hillyer (Leicester, UK, and Downers Grove, IL, 1980).

38. How the believer's present life is, in different respects, implicated in both of these spheres I address in Ellis (note 31), 35-48.

in the flesh	in the Spirit (Rom 8:8f.)
in the body [of Adam]	away from the body [of Adam] (2 Cor 5:6ff., 10)
the natural body	the spiritual body (1 Cor 15:44f.)
the mortal [body]	immortality (1 Cor 15:53; cf. 2 Cor 5:4)
the corruptible [body]	incorruption (1 Cor 15:53)
the body of humiliation	the body of glory (Phil 3:21)
the body of the flesh	the body of Christ (Col 2:11; cf. 2:17ff.)
the body of death	the body of Christ (Rom 7:24f.; 7:4; Col 1:22)
the body of sin	life in Christ (Rom 6:6, 11; cf. 7:4; 12:5)
earthly house	house from God (2 Cor 5:1)

The sharp discontinuity that the Apostle places between the world "in Adam" and the body of Christ is in two respects an important presupposition for his teaching on ministry in that world. (1) First, ministry facilitates a shift of people's identities from the sphere of Adam to the sphere of Christ, from the old humanity to the new, and a building up or individual actualization of their new corporate identity. That is, in traditional terms, ministry facilitates regeneration and sanctification. Thus, the ministry of "reconciling the world" to God is presented as a ministry of evangelism:

> If anyone is in Christ, he is a new creation.
> The old has passed away; behold, the new has come.
> All this is from God, who through Christ reconciled us
>   to himself
> And gave us the ministry of reconciliation;
> That is, in Christ God was reconciling the world to himself,
> Not counting their trespasses against them,
> And entrusting to us the message of reconciliation.
> So we are ambassadors for Christ, God making his appeal
>   through us.
> We beseech you on behalf of Christ, be reconciled to God.
>   2 Cor 5:17-20

13

In this context "the world" appears to be the aggregate of individual sinners who are to be reconciled as believers have been, by being delivered "from the present evil age" and by being incorporated into the body of Messiah through faith in him.[39]

Throughout Paul's letters Christian ministry has its locus in the body of Christ, the church, and usually it is represented as taking place there. When it reaches out into the world as God's instrument of reconciliation, as in evangelism, it has the purpose and the effect of drawing people into the body. It may build up the body through acts of loving service, as is pointedly illustrated in Paul's letters by the collection for the Christian poor of Jerusalem.[40] More often, as we shall observe in detail later, ministry has to do with building up the body by gifts of inspired speech, of prophetic discernment, of administration, and of healing. Briefly stated, ministry is of the body, for the body, and by the body.

(2) A second aspect of the discontinuity between the corporate communities "in Adam" and "in Christ" is at first sight rather shocking. It is that the present world-order, society "in Adam," is not as such the object of God's redemption and therefore not the concern of Christian ministry. It "is passing away," is the object of God's condemnation, and at the parousia it will be destroyed.[41] Here one observes in its starkest form the catastrophic discontinuity that the Apostle sees between the present age and the kingdom of God. William Shakespeare captures in poetic form something of the dark side of this prospect:

---

39. Gal 1:4; Rom 5:1f., 10f.; cf. 11:23, 15. Prophetic proclamation within the community may also have the effect of "convicting" and converting unbelievers who are in attendance (1 Cor 14:24f.).

40. Rom 15:25f.; 2 Cor 9:1; cf. Acts 24:17. Interestingly, this is viewed as a ministering of "fleshly things" (Rom 15:26f.), that is, benefits relating to the needs of the present age within which believers still live.

41. Cf. 1 Cor 7:31; 2 Thess 2:8-12; 2 Cor 7:10; Eph 2:3; 5:5-8; Col 3:6. To be "condemned" is to be "destroyed"; cf. F. Büchsel, "κατακρίνω," *TDNT* 3 (1965), 951f. Cf. the Qumran document, "The War of the Sons of Light against the Sons of Darkness," which shares Paul's conflict-perspective but develops it differently.

> The cloud-capp'd towers, the gorgeous palaces,
> The solemn temples, the great globe itself,
> Yea, all which it inherit, shall dissolve,
> And, like this insubstantial pageant faded,
> Leave not a rack behind. We are such stuff
> As dreams are made on; and our little life
> Is rounded with a sleep.   *The Tempest*, IV, 152-58

Paul puts the accent on a twofold note, destruction and salvation:

> When we are judged by the Lord, we are chastened
> So that we may not be condemned along with the world.
>   1 Cor 11:32

> When the Lord Jesus is revealed from heaven
> With his mighty angels in flaming fire,
> He will inflict vengeance upon those who do not know God
> And upon those who do not obey the gospel of our Lord Jesus.
> They shall suffer the punishment of eternal destruction
> From the presence of the Lord and from the glory of his might.
>   2 Thess 1:7ff.

> The day of the Lord will come like a thief in the night.
> When they say, "Peace and security,"
> Then sudden destruction will come upon them . . .
> And there will be no escape.
> But you are not in darkness, brothers,
> For that day to surprise you like a thief.
> For you are all sons of light and sons of the day.   1 Thess 5:2-5

The picture of the eschatological and christological context of ministry that has been briefly sketched here is congruent with Paul's teaching elsewhere and has, I believe, a continuing validity for Christian ministry today. It has close affinities with first-century Jewish apocalyptic conceptions, particularly those disclosed by the Qumran library, as they were elaborated and modified by the teachings of Jesus.[42]

42. In the New Testament the prospect of a final divine destruction of the wicked by fire (1 Cor 3:13ff.; 2 Thess 1:7-10; Heb 12:29; Rev 20:9-15; cf. 1 Pet

Several factors suggest that this perspective was not occasioned by nor dependent upon an expectation of a near-term glorious parousia of Jesus and thus made obsolete by the passage of the centuries. (1) In 1 Thess 4–5 and 2 Thess 1–2 Paul was apparently informed to some degree by Jesus' apocalyptic discourse (Mt 24–25; Mk 13) in which imminence in expectation was combined with chronological uncertainty regarding the time of the parousia of Jesus and end of the age.[43] (2) The coming of the kingdom of God in the resurrection of Jesus and in the activity of the Holy Spirit in the church effectively diminished the importance of the precise time of its final consummation. While "the delay of the parousia" was a problem for early twentieth-century Christian scholars, there is little if any evidence that it was a significant problem for the early church.[44] (3) From the beginning Paul considered the parousia expectation to be equally relevant for believers who were alive and for those who had fallen asleep in death and could, indifferently, identify himself with either group.[45] In one text he writes:

1:7) and even a cosmic conflagration (2 Pet 3:7, 10f.) has part of its background in a "Sodom" typology (Jude 7). Cf. Gen 18:24; Isa 34:4; 66:24; Zeph 1:18; 3:8; Mal 4:1 = 3:19 MT; 1 Enoch 1:3-6; Jubilees 16:5f.; R. Mayer, *Die biblische Vorstellung vom Weltbrand* (Bonn, 1956); C. P. Thiede, "A Pagan Reader of 2 Peter," *JSNT* 26 (1986), 79-96. At Qumran cf. 1QH 3:26-36; 15:17-21; 1QS 4:12-14; 1QpHab 13:2-4; H. W. Kuhn, *Enderwartung und Gegenwartiges Heil* (Göttingen, 1966), 38-43.

Among Stoic philosophers cf. Epictetus, *Discourses* 3.13.4f. For Stoic parallels with Paul's eschatology cf. H. C. Kee, "Pauline Eschatology," *Glaube und Eschatologie,* ed. E. Grässer (Tübingen, 1985), 135-58.

In that last day of the present age not only will there be revealed the discontinuity between the present and the new creations in bringing Adamic society and its adherents to their ultimate end but also the continuity between them in the resurrection and/or transformation to immortality of those in Christ (1 Cor 15:51-55; Phil 3:21) and in the subsequent transfiguration of the natural creation (Rom 8:19-23; cf. O. Cullmann, *Christ and Time* [London, 1952], 102f. [GT: 89]).

43. Cf. D. Wenham, *The Rediscovery of Jesus' Eschatological Discourse* (Sheffield, UK, 1984), 282ff., 295f., 304ff., 366f.; A. L. Moore, *The Parousia in the New Testament* (Leiden, 1966), 191-206.

44. Cf. Cullmann (note 16), 166-85, 241f.; S. S. Smalley, "The Delay of the Parousia," *JBL* 83 (1964), 41-54.

45. Rom 14:8f.; 2 Cor 4:14; 1 Thess 5:10; see Ellis (note 31), 47f.; cf.

Since we believe that Jesus died and rose again,
So too those who sleep in Jesus:
God will bring them to life with him . . .
We who are alive, who remain until the coming of the Lord,
Will not precede those who have fallen asleep. . . .
The dead in Christ shall rise first.   1 Thess 4:14ff.

In the light of the above observations we may conclude that the Pauline conception of ministry rests upon a salvation-history perspective with an orientation on the parousia as the next, and therefore impending, decisive salvation event. With its focus upon the kingdom of God and the body of Christ, ministry for Paul has to do with the believers' relationship to the new age and is not directed toward their responsibilities in the οἰκουμένη or, in today's parlance, the secular world. Since this proposition is much disputed, it demands that we look in more detail at this aspect of the matter.

MINISTRY AND THE SECULAR WORLD

The relationship of ministry to secular society is part of the larger theme of early Christianity and the world order, which will be considered in a subsequent chapter. However, it is also important for understanding Paul's conception of ministry. The question is not whether believers, including ministers, have obligations and responsibilities in the present world but whether the fulfillment of such responsibilities constitutes Christian ministry in the Pauline

---

C. E. B. Cranfield, "New Testament Eschatology," *SJT* 35 (1982), 505, 510; O. Cullmann, *Immortality of the Soul or Resurrection of the Dead?* (London, 1958), 41-45. In Pauline perspective, the transition from death to resurrection is equivalent to the transition from non-being to being (Rom 4:17); thus, for the unconscious dead the parousia of Jesus Christ is immediately imminent, only one moment into the future, and thus for the living that moment is never very far (chronologically!) into the future. Living in the imminence of Christ's return is, therefore, the privilege and the proper stance toward life of every generation of Christians. On the centrality of apocalyptic in Paul's theology cf. J. C. Beker, *Paul's Apocalyptic Gospel* (Philadelphia, 1982), 44-53, 106-21; idem (note 14), 354-67. Cf. B. Reichenbach, "Resurrection. . . ," *JTSA* 21 (1977), 33ff.

sense of the word. That is, does Christian ministry in Paul's view include activities designed to serve the present world-order—to resolve its problems, to improve its structures, and otherwise to engage in humanitarian enterprises and pursuits?

Is Sociopolitical Action Ministry?

The question takes on added significance today since some movements in the church do identify the facilitation of social and political change with Christian ministry. It may perhaps be addressed best by sketching something of the background and current expression of this viewpoint and then by comparing and contrasting it with Paul's teachings.

The identification of Christian ministry with the reform of society appears to have arisen from a convergence of two traditional Christian convictions. The first is the obligation of believers, which none I think would deny, to be "light" and "salt" in the world so that others "may see your good works and glorify your Father who is in heaven."[46] The second is a more questionable belief that the secular world will, over time, be transformed toward the kingdom of God before the final revelation of Christ at his glorious parousia. The latter view, traditionally known as postmillennial eschatology, has exercised a considerable influence in the modern church.[47] It has a number of roots, including the relatively modern idea of "progress" that flourished during the Victorian era. Among evangelicals it meant the evan-

46. Mt 5:13-16.
47. The postmillennial theory apparently began with Daniel Whitby, "A Treatise of the True Millennium" (1706), in S. Patrick et al., *Commentary and Paraphrase on the Old and New Testaments and Apocrypha*, 6 vols. (London, 1822), VI, Appendix. In the nineteenth century this eschatology seems to have been dominant in almost all Protestant churches. As an issue the millennium was significant enough to be the subject of the Oxford University Bampton Lectures for 1854: S. Waldegrave, *New Testament Millenarianism* (London, 1855). For postmillennial writings in the eighteenth and nineteenth centuries and their influence cf. the convenient annotated references of L. Froom, *The Prophetic Faith of our Fathers*, 4 vols. (Washington, 1950-54), II, 649-55; IV, 89f., 121-25, 412ff.

gelization of the world, clearly a mandate of Christ and a primary ministry of Paul, and in the last century it became a spur to the worldwide missionary movement of the church.[48] But while Christ and Paul viewed the proclamation of the gospel as a witness to the nations,[49] many of these evangelicals thought the missionary enterprise had the goal of conforming the nations themselves toward the kingdom of God, so that "the earth may be filled with the glory of God as the waters cover the sea."[50]

In early twentieth-century Protestant liberalism, particularly in America, the transformation of the world toward the kingdom meant changing the structures of society so as to implement "the righteousness of the kingdom." In effect, its advocates gave the works of love enjoined by Christ a redemptive, eschatological significance for society and, thereby, again promoted as "the social gospel"[51] the ancient flattery of salvation by works which, at the individual level, had been vigorously combated by Paul and the Reformers. One of them, who was not atypical, titled an essay "Salvation by Education" and indexed a book with the entry "Kingdom of God, see *Democracy*."[52] In general, these liberal Christians seem to have been less guided by New Testament eschatology than by the vision of William Blake:

---

48. Mt 28:19f.; Rom 15:18f.; 2 Cor 5:18ff. On the missionary movement cf. K. S. Latourette, *The Expansion of Christianity*, 6 vols. (London, 1945), IV, 150-72, 381-423 passim; VII, 500 passim.

49. E.g., Mk 13:10; Acts 1:8; Rom 15:19.

50. A paraphrase of Hab 2:14, incorporated into the popular missionary hymn "God is Working his Purpose Out," by A. C. Ainger († 1919). Cf. Isa 11:9.

51. Cf. the posthumous publication of W. Rauschenbusch, *The Righteousness of the Kingdom* (Nashville, 1968); K. Cauthen, *The Impact of American Religious Liberalism* (New York, 1962), 84-107, 147-68. In criticism cf. H. J. Cadbury, *The Peril of Modernizing Jesus* (New York, 1937); J. G. Machen, *Christianity and Liberalism* (Grand Rapids, 1946).

52. G. A. Coe, "Salvation by Education," *American Protestant Thought: the Liberal Era*, ed. W. R. Hutchinson (New York, 1968), 117-25; idem, *A Sociological Theory of Religious Education* (New York, 1917), 359. For a brief sketch of other participants cf. J. Macquarrie, *Twentieth-Century Thought* (London, ²1981), 162-65.

I will not cease from mental fight
Nor shall my sword sleep in my hand
Till we have built Jerusalem
In England's green and pleasant land.[53]

Today this kind of eschatology, what George Will has termed "the myth of collective salvation through political action," continues to be implicit in the liberation theology that is influential in the World Council of Churches and among some Latin American theologians. Here the sign of the kingdom and thus the task of Christian ministry is seen to be not so much social reform as Marxist revolution that will bring about the economic-political "liberation" of the poor.[54]

It is beyond the scope of these remarks to explore the fundamental questions raised by liberation theology—for example, the legitimacy of interpreting the Gospel of Mark by the gospel of Marx and the "judaizing" of the message of salvation that is implicit in imputing—à la Bar Kokhba's revolt—a redemptive significance to political revolution.[55] But it may be worthwhile for our present theme to note briefly two basic differences between Paul's conception of ministry and that which is prevalent in much of liberation theology. First, as we have seen, for Paul the locus

---

53. From the poem, "Jerusalem," by William Blake (†1827), which has been included in many hymnals.

54. Cf. George Will, "Whittaker Chambers: Upon a Winding Staircase," *National Review* 37, 25 (31 December 1985), 63-68, 66. For a useful survey and critique of "liberation theology" cf. J. A. Kirk, *Liberation Theology* (London, 1979); for a more critical appraisal cf. H. T. Hoekstra, *Evangelism in Eclipse: World Mission and the World Council of Churches* (Exeter, 1979) (American title: *The World Council of Churches and the Demise of Evangelism*); E. R. Norman, *Christianity and the World Order* (Oxford, 1979); R. T. France, "Liberation in the New Testament," *EQ* 58, 1 (1986), 3-23. On the revolutionary character of some "liberation theology" cf. "The Kairos Document," in *Crisis in Christian Teaching and the Struggle for Justice in Africa,* edd. P. and T. Colvin (Geneva, 1985), 17-39, 36: "[We] must endeavour to love [our enemies].... But ... the most loving thing we can do ... is to ... remove the tyrants...."

55. I address this hermeneutical question briefly in a foreword to L. Goppelt, *TYPOS: The Typological Interpretation of the Old Testament in the New* (Grand Rapids, 1982), xiiff.

of ministry is in and through the body of Christ, the church. For liberation theology, as expressed, for example, in a World Council of Churches report, "God's primary relationship is to the world, and it is the world and not the Church that is the focus of God's plan [of redemptive work]."[56] One observes in this statement no awareness of the Pauline distinction between the world that is destined to be destroyed and the world that will be redeemed. Second, for Paul the presupposition for ministry is the radical distinction between existence in Adam and existence in Christ and, consequently, the distinction between salvation history and general secular history. Liberation theology usually rejects these distinctions. One writer puts it thus: "There are not two histories, one profane and one sacred. . . . Rather there is only one human destiny, irreversibly assumed by Christ. . . . The history of salvation is the very heart of human history"; ". . . building the temporal city is not simply 'pre-evangelization. . . .' Rather it is to become a part of the saving process which embraces the whole of man and all human history."[57] But what has this point of view in common with Paul's conception of salvation?

Although Paul doubtless knew that his ministry within the body of Christ — his exhortations to Christian masters and servants, for example — would have its influence in society, he nowhere suggests that serving or changing society is an aspect, much less a goal, of Christian ministry. From a Pauline perspective this view of the matter is defective on two counts. It fails to perceive the difference between the task of ministry and its effects and, equally mistaken, it falls into a fatal confusion of the church with the world, the body of Christ with the body of Adam. Also foreign to the Apostle's thought is the idea that secular society will somehow be incorporated or caught up in the new creation or that

56. "The Church for Others," *World Council of Churches Report* (Geneva, 1967), 16f., cf. 78, cited in Hoekstra (note 51), 59, cf. 69.

57. G. Gutiérrez, *A Theology of Liberation* (London, 1974), 153, 160; apparently also J. P. Miranda (*Marx and the Bible* [New York, 1974], 254f.), whose clarity, however, does not match his intensity. For other less revolutionary currents in liberation theology cf. J. E. Weir, "Liberation Theology Comes of Age," *ET* 98, 1 (1986-87), 3-9.

man's existence in Adam is a hidden but real existence in Christ.[58] These suppositions are, as far as I can see, alien to Pauline theology in several respects. They ignore the role of faith in Jesus Christ as the essential prerequisite for salvation and the indispensable means by which one is transferred from the sphere of Adam to the sphere of Christ.[59] Also, as has been observed, they fail to do justice to the element of standing discontinuity that Paul sees between the present world and the new age of the kingdom of God. According to Paul the Adamic world order will remain in opposition to God until the parousia of Jesus Christ, and nothing has happened in the past two millennia to cast the slightest doubt upon the truth of this teaching. Although the present natural creation is to be redeemed, secular society is never represented in this way. Emil Brunner long ago stated the matter quite correctly:

> Nowhere in the New Testament do we find any expectation that in the course of the centuries mankind will become Christian, so that the opposition between the world and the Church would be overcome in historical time. But the contrary is true: the Christian community or Church will be a minority until the end, and therefore the battle between the dark powers and the powers of Christ goes on until the day of judgment. If there is any truth in the apocalyptic pictures which we find in the New Testament, we have to say even more. The apocalyptic visions are unanimous in depicting the end of time, the last phase of human history before the coming of the day of Christ, as a time of uttermost tension between light and darkness, the Church and the world, Christ and the Devil.[60]

As a reality of the resurrection age Christian ministry has for Paul an evangelical, Christ-imparting relationship to the commu-

---

58. *Pace* K. Barth, *Christ and Adam* (New York, 1956), whose exegesis was rightly criticized by R. Bultmann, "Adam and Christ according to Romans 5," *Current Issues in New Testament Studies,* edd. W. Klassen and G. F. Snyder (New York, 1962), 143-65.

59. Note the qualifiers in Rom 5:17 ("those who receive"; cf. Gal 3:2) and in 1 Cor 15:23 ("those who belong to Christ").

60. E. Brunner, *The Scandal of Christianity* (Philadelphia, 1951), 110. See above, notes 33, 41 and 42.

nity of the dying. Evangelical theology has always underscored this truth as the essence of the ministry of the word of God in the secular world. Sacramentalist theology also, which understands the sacraments to impart this reality to the recipient, has rightly seen the essentially supernatural, that is, eschatological character of Christian ministry. Unfortunately, other elements in the church's theological spectrum have not always been alert to this aspect of Pauline thought.

Christian Obligation in the World

While Paul regards the Christians' true commonwealth as the kingdom "in the heavens" (Phil 3:20), he is not indifferent to their obligations to the present world. While he does not identify such activities with Christian ministry, he does exhort believers concerning them. Ordinarily he does this in rather general terms of responsibilities to do "what is good," to live peaceably with all, and to render obedience and respect to the governing authorities.[61] Although the Apostle never encourages humanitarian programs of social change, much less political revolution,[62] he does recognize that Christian ministry, such as his own ministry of exhortation, will have its effects on the behavior of believers. This behavior will itself have effects in society and is to reflect those virtues that even pagan moralists would find commendable.

The Christian's obligation to society does not belong, then, to Paul's theology of ministry but to his theology of ethics, specifically to the command to love one's neighbor (Rom 13:8ff.). Love toward one's neighbor is the second of two commandments summing up the Mosaic law, the good work that all are under obligation to observe. Such acts of love, which are common to Christians, Jews, and noble pagans, can bring and have brought

---

61. Rom 12:17f., 20; 13:1-7; Gal 6:10; Eph 5:9; 1 Tim 2:1f.; 6:18; Tit 3:1.
62. Even S. G. F. Brandon and R. Eisler, who made the most thorough (albeit unsuccessful) efforts to set forth a politically activist picture of early Christianity, recognize that it did not apply to the Pauline church. Cf. S. G. F. Brandon, *The Fall of Jerusalem and the Christian Church* (London, ²1957), 200, 204f.; R. Eisler, *The Messiah Jesus* (London, 1931), 364, 552f. See below, 154ff.

significant transformations in both personal and societal relationships within the present age. But in Paul's teaching they are not represented as a means of creating new-age "kingdom of God" realities in the recipients, that is, a means of salvation, either personal or societal. For Christians this neighbor-love is part of what Paul called "the fruit of the Spirit" (Gal 5:22f.); it should therefore be manifested with different motives and to a greater degree by those who have received the Spirit of Christ. But it is distinguished from "the gifts of the Spirit," which constitute Christian ministry and which do mediate such realities.

Are we drawing too fine a line here? The fruit of the Spirit is as much a part of the "kingdom of God" role of the Spirit as are the gifts, and at least one of the listed gifts, "acts of mercy" (Rom 12:8), seems to be very close to "acts of love." The differentiation between works of love and ministry has similarities with the Reformation debate about the difference between good works and faith. While perhaps a fine distinction, it is, I believe, a necessary one if Paul's theology is to be rightly apprehended.[63]

The relation of ministry and societal responsibilities has a broader significance than has been suggested by the topics raised here, and we shall consider later the Pauline perspective on it. But the above observations have shown, I hope, that the two activities cannot be identified. Clearly, Christians will fulfill their social role in the secular society with more realism and therefore with more true optimism when they recognize the true nature of the present world-order as it is taught us by Christ's Apostle.

In conclusion, Paul's distinction between the present and the coming age and between the world and the church, society in Adam and society in Christ, and his conviction of the coming destruction of the present world do not occasion either a cynical attitude toward the world or a pharisaical aloofness from it. It is rather a perspective that gives urgency to his preaching, for he knows that the gospel is not only an odor "from life to life" but also "among those who are perishing . . . an odor from death to

63. Cf. B. G. Webb, ed., *Christians in Society* (Homebush West, AUS, 1988).

death" (2 Cor 2:16). In his ministry, both in his evangelism to outsiders and in his teaching and exhortation to his churches, the word of judgment is the backdrop and alternative to his message of life in Christ. Only when that alternative is present does Christian ministry, even in its positive aspects, fully correspond to a Pauline conception.

The community of Adam is going to its death as a river goes to the sea—sometimes quietly, sometimes stormily, but always inevitably. For the present world no less than for each individual life the paths of glory lead but to the grave. In the present-day Western world believers individually and organized churches collectively are able by their good works to ameliorate some social evils and to promote a more equitable society. This is not a small thing, as those who have lived in cultures lacking Christian influence can testify. But they also have the tasks of calling people from citizenship in the community of Adam to citizenship in the community of Christ and of building them up in their new-world identity. Only when mediating these realities in the church and in the world do Christians truly exercise ministry through our Lord Jesus Christ, who gave himself for our sins to deliver us from the present evil age, according to the will of our God and Father, to whom be the glory forever and ever. Amen.

- II -

The Spirit and the Gifts

It has been observed above that for Paul Christian ministry is an activity of the Holy Spirit. This observation gives rise to further questions. How, one may ask, does the activity of the Spirit in ministry differ from his role in the present natural created order? How does it differ from other activities of the Spirit within the church? To answer these questions we shall (1) distinguish the role of the Spirit in the Old Testament from his role in the ministries of Jesus and Paul. From the Pauline letters we will then set forth (2) the functions of the Spirit and (3) the characteristics of his gifts of ministry, and observe (4) how the gifts are to be implemented in the church and (5) why Paul considers the fruit of Spirit in the Christian life to have a certain priority over his gifts.

According to the Old Testament the Spirit of God had both a prophetic and a creative role. Through the Spirit God inspired the prophets.[1] By the same means he made the heavens and "renews the face of the ground," and should God withdraw his Spirit "all flesh would perish together."[2] A distinction between

---

1. Exod 11:29; Judg 3:10; 2 Chron 15:1f.; Ezek 2:1-7; Hos 9:7; Mic 3:8; Zech 12; cf. F. Baumgärtel, "πνεῦμα," *TDNT* 6 (1968), 362f. The πνεῦμα ("spirit") has little or no role in Greco-Roman conceptions of inspired prophecy according to D. Aune, *Prophecy in Early Christianity and the Ancient Mediterranean World* (Grand Rapids, 1983), 34.

2. Ps 33:6; 104:30; Job 33:4; 34:14f.; cf. Gen 1:2.

God and his Spirit is at best difficult to discern, and the contemporary activity of the Spirit is, apart from Isaiah and Ezekiel, not explicitly stated very often. When it is mentioned, it ordinarily concerns (1) the creation and maintenance of the present order of nature, (2) the mediation of God's word for the present age,[3] and (3) the source of transitory "this age" benefits[4] and judgments.[5] The Spirit's future eschatological action, the few times it is touched on, appears as an escalated form of his present role, that is, a final word of warning and of salvation followed by a final destruction of God's enemies and by a redemption of God's people and regeneration of the natural world.[6] At times the Old Testament prophetic description represents the Spirit's present work as an anticipation or type of his future eschatological role.[7]

In the New Testament the Spirit is identified with the same Spirit of God,[8] whose activity continues to have similar prophetic and creative aspects. However, in several respects his work is represented as a new and radically different one from that in the Old Testament. Specifically, (1) the new work is mediated exclusively through Jesus the Messiah. (2) With respect to its *creative* aspect it is directed not toward sustaining the present creation but toward bringing to birth the "new creation" of the kingdom of God, the eschatological age to come characterized by an immortal and transfigured resurrection life. (3) With respect to its *prophetic* aspect it primarily concerns the communication of the truths, demands, conditions, and promises of this resurrection life.

3. Neh 9:20; Mic 3:8-12.

4. Isa 63:11-14; Zech 4:6-10.

5. Job 4:8f.; Isa 30:28. This perception continues in the rabbinic writing, the Mekilta. Cf. Mekilta on Exod 15:9f.; W. D. Davies, *Jewish and Pauline Studies* (Philadelphia, 1984), 81ff.

6. Isa 11:1-9; 32:15-20; Joel 2:28-32; cf. Isa 4:2-5; 66:22-24.

7. Cf. Isa 42:1–49:6; 61:1f.; Ezek 37:14.

8. This is evident from passages in which the Spirit that is active in the ministry of Jesus (Mt 12:18 = Isa 42:1; Lk 4:18 = Isa 61:1) or in the early church is identified with the Old Testament Spirit of the Lord (Acts 2:16f. = Joel 2:28). Cf. Mk 12:36 with 13:11; Lk 4:17f., 21; 2 Cor 3:15-18; Tit 3:5f.; 1 Pet 1:10f.

THE SPIRIT'S NEW ROLE

The new role of the Holy Spirit is, according to the Gospels, initiated through Jesus, in whose prophetic words and miraculous works the future kingdom of God was manifested in the present.[9] Jesus states this most explicitly of his exorcisms (Mt 12:28), but he makes essentially the same claim for his preaching and teaching[10] in his inaugural sermon on Isa 61 in the synagogue at Nazareth:

> "The Spirit of the Lord is upon me,
> Because he anointed me
> To evangelize the poor . . ." (Isa 61:1).
> Today this scripture is fulfilled in your ears.   Lk 4:18, 21

Although the role of the Holy Spirit in connection with Jesus is not mentioned frequently in the Gospels,[11] its importance can be inferred from the manner in which it occurs. It frames the beginning and the end of the Gospels' picture, appearing at Jesus' birth and baptism and again at his promise (or impartation) of the Spirit to his disciples at the close of his earthly ministry.[12] It is implicit

---

9. Mt 3:16; 4:23; 12:28; Lk 4:43; 16:16. Cf. E. E. Ellis, *Eschatology in Luke* (Philadelphia, 1972), 11ff. W. G. Kümmel, *Promise and Fulfilment* (London, 1957), 105-40. H. Leisegang (*Pneuma Hagion* [Leipzig, 1922], 3f.) rightly gives priority to the Gospels (and not to Paul) for understanding the beginnings of the new role of the Spirit in Christianity, but his development of this thesis is less persuasive.

10. Matthew (12:18 = Isa 42:1) interprets Jesus' preaching similarly. The sermon at Nazareth is found only in Luke's Gospel (4:14-30) but is not for that reason to be discounted. Contrary to the conclusions of the early form-critical studies, the traditions of Jesus' earthly ministry were carefully transmitted within apostolic circles, and a proper critical method will place them there unless it can be shown that they were postresurrection elaborations or creations. Cf. E. E. Ellis, "Gospels Criticism: A Perspective on the State of the Art," *Das Evangelium und die Evangelien,* ed. P. Stuhlmacher (Tübingen, 1983), 27-54. On the importance of Isaiah for Jesus' understanding of his ministry cf. W. Grimm, *Die Verkündigung Jesu und Deuterojesaia* (Frankfurt, ²1981).

11. Cf. C. K. Barrett, *The Holy Spirit and the Gospel Tradition* (London, 1958), 117-20.

12. Mt 1:20; 3:11, 16; 4:1; Mk 13:10f.; Lk 11:13; 12:12; 21:15; Jn 7:39;

in the authority (ἐξουσία),[13] the charisma, and even ecstasy[14] that characterized his ministry. All the indicators (and they were considerable) that marked Jesus off as a prophet in the eyes of many also testified to his empowerment by the Holy Spirit[15] since, in Jewish tradition, the Holy Spirit is the spirit of prophecy.[16] Indeed, Jesus on occasion spoke of himself as a prophet without, of course, excluding other more exalted claims.[17]

In the light of this one may say that it was not so much that Jesus brought the Spirit in his new eschatological role but that the Spirit in his new role brought Jesus.[18] During his earthly ministry Jesus was, like a prophet, at the disposal of the Holy Spirit. After his resurrection, however, the order is reversed. The Spirit is now at the disposition of the exalted Jesus. It is in this context that Jesus is represented as the one who, as the exalted Lord, sends the Spirit and his gifts to the Christian community.[19] This is perhaps best seen in the Pauline letters in the quotation-exposition of Ps 68:18 at Eph 4:8:[20]

14:17, 26; 15:26; 16:13. At Jn 20:21ff., in a kind of proleptic Pentecost, Jesus imparts the Spirit to his disciples as he commissions them.

13. Cf. Mt 21:23 with 21:25f. parr; cf. 7:29; Mk 1:27 par.

14. Mk 3:21: "They were saying, he is beside himself" (ἐξέστη). While the interpretation of his hearers was mistaken, Jesus' conduct must have reflected a spiritual charisma sufficient to evoke such a reaction. Cf. Lk 10:18, 21; M. Hengel, *The Charismatic Leader and His Followers* (New York, 1981), 63-66.

15. Mt 21:11, 46; Mk 6:14f.; 8:28; 14:65; Lk 7:39; Jn 4:19; cf. J. D. G. Dunn, *Jesus and the Spirit* (Philadelphia, 1975), 82ff.; G. Friedrich, "προφήτης," *TDNT* 6, 843ff.

16. Cf. J. Lindblom, *Prophecy in Ancient Israel* (Oxford, 1962), 174-82; E. E. Ellis, *Prophecy and Hermeneutic* (Tübingen and Grand Rapids, 1978), 27f.

17. Mk 6:4; Lk 4:24; 13:33; Hengel (note 14).

18. Altering the memorable comment of R. Otto (*The Kingdom of God and the Son of Man* [London, ²1951 (1938)], 103): "It is not Jesus who brings the kingdom . . . ; on the contrary, the kingdom brings him with it." For an analysis and critique of Otto's views cf. G. Lundström, *The Kingdom of God in the Teaching of Jesus* (Richmond, VA, 1963), 172-99.

19. Mt 3:11; Acts 2:17f., 33; cf. 1 Cor 12:5; Eph 4:8-11. See above, 5ff.

20. Eph 4:7-16 appears to be a preformed midrash, that is, commentary on Ps 68:19 that Paul has here employed.

Having ascended on high,
[Christ] took captivity captive
And gave gifts to men.

Indeed, it is remarkable how Paul can equate the Spirit of God or the Holy Spirit with the Spirit of Christ[21] and occasionally with Christ himself.[22] His discussion of the functions of the Holy Spirit in the life of believers is, therefore, totally bound up with the activity of Christ himself.

FOUR FUNCTIONS OF THE HOLY SPIRIT

In the writings of the Apostle at least four functions of the Spirit may be distinguished: baptism in the Spirit, the fruit of the Spirit, the gifts of the Spirit, and the final regeneration of the individual believer and of the natural creation at the end of the age through the Spirit.[23] The first function, baptism in the Spirit, is that which brings a person into the church, the body of Christ. Paul puts it in these words:

In (ἐν) one Spirit we all were baptized
Into one body.   1 Cor 12:13

The initial coming of the Spirit results in an indwelling that sets God's seal upon the believer and gives assurance that he belongs to Christ.[24] It is apparently conceived "spatially" and may be expressed either as the individual's baptism *in* the Spirit or the Spirit's presence *in* the individual or *in* the Christian community.[25] The conception of "baptism in the Spirit" is very similar, if

21. Cf. Rom 8:9; 1 Cor 2:11, 14, 16; H. Gunkel, *The Influence of the Holy Spirit* (Philadelphia, 1979 [1888]), 113-16; A. Deissmann, *Paul* (New York, 1957 [²1927]), 138f.; Ellis (note 16), 63-71.

22. 1 Cor 15:45; cf. 6:17; Rom 9:1; 2 Cor 3:17.

23. Rom 8:11, 18-23. It is possible that the Spirit may also be viewed as the instrument of the divine destruction of the present world-order (2 Thess 2:2). For a somewhat different enumeration of the functions of the Spirit cf. M. Green, *I Believe in the Holy Spirit* (Grand Rapids, 1975), 76-99.

24. Rom 8:15f.; 2 Cor 1:22; 5:5; Eph 1:13f.; 2 Tim 1:14.

25. 1 Cor 3:16; 6:16; 12:13.

not identical, to "baptism into Christ" and to the believer's existence "in Christ" or "Christ in him."[26] To belong to Christ means by definition "to have the Spirit" (ἔχειν πνεῦμα).[27]

A similar description of the initial work of the Spirit in the Christian life is found in 1 Cor 6:11: "You were washed . . . in the Spirit of our God." A third and more interesting text is Tit 3:5f., one of a number of traditional "faithful sayings" that Paul incorporated into his Pastoral letters:[28]

> [God] saved us through the washing
> Of regeneration and renewal
> In the Holy Spirit.

This passage is sometimes taken to refer to two distinct events, that is, "the washing of regeneration, and the renewal of the Holy Spirit." Translated thus, it may be used to support (1) two successive comings of the Spirit to the believer, first in regeneration and later in renewal, or (2) an initial water baptism followed later by the baptism in the Spirit. The first interpretation is not impossible, but the Old Testament allusions in Tit 3:6 to "pouring out" the Spirit suggest that the renewal, like that in the account of Pentecost in Acts 2, refers to the initial endowment of the Spirit to the believer.[29]

The second interpretation is even more problematic. In its favor are certain passages in the Gospels and Acts in which water baptism and the coming of the Spirit are closely associated and yet clearly distinguished. The baptism of Jesus and, in Acts, the baptism of Paul, Cornelius, and the Samaritan and Ephesian believers are instances of this.[30] However, neither these texts nor Paul's teachings suggest that regeneration can occur apart from

26. Rom 6:3; 8:1, 10; 2 Cor 5:17; 13:5; Gal 3:27.

27. Rom 8:9; cf. Jude 19. However, this is not to be equated with "being a spiritual person" or "a pneumatic" (εἶναι πνευματικός, 1 Cor 14:37) or with "having the Spirit" in the sense of a prophetic revelation (cf. 1 Cor 7:40). See below, 116f.

28. On the authorship and historical setting of the Pastoral epistles see below, 102-11.

29. Joel 2:28; Isa 44:3.

30. Mt 3:16f.; Lk 3:21ff.; Acts 8:14-17; 9:17ff.; 10:45ff.; 19:5ff.

the Holy Spirit,[31] so it is doubtful that the "washing of regeneration" in Tit 3:5 refers merely to water baptism. May it, however, refer to baptism as the rite that conveys the Spirit?

Such a sacramental understanding of Tit 3:5 is widely accepted,[32] but it is difficult to reconcile with the sharp distinction drawn elsewhere in the New Testament between water baptism and the coming of the Spirit. More significantly, it is doubtful that Paul would use unaltered a "faithful saying" so at odds both with his own lack of interest in baptizing people and with his teaching that the Spirit is received "from the hearing of faith."[33] Moreover, Paul views the Spirit as the author of faith, and since in the New Testament faith is the prerequisite for water baptism, the Apostle's references to baptism as a "putting on" or being "buried with" Christ either refer to baptism in the Spirit or are representational, symbolic statements. As Karl Barth has argued, these texts are concerned with the acts of the Holy Spirit[34] and do not suggest that water baptism in itself effects the believer's incorporation into Christ or that it is necessary for that union, although it is not unimportant in other respects. Incor-

31. Cf. Rom 8:9; 2 Cor 3:6; Gal 4:6; cf. Jn 3:3-8; 7:38f.

32. Cf. G. R. Beasley-Murray, *Baptism in the New Testament* (Grand Rapids, 1962), 211-16; O. Cullmann, *Baptism in the New Testament* (London, 1961), 48f.; A. Richardson, *The Theology of the New Testament* (New York, 1958), 36, 337f. Early in this century Tit 3:5 was thought by some to reflect mystery-religion conceptions (cf. M. Dibelius–H. Conzelmann, *The Pastoral Epistles* [Philadelphia, 1972 ([1]1931)]). However, this view was refuted by linguistic and substantive differences between Paul and the mysteries and by the later date of the evidence for these conceptions in the mystery religions. Cf. J. G. Machen, *The Origin of Paul's Religion* (Grand Rapids, 1947 [1921]), 279-90; A. D. Nock, "Hellenistic Mysteries and Christian Sacraments" (1952), *Essays on Religion and the Ancient World*, 2 vols. (Oxford, 1972), II, 791-820.

33. 1 Cor 1:14, 17; Gal 3:2, 14; Eph 1:13f.; cf. Rom 10:17; Acts 15:8f. Cf. J. D. G. Dunn, *Baptism in the Holy Spirit* (London, 1977), 105-11, 151, 170ff.

34. Gal 3:27; Rom 6:4; Col 2:12; cf. Eph 4:24; Col 3:10. Cf. the discussion of K. Barth, *Church Dogmatics*, 4 vols. (Edinburgh, 1936-1969), IV/iv, 6-10, 115-22. On the Spirit as the author of faith cf. Rom 8:15f.; 10:17; Gal 5:5, 22; F. L. Godet, *Commentary on First Corinthians* (Grand Rapids, 1977 [1886]), 129 (on 1 Cor 2:4f.): The Spirit acts "at once in him who speaks and in him who hears, in such a way as to make the light pass . . . from the mind of the one into the mind of the other."

poration into Christ is, rather, the first function of the Spirit in the life of the believer, and that function is sometimes described by Paul, as it is elsewhere in the New Testament, as a baptism or a washing.

The initial coming of the Spirit, also called "the firstfruits" (ἀπαρχή) or "sealing" (σφραγίζειν) or "down-payment" (ἀρρα- βών), anticipates and assures the final work of the Spirit at the last day.[35] The connection between these two events is first seen in the individual person of Jesus. The Spirit who came upon Jesus after his baptism was apparently also considered to be active in his resurrection from death in which Jesus' body became the first bit of earth to be transformed into immortal-living matter.

In 1 Cor 15 Paul teaches that the resurrection of believers is implicated in, dependent upon, and derivative from the resurrec- tion of Christ, and in Rom 8:11 he specifies the role of the Spirit in both events:[36]

> If the Spirit of him who raised Jesus from among the dead
> Dwells in you,
> The one who raised Christ from among the dead
> Will also make alive your mortal bodies
> Through his Spirit who dwells in you.

Thus, the first act of the Spirit, the down-payment, will be complemented and fulfilled when the resurrection life of the new age is actualized in the individual bodies of the faithful as they are called forth from the earth. For the Spirit who, as we saw earlier,[37] gives believers a corporate participation in Christ's resurrection in the present, will at the last day of this age also effect in them an

35. Rom 8:23; 2 Cor 1:22; 5:5; Eph 1:13f.; 4:30. Cf. C. F. D. Moule, *The Holy Spirit* (Grand Rapids, 1978), 34ff.

36. Cf. Rom 8:23; 1 Cor 15:12-19, 45; Gal 6:8; Jn 6:63. On the connec- tion between the resurrection of Christ and the resurrection of Christians see also 1 Cor 6:14; 15:20-23; 2 Cor 4:14 with 1 Thess 4:14; Phil 3:20f. The Spirit's role in the resurrection of believers as seen in Paul's writings may be compared with the imaginative description of the newborn world of Narnia in C. S. Lewis's *The Magician's Nephew.* There the animals respond to the creative song by taking form and leaping forth from the earth as out of a cocoon.

37. See above, 10f.

individual actualization of that resurrection. He mediates these creative changes to the believer by a word, the first a word through an evangelist and the second a death-destroying word of the Son of God.[38]

Between the first and final acts of the Spirit are his intermediate functions, the fruit and the gifts. The fruit is the evidence of Christ's *character* that is increasingly made manifest in believers' attitudes and conduct and finally abides forever in the perfected people of God. It is summarized in Gal 5:22:[39]

> The fruit of the Spirit is
> Love, joy, peace,
> Patience, kindness, goodness,
> Faith, gentleness, self-control.

To manifest this fruit in one's life is, in Paul's language, to walk "in the Spirit" or "according to the Spirit" and "to think the things of the Spirit."[40]

The gifts of the Spirit are the function of the Spirit that Paul identifies with Christian ministry. They enable believers to fulfill the *mission* of Christ. Also a part of the firstfruits of the new creation, the gifts are transitional and come to an end at the second coming of the Lord. They may be exercised when one is "filled with the Spirit" or "rekindles the charism."[41] While the Apostle provides a list of gifts at several places in his letters, he treats them most extensively in 1 Cor 12–14. We must, then, examine that passage in more detail.

---

38. Rom 10:8, 14-17; Eph 1:13; 1 Thess 4:16; cf. Jn 5:25, 28f.

39. Cf. 1 Cor 13:8-13; Rom 5:5; 8:13f.; Gal 5:25f.; 1 Thess 1:6; 4:7; 2 Thess 2:13. See below, 50ff.

40. Gal 5:16, 25; Rom 8:4f.

41. 1 Cor 13:10; Eph 5:18; 2 Tim 1:6; cf. 1 Tim 5:19f.; Lk 1:41, 67; Acts 2:4; 4:8; 6:5. Further, on the gifts, cf. E. E. Ellis, "Prophecy," "Spiritual Gifts," "Tongues," *IDBS,* 700f., 841f., 908f.

THE NATURE OF THE GIFTS OF THE SPIRIT

Characteristics of the Gifts

1 Cor 12 sets forth several aspects of the Apostle's teaching on the gifts of the Holy Spirit—specifically, (1) their christological focus, (2) their divine origin, (3) their twofold classification, (4) their sovereign distribution, and (5) their churchly purpose. The chapter opens with the basic principle that "no one speaking in the Spirit of God ever says, 'Jesus be cursed'; and no one is able to say 'Jesus is Lord' except in the Holy Spirit" (12:3). With these words Paul sets forth the essential test of the genuineness of a Christian ministry, that is, *a focus upon Jesus Christ* within the confessional affirmation that he is Lord. In 1 Cor 12:3 the test is applied to a verbal prophetic-type ministry, as it is in Rev 19:10, where it is stated that "the Spirit of [true] prophecy is the testimony to Jesus." But the christocentric principle applies as well to other types of ministry that are done in Christ's name.

The second section of the chapter (1 Cor 12:4-11) further defines *the divine origin* of the gifts of ministry. Probably a teaching-piece used previously in the Pauline circle,[42] it is unusual in attributing the gifts to the divine triad—Spirit, Lord, God (12:4-6), a formulation that with variations appears in other Pauline texts[43] and that foreshadows later, more definitive trinitarian expressions. The gifts appear to be designated generally as charisms (χαρίσματα) of the Spirit and then specified as (1) prophetic-type ministries (διακονίαι) associated particularly with the Lord Christ and (2) miraculous powers (ἐνεργήματα) associated particularly

42. Supporting a preformed tradition at 1 Cor 12:4-11 are (1) its carefully framed unity, (2) its independence from its context, and (3) the number of peculiar words and expressions for the gifts of the Spirit that are different from Paul's usage elsewhere in 1 Corinthians and in his other letters. Cf. Ellis (note 16), 24n.

43. Cf. also 2 Cor 13:13; cf. 1:21f.; Gal 4:6; G. D. Fee, *The First Epistle to the Corinthians* (Grand Rapids, 1987), 588. Eph 4:4ff. is somewhat similar. Elsewhere in Paul's writings the gifts are ascribed to "God's appointment" (1 Cor 12:28; cf. Tit 3:6) or to Christ's gift (Eph 4:7; cf. Acts 2:33). Cf. Eph 2:18.

with God the Father.[44] This specification represents *a twofold classification* of the gifts that is present elsewhere in Paul. As an activity of the risen Christ it appears, for example, in a chiastic pattern at Rom 15:18f., where the ministry of "word" is associated with the (prophetic) Spirit and the ministry of "deed" with miracles:[45]

> Christ has worked through me . . .
> By word and by deed,
> By the power of signs and wonders,
> By the power of the [prophetic] Spirit.

The remainder of the section (12:7-11) delineates the gifts in greater detail and focuses upon the role of the Holy Spirit as the mediator of them. It is the Spirit who "empowers all the charisms and distributes them to each one as he wills."[46] The Spirit's *sovereign distribution* of the gifts is described in two ways. First (1), he distributes the gifts severally, a gift to a particular person and another to someone else. This means that no individual believer receives all the gifts and no one gift is imparted to all. Later in the chapter Paul underscores this diverse character of ministry.[47]

Second (2), the Spirit endows individuals with gifts not to serve their own personal interests but *"for the common good"* (12:7) of the Christian community. It was precisely at this point that some Corinthian charismatics came under the Apostle's

---

44. In Rom 12:7f. ministry (διακονία) is further specified as consisting of one who teaches (διδάσκειν) or exhorts (παρακαλεῖν). As a collective for gifts of inspired speech it is appropriately associated with Christ, who, as the "wisdom" of God, mediates his mind to his ministers (cf. 1 Cor 1:24, 30; 2:16; Ellis [note 16], 59-62). The ministry of service (διακονία τῆς λειτουργίας) is somewhat different. Cf. 2 Cor 9:1, 12. The term ἐνέργημα, found only here in the New Testament, is in cognate forms used often, though not exclusively, for healing and other miracles (cf. Mk 6:14; Gal 3:5; Eph 1:20; Phil 3:21; but see Gal 2:8; Phil 2:13; Col 1:29; 1 Thess 2:13).

45. Cf. also 2 Cor 8:7, where "faith" (πίστις) may refer to miracles, "word and knowledge" (λόγος καὶ γνῶσις) to inspired speech.

46. 1 Cor 12:11; cf. Heb 2:3f.

47. 1 Cor 12:17, 29f.

severe criticism because they had not used their gifts for the benefit of the church but had allowed them to become a source of self-centered pride and arrogance.[48]

The gifts of ministry specified in more detail at the end of the section (12:8-10) may still be broadly arranged in the twofold classification of miraculous works and of inspired speech and discernment. However, other lists of gifts in the Pauline letters show greater diversity and require an expanded classification. Using the longest list as the base, they may be compared as follows:

1 Cor 12:8ff.	1 Cor 12:28ff.	Rom 12:6ff.	Eph 4:11
	1. apostles		1. apostles
1. word of wisdom			
2. word of knowledge			
6. prophecy	2. prophets	1. prophecy	2. prophets
	3. teachers	2.3. ministry:	4. shepherds
		teaching	and
		exhortation	teachers
			3. evangelists
3. faith			
5. miracle working	4. miracle working		
4. gifts of healing	5. gifts of healing		
7. discernment of	6. discernment[49]		
spirits			
		4. distributing[50]	
	7. piloting	5. leading	
		6. showing mercy	
8. varieties of	8. varieties of		
tongues	tongues		
9. interpretation	9. interpretation		
of tongues	of tongues		

48. Cf. 1 Cor 3:1-3; 4:6-21; 11:21f.

49. The term ἀντίλημψις (1 Cor 12:28), found only here in the New Testament, may mean "grasp of mind" or "perception." Cf. H. G. Liddell–R. Scott–H. S. Jones, *A Greek-English Lexicon* (Oxford, [9]1961), 158; A. P. Stanley, *The Epistles of St. Paul to the Corinthians* (London, 1876), 221 (on 1 Cor 12:28): Ἀνάλημψις "would well express the various helps rendered by those who had the gift of interpretation."

50. The term μεταδιδόναι may refer to "distributing" the church's charities or to "contributing" one's own offerings. Cf. C. E. B. Cranfield, *The Epistle to the Romans,* 2 vols. (Edinburgh, 1979), II, 624f.

Different Kinds of Gifts

In these lists the gifts fall into a number of well-defined categories. In addition to gifts of inspired speech and discernment and those of miracle working there are gifts of leadership and, in Rom 12:8, divine powers of empathy and sympathy, prompting care for those in need. None of the lists is exhaustive, and they suggest that the kinds of gifts may vary from place to place and time to time. For example, 1 Cor 14:15 and Col 3:16 imply that the verbal gifts may be extended to include music. We may here survey briefly four types of gifts: inspired speech, discernment, leadership, and faith.

The *gifts of inspired speech* seem to be given a special prominence by Paul. In the list at Eph 4:11 they alone are mentioned. At 1 Cor 12:28ff. they are given pride of place — first apostles, second prophets, third teachers. All three are gifts of inspired speech or at least include such a gift. The gift of "apostle of Jesus Christ" was conferred by the personal appearance and commissioning of the risen Lord and was unique to the first generation of Christians.[51] Prophecy and tongues were prominent in the worship of the Pauline congregations, as we shall detail below in the chapter on church order, but in the succeeding centuries they have been at most occasional gifts in the church.[52] However, faithful teachers, whose gift overlaps that of the prophet, and those with other verbal charisms have been granted to the church in every generation.

51. Cf. 1 Cor 1:1; 9:1-3; Gal 1:1; 1 Pet 1:1; Jude 17. The designation "apostles of the churches" (2 Cor 8:23; Phil 2:25) is quite different, of course, and may refer to any authorized and commissioned missionaries. Cf. P. R. Jones, "I Corinthians 15:8: Paul the Last Apostle," *TB* 36 (1985), 3-34.

52. In the patristic church, prophecy is mentioned, for example, by Justin Martyr (*Dialogue with Trypho* 82.1) and by Irenaeus (*Against Heresies* 2.32.4; 5.6.1). On reported prophetic phenomena in the modern church compare, for example, J. Lindblom, *Prophecy in Ancient Israel* (Oxford, 1962), 13-18 (Scandinavia); the autobiography of A. Blessitt, *Turned On to Jesus* (New York and London, 1972), 90-95, 130 (USA); G. M. Haliburton, *The Prophet Harris* (London, 1971); idem, "Walter Matitta . . . Prophet . . . in Lesotho," *Journal of Religion in Africa* 7 (1975), 111-23 (Africa). Further, cf. E. E. Ellis, "Prophecy in the New Testament Church—and Today," *Prophetic Vocation in the New Testament and Today*, ed. J. Panagopoulos (Leiden, 1977), 46-57.

The same constancy in the life of the church has characterized the closely related *gift of discernment* (διάκρισις, 1 Cor 12:10). The term generally means the evaluation of a matter by distinguishing the factors involved. In Heb 5:14 it is the moral "discernment" between good and evil, regarded as the mark of mature believers who are competent to teach. The meaning "discernment" or (as a verb) "to discern" also best fits the term in 1 Cor 6:5, where it means to give a word of wisdom,[53] that is, to evaluate and "decide" the merits of a dispute between Christians. In 1 Cor 14:29 it is to "weigh" or "test" (διακρίνειν) prophetic messages. Here it can hardly mean merely to "interpret" them in the sense of translation since throughout the chapter prophecy is commended because, unlike the gift of tongues, it needs no "interpretation."[54]

What, then, needs to be discerned in prophetic messages? Other verses in 1 Cor 12–14 point to the answer. (1) The prophet perceives divine knowledge only "in part" (13:9, 12) and may need to have his message clarified. But even more, (2) prophets are considered to have the ability and the task to confirm which messages of another prophet are "a command of the Lord" and which are only human impulses or judgments (14:37f.; cf. 7:40). In Paul's view a prophet in a congregation is never the sole judge of his own message. Finally, (3) an erring or pseudo-prophet may give voice in the assembly to false prophecy inspired, apparently, by a beguiling demonic spirit (12:3). These expressed limitations and problems of prophecy give to the closely related gift of "discernment of spirits" (12:10) more specific connotations. It is a gift not only of clarifying true prophecy but also of distinguishing it from the prophet's human opinions and from demonic aberrations.[55] And

53. Cf. 1 Cor 12:8; 1 Kings 3:9, 12, 28.

54. Cf. 1 Cor 14:5f., 13, 24-27. Otherwise: G. Dautzenberg, *Urchristliche Prophetie* (Stuttgart, 1975), 122-48. His view is summarized and critiqued by W. A. Grudem, *The Gift of Prophecy in 1 Corinthians* (Washington, D.C., 1982), 263-88.

55. Cf. 1 Cor 2:6-16; 1 Jn 4:1-4; Rev 19:10; Ellis (note 16), 25ff., 30-44, 69ff. *Pace* D. Hill (*New Testament Prophecy* [Atlanta, 1979], 135) similar problems of discernment and ratification were present in Old Testament prophecy (Deut 13:1-3; 1 Kings 13:11, 18-25; 22:6, 13-22; 2 Chron 18:4-27; Isa 9:14f.; 28:7; Jer 23:11-16, 28; 28:1-17; Hos 4:5; 9:7). The prophecies in our Old Testa-

it may be applied more broadly to teaching and other charisms and to various issues within the life of the congregations.

Gifts of leadership also have been continually present in the church, but they are not emphasized in the major letters of Paul. The Apostle usually underscores the verbal gifts, both in his lists of charisms and elsewhere.[56] This is true also when, as in 1 Cor 14, he is concerned about church order. In the last years of his ministry, after his churches had been increasingly threatened and sometimes ravaged by false teachers, Paul did pay more attention to the gifts of oversight and administration.[57] But even then, in the Pastoral letters, he treats these charisms in combination with gifts of teaching. We shall look in detail at the gifts of leadership in the chapter on Pauline church order.

The *gift of faith* (πίστις) is of particular interest since in Gal 5:22 it is listed as the *fruit* of the Spirit. Apparently the latter is the faith that saves, the grace common to all Christians as the medium through which the Spirit engrafts one into Christ. The *gift* of faith, on the other hand, seems to be that endowment enabling one to invoke or to receive a miracle, not only of physical healing[58] but also of incredible feats of ministry.[59] In 1 Cor 13 faith is apparently used both in the sense of gift (13:2) and of fruit (13:13).

THE GIFTS AND THE BODY OF CHRIST

General Considerations

As has been observed above,[60] Paul regards Christians as living in a corporate sphere of existence that may be termed "the body

---

ment are precisely those that were ratified and affirmed by the prophetic circle that (collected and) first transmitted them.

56. Cf. Gal 6:6; Eph 5:19; Col 3:16. However, references to leadership roles also appear, for example, in 1 Cor 16:15f.; Phil 1:1; Col 4:16; 1 Thess 5:12f.

57. 1 Tim 3:1-15; Tit 1:5, 10f.

58. For example, Mt 9:2, 22; Acts 14:9; Gal 3:5.

59. For example, Rom 1:8. Cf. A. Bittlinger, *Gifts and Graces* (London, 1967), 32ff.

60. See above, 8-14.

of Christ." He draws an analogy between it and the corporate body created by the sexual union:

> Your bodies are members of Christ.
> Shall I take members of Christ and make them members
>   of a prostitute? . . .
> He who is united to a prostitute is one body [with her].
> For it says, "the two shall be one flesh" (Gen 2:24).
>
> 1 Cor 6:15f.

The same imagery is later employed to describe the husband as "the head of the wife" (1 Cor 11:3). In Ephesians it is more comprehensive but reflects the same conception:

> The husband is head of the wife
> As Christ is head of the church,
> The Savior of the body.   Eph 5:23

The imagery is not "head and torso"[61] but rather the leader or ruler and the "body" that is distinct from him but that is nonetheless subject to his lordship and included under the umbrella of his corporate person. The term "head" is used this way not only of the husband as head of the family but also, in the Old Testament, of the tribal or national ruler[62] and of the future messianic king.[63]

The conception of the wife as the "body" of the husband becomes more explicit and elaborate later in the same chapter:

> Husbands ought to love their wives as [being] their own bodies.
> He who loves his wife loves himself.

61. For that imagery cf. Seneca, *On Mercy* 2.2.1. But it is not found in Paul, not even in Eph 4:15f. (cf. Col 2:19), which is to be understood in terms of Eph 5:21-31.

62. Judg 11:11; 1 Chron 5:15; 1 Sam 15:17; Ps 18:43; Isa 7:8f. The denomination of Christ as "head" or "ruler" of the demonic powers (Col 2:10), and of the whole cosmos that consists in him (Col 1:16f.; Eph 1:22), appears to have a similar conceptual basis. Cf. also Philo, *Special Laws* 3.131. For a somewhat different conception, in other Jewish and Greco-Roman literature, of society as a corporate or collective body cf. Josephus, *The Jewish War* 5.279 = 5.6.4; Dio Cassius, *Roman History* 4.17 (Livy, *The History of Rome* 2.32); cf. C. F. D. Moule, *The Origin of Christology* (Cambridge, 1978), 83-87.

63. Hos 1:10f. The Apostle was aware of this usage (cf. Rom 9:26).

For no one ever hated his own flesh,
But nourishes and cherishes it,
As Christ does the church,
For we are members of his body:
"On account of this . . . shall a man be united to his wife,
And the two shall be one flesh" (Gen 2:24).

Eph 5:28-31

The closing quotation from Genesis makes clear that the "flesh" or "body"[64] of the husband in verses 28 and 29 includes and, in the present context, specifically refers to his wife. This Genesis text, moreover, appears to provide the biblical rationale and the conceptual foundation for the Apostle's understanding, throughout his letters, of the church as the body of Christ.[65]

Just as the sexual union is not merely a metaphor but creates an ontological reality, so also does the union of Christ and his followers. For Paul this "body of Christ" corporeity (unlike some philosophical realism) does not exclude the equal reality of the individual bodies of believers and of Christ, and (unlike philosophical nominalism) it is not merely a mental concept or a name for a group of individual realities. If Christ and the church—like husband and wife—form one body, how is such a reality conceived? In what does its organic unity consist?

The Apostle may give a clue to his thought when he contrasts the "body" formed by the sexual union as "one flesh" with the "body" formed by the union of Christ and believers as "one Spirit" (1 Cor 6:17) and, using different imagery to express the same idea, when he describes the Christian community as the temple of God in which God's Spirit dwells.[66] In addition, Paul regularly employs the idiom "the body of Christ" to describe the

---

64. For the Apostle's use of "flesh" (σάρξ) and "body" (σῶμα) as equivalent terms elsewhere cf. 1 Cor 6:16; 15:38ff.; 2 Cor 4:10f.; Gal 4:13 with 6:17; 1 Cor 5:3 with Col 2:5. Cf. H. Ridderbos, *Paul: An Outline of his Theology* (Grand Rapids, 1975), 115ff., 229ff.

65. See note 64. Cf. E. E. Ellis, "Traditions in 1 Corinthians," *NTS* 32 (1986), 487f.

66. 1 Cor 3:16f.; cf. 2 Cor 6:16; Eph 2:22; 1 Pet 2:5.

church when he discusses the gifts of the Spirit.[67] In this context Eph 4 appears to offer the most illuminating comment on the role of the Spirit in sustaining the unity of the body of Christ. After exhorting believers to "preserve the unity of the Spirit," the passage defines their individual ministries "according to the measure of the gift of Christ given to each of us" "for the upbuilding of the body."[68] It concludes with the words:

> Christ,
> From whom all the body
> —Being joined and knit together through every joint
> By [God's] powerful supply
> In proper measure for each individual part—
> Makes for the growth of the body
> Unto its upbuilding in love. Eph 4:15f.

The most significant point of this passage concerns the "powerful supply" (ἐπιχορηγίας κατ᾽ ἐνέργειαν) and the bodily "growth."[69] Elsewhere Paul speaks of the "supply of the Spirit" that is given to believers,[70] and very probably he uses the term "powerful supply" in Eph 4 also with reference to the role of the Spirit or, specifically, of the spiritual gifts.[71] The unity (4:4), "growth," and "upbuilding" of the body, which the supply of the Spirit makes possible, is assured as each gifted member receives and exercises his ministry in its "proper measure" and in the edifying context of "love," which is the fruit of the Spirit.[72] The relation of ministry to the body of Christ, which is summarized in Eph 4, appears in more detail in Paul's message to the Corinthian Christians in 1 Cor 12:12-27.

Stoic philosophical writings, in language not unlike St.

---

67. Rom 12:4f.; 1 Cor 12:27; Eph 4:12, 16; elsewhere: Eph 1:23; 5:23, 30 (cf. 3:6); Col 1:18; 2:19; 3:15; perhaps, 1 Cor 11:29.

68. Eph 4:3, 7, 12, 16; cf. Rom 12:3; 1 Cor 7:7, 17 (μερίζειν); Jn 3:34.

69. The point is not the role of the "joints" and "ligaments" (cf. Col 2:19); the terms serve simply to enhance the "body" imagery.

70. Phil 1:19; cf. Gal 3:5; 2 Cor 9:10.

71. 1 Pet 4:10f. is remarkably similar.

72. Gal 5:22; cf. Rom 12:3-9a; 15:30; 2 Tim 1:7; 1 Jn 4:12f.

Paul's, refer to God and mankind as "one great body"[73] or to mankind as members of one social body.[74] In more modern dress these ideas are reflected in Alexander Pope's *Essay on Man* (1.9):

> All are but parts of one stupendous whole
> Whose body nature is, and God the soul.

But if the idiom and the analogies from nature are similar, the pantheistic ideas of the Stoics have little in common with Paul's thought. The significant background for his conception of the "body" is that to which he himself appeals. It is the Old Testament conception of corporate personality and, specifically, the analogy between Adam and Christ[75] and consequently between Eve, the body of Adam, and the church.[76] As we have seen above, this Old Testament–based analogy is presented most explicitly in Ephesians.[77] But it is found also in 1 Cor 12:12:

> Just as the body is one
> And has many members,
> And all the members . . . are one body,
> So also is Christ.

The analogy is then employed to teach the Corinthians the meaning and the proper use of the charisms.

---

73. Seneca, *Epistles* 95.52. For further texts cf. H. Lietzmann–W. G. Kümmel, *An die Korinther I–II* (Tübingen, 1949), 62f., 187.

74. Marcus Aurelius, *Meditations* 7.13; cf. Epictetus, *Discourses* 2.10.3f. In early Christian writings cf. 1 Clement 37:5; Justin Martyr, *Dialogue with Trypho* 42.3. Cf. H. Conzelmann, *1 Corinthians* (Philadelphia, 1975), 211.

75. 1 Cor 15:22, 45; Rom 5:12-20. Further, cf. Ellis (note 16), 170ff. See above, 10-14.

76. Cf. 2 Cor 11:3.

77. Even if Ephesians had been written after Paul's death by his "disciples," as some have supposed, it would still provide a better key to his thought than, say, Greek philosophical ideas in which he shows no interest and may not even have known.

Ministry in the Body

In 1 Cor 12:12-27 the body of Christ with its variously gifted members is compared with the parts of the human body. In 1 Cor 12:12-13 "the body" is the corporate Christ, including Jesus and his church,[78] on the analogy used earlier in the letter of Adam and Eve's forming "one body" or "one flesh."[79] It is the "one body" into which the regenerating Spirit has incorporated every believer, so that to be baptized "into one body" (εἰς ἓν σῶμα βαπτίσθηναι, 12:13) is precisely the same as "to be baptized into Christ Jesus" (βαπτίσθηναι εἰς Χριστὸν Ἰησοῦν) or "to put on (ἐνδύσασθαι) the Lord Jesus Christ" or "the new man."[80] Like the marriage union, the corporate body of Christ is for Paul not a metaphor but is viewed as an ontological reality alongside the equally real individual Christ and individual Christian.[81]

In his exposition of this conception at 1 Cor 12:14-30 "the body" represents only the church, as 12:27-28 shows.[82] Here the "body of Christ" is compared with parts of the physical body, which represent and by implication are allegorically identified with gifted individuals in the church.[83] Within this framework the Apostle sets forth two important principles for the use of the gifts of ministry in the body of Christ.

1. The first is the principle of diversity. As the bodily organs differ in status, importance, and function, so also believers differ in accordance with their particular spiritual gifts. The Corinthians had observed this and, on the one hand, had become proud of their

---

78. Cf. R. P. Shedd, *Man in Community* (London, 1958), 159-65; S. Hanson, *The Unity of the Church in the New Testament* (Lexington, KY, 1963 [1946]), 73-98; C. F. G. Heinrici, *Das erste Sendschreiben des Apostel Paulus an die Korinther* (Berlin, 1880), 398f., citing 2 Sam 5:1. Otherwise: E. Fascher–C. Wolff, *Der erste Brief des Paulus an die Korinther* 2 vols. (Berlin, 1980, 1982), II, 107f., 110-14.

79. This exegesis of Gen 2:24 is explicit in 1 Cor 6:15ff.; cf. Eph 5:31f.

80. Rom 6:3; 13:14; cf. Gal 3:27; Eph 4:24; Col 3:10.

81. Cf. Shedd (note 78), 163ff.

82. This is also the case in Romans and Ephesians; cf. Rom 12:4f.; Eph 4:12-16; 5:23-32.

83. For example, 1 Cor 12:16, 21.

superior status or, on the other hand, had concluded that their lesser status made them of no importance.

The Apostle does not contest the element of inequality, as readers from our more egalitarian age might expect him to do. Even when he elsewhere affirms that in Christ "there is neither Jew nor Greek, . . . no male and female," he does not conclude that differences in order and role between these groups are thereby eliminated; for he gives Jews a priority in salvation history and, as we shall detail later, distinguishes the roles of husband and wife in the family.[84] So also in 1 Cor 12 Paul recognizes that in the one body of Christ, the church, diverse gifts confer differences in status upon the various members of the body: "first apostles, second prophets, third teachers" (12:28). Thus, unity in Christ, as in the human body, is a unity in diversity.

But the Apostle does contest in three ways the conclusions that the Corinthians apparently had drawn from the observed diversity in their gifts. First (1), he underscores the sovereignty of God in "placing" (τιθέναι) the members in the body "as he willed."[85] If this is so, there can be no place for self-disparagement among those with a lower status (12:15) or for prideful autonomy among those with a greater (12:21). Although one should seek "the higher gifts" (12:31), one is to affirm and exercise the role and rank of ministry "according to the measure of faith that God has assigned him."[86]

Second (2), Paul affirms the importance of all members of the body. In the physical body organs that appear to be "weaker" may in fact be indispensable (12:22). If there are inequalities in status, no bodily part is without value. The ankles or ears, for example, may be neither attractive nor particularly efficient, but if they cease to function, their importance suddenly becomes apparent. So in the body of Christ those whose ministries appear to be incidental are nonetheless very significant for the healthy functioning of the total congregation.

84. Gal 3:28; cf. Rom 1:16; 2:9f.; 11:24, 28; 1 Cor 14:34f. See below, 58-61, 64.
85. 1 Cor 12:18; cf. 12:11, 24, 28; 3:5f.
86. Rom 12:3, 4-8.

Third (3), a law of compensation is at work that tends to balance out the inequalities between those with different gifts. In the natural body it manifests itself in the way that the whole body attends to and cares for the less attractive or the needy parts. If one has good eyes and unbecoming (ἀσχήμων) teeth, one will give priority to dental care. If the piano drops on a big toe, there will be no hesitation or debate about what bodily part should receive the greatest respect and attention (cf. εὐσχημοσύνη, 12:23).

This natural law of compensation, Paul implies, is a key to proper Christian conduct. Special concern or care should not go to those whose ministry in itself confers honor because they "have no need" (12:24). Rather it should go to those whose ministry is not prominent or is in need of support and nurture. Thus, diversity in the body of Christ is not there to promote further diversity but to serve the unity, mutuality, and benefit of the whole.

2. The second important principle in the comparison between the physical body and Christian ministries is that of unity. As the human body shows, unity does not exclude diversity but incorporates it and determines its purpose and goal. It is, then, the more important principle in the "body" imagery in 1 Cor 12. Unity in diversity means harmony and mutuality, or, in Paul's idiom, "that there be no discord" (σχίσμα) and that "the members have the same mutual care for one another" (12:25). In application, it means that those with lesser ministries are not to opt out because of discouragement or envy (12:15f.) and that those with greater ministries are not to exercise them in disregard of the community or in disesteem or disdain for its less endowed members (12:21-24), whose interest their gifts are meant to serve. Just as the physical body can function well only when each part is healthy and working in unity, so also with the gifts of the Spirit in the life of the body of Christ.

Three Aspects of Ministry

Further implications may be drawn from three aspects of Christian ministry mentioned in the previous chapter, that is, its eschatological, charismatic, and diverse character. First, the gifts

47

of ministry are for Paul an *eschatological* phenomenon, a reality of the resurrection age being manifested in the present.[87] Therefore, while they may build upon "natural" talents, they are not to be identified with them. On the same grounds ministry is to be distinguished from occupation. Paul himself offers the best illustration of this distinction. He was both an apostle and a tentmaker (Acts 18:3), and in the latter occupation he certainly performed a good work and benefited the society of his day. But in this he did nothing more or different than the conscientious pagan working beside him. Thus, it is doubtful that he would have regarded that activity as ministry, which in his view involved the mediation of uniquely Christian realities of the new age into the present.

Second, the *charismatic* or "gift" character of ministry also has important implications, signifying above all (1) that the gifts are not the products of one's own efforts or of institutional actions. Again, Paul's own case provides the model: he was an apostle because he had been commissioned and gifted by the risen Lord; he was not gifted because he had been approved by the church as an apostle. As we shall see in a subsequent chapter, Paul affirmed the church's role in recognizing and implementing the charisms within its structures, but not in creating them. Also, while he urged that the "higher charisms" be sought by prayer, he recognized that a particular gift could not be demanded or necessarily expected from God.[88] When a gift is granted, (2) it is not, Paul emphasizes, simply at the disposal of the recipient but is to be used as a means

87. See above, 4-7.
88. Cf. 1 Cor 12:11, 29f. The phrases "strive for the more valuable gifts" (τὰ χαρίσματα τὰ μείζονα, 1 Cor 12:31) and "strive for the spiritual gifts" (14:1) bracket the inserted 1 Cor 13 and are equivalent idioms. Paul has already identified which gifts are more valuable (12:28) and in 1 Cor 14 gives prophecy a special recommendation for public worship (14:6, 12, 24, 39). The verb "strive" (ζηλοῦτε) in 12:31 and 14:1, 39 is imperative; if it were indicative, 1 Cor 14:1 would be a meaningless opening for that chapter. It was precisely because the Corinthians were not striving "especially" (μᾶλλον) for the spiritual gift of prophecy that Paul wrote 1 Cor 14. Also, 12:31 would lose any meaningful relationship to 12:28ff. if it were indicative. Otherwise: R. P. Martin, *The Spirit and the Congregation* (Grand Rapids, 1984), 33, 66.

of "building up the body of Christ."[89] If the charisms become a source of boasting[90] or a means merely to indulge a desire for self-assertion or for an emotional "high," as they apparently did in the church at Corinth, they are being misused.[91]

Finally (3), charismatic is not to be equated with ecstatic. The gifts of inspired speech were sometimes exercised by the early Christians in an ecstatic manner, that is, in an exalted mood in which the speaker appears to be borne along as a vehicle of the Spirit speaking through him.[92] However, while such utterance was doubtless impressive, the gifts were not necessarily more effective or more powerful when manifested in such an ecstatic state. For example, in Paul's case the abiding form of the prophetic word was deliberately formulated in letters. In the post-Reformation era one recalls the sermon of Jonathan Edwards, "Sinners in the Hands of an Angry God," which sparked a widespread revival in New England and which can hardly be viewed by Christians other than as a manifestation of spiritual power. Yet the sermon was largely read from a manuscript and, it is said, delivered in a rather low tone of voice.

Third, the gifts of the Spirit in the Pauline letters are *diverse* in status and in kind. They may be verbal and nonverbal, and certain gifts are accorded a distinct priority.[93] Also, they are diverse in their direction and implementation. Most are directed toward the congregation, but evangelistic gifts, which may include apostleship and miracles and healings, are directed toward the world. Prayer, including some manifestations of tongues, is directed toward God. In their implementation they may remain "free" and unstructured or, as we shall see below, they may be "or-

89. Eph 4:12; cf. 1 Cor 12:7; 14:4f.
90. Cf. Col 2:18; 1 Thess 2:5; Tit 1:11.
91. 1 Cor 3:1-3, 16f.; 4:7, 18ff.; 14:30-33; 2 Cor 5:12; 10:12f.
92. 1 Cor 14:15f., 23; 2 Cor 12:1-4; Eph 5:18f.; Acts 2:13, 15-18; cf. Lk 10:21f.; 2 Pet 1:21. In other first-century Jewish writers ecstatic experiences are also mentioned, for example, in Philo (*On Cherubim* 27) and, perhaps, among the wise teachers *(maskilim)* in the Qumran Hymns (1QH 12:11ff.). Cf. Ellis (note 16), 58f.
93. For example, 1 Cor 9:1; 12:28; 14:1; Gal 1:1, 11f.; Eph 2:20; 3:5; cf. Rom 16:26; Lk 11:49; Rev 18:20. See above, 38ff.

dered" within the institutional church. All the gifts, however, had an outworking within the Christian community. In all respects the eschatological, charismatic, and diverse character of the gifts served not only to define their nature but also to clarify their application in the life of the Pauline church.

THE GIFTS AND THE FRUIT OF THE SPIRIT

In the midst of his discussion of the gifts the Apostle suddenly, in 1 Cor 13, turns to the praise of love as the "more excellent way" to unite the body of Christ. Three questions immediately present themselves. What is the reason for the change of topic? Why is love the "more excellent way"? What is the relationship between the charisms and love?

1 Cor 13 is a self-contained passage that carries its message quite apart from the context of chapters 12 and 14. Probably it was a "hymn" composed independently by Paul or his coworkers and then adapted and incorporated into the present context when 1 Corinthians was being written.

The love (ἀγάπη) that is praised here is not a general concept nor a human attribute[94] but, like the charisms, a work of the Holy Spirit. This is indicated primarily (1) by the designation elsewhere of love as the fruit of the Spirit.[95] (2) Although the terms Spirit and Christ do not appear in 1 Cor 13, allusions to both may be discerned from the way in which Paul elsewhere associates the Spirit and Christ with love. He can speak, apparently interchangeably, of putting on love or Christ,[96] of being rooted in love or in Christ,[97] of walking in love or in Christ or in the

---

94. One finds this theme in other ancient writings with some stylistic affinities with 1 Cor 13, for example, in Plato's (*Symposium* 197) encomium of love (ἔρως) and in a Jewish writer's praise of truth (1 Esdr 4:33-40).

95. Gal 5:22; cf. Col 3:12ff. Of the ninefold fruit of the Spirit listed in Galatians, four appear in 1 Cor 13: patience (4, 7), kindness (4), joy (6), faith (7, 13).

96. Col 3:14; Rom 13:14.

97. Col 2:7; Eph 3:17. Cf. 1 Thess 5:12f.

Spirit.[98] Also (3), in Romans and Ephesians Paul brings his teaching on the gifts of ministry into connection with comments on the fruit of the Spirit, particularly that of love.[99] This shows that the theme of 1 Cor 13 is not out of place in its present context, but it does not explain why the theme is given a greater emphasis here than in the other letters. The explanation appears to lie in the special needs of the church at Corinth and, especially, the aberrations of certain charismatics in that church.

Paul sometimes calls prophetic-type gifts of inspired speech and discernment "spiritual gifts" (πνευματικά)[100] and names the charismatics manifesting them "spirituals" or pneumatics.[101] Earlier in 1 Corinthians he refused to recognize certain Corinthian charismatics as true pneumatics because their gifts, not accompanied by the fruit of the Spirit, had become distorted by jealousy, strife, false wisdom, and arrogance.[102] Such a state of affairs did not contribute to the unity of the church. In 1 Cor 13, no doubt with the same problem in mind, he lays down a general principle that without love the gifts also do not profit the recipient (13:1-3).

The Apostle does not here deny the genuineness of such gifts. But as he shows elsewhere,[103] Paul does believe that the charismatic who loses a focus upon Jesus and who lacks the fruit of the Spirit may in a subtle self-distortion become the mouthpiece of "another spirit," an erring demonic spirit. This perceived danger may have contributed to his strong emphasis upon the importance of love as the necessary complement to the gifts of the Spirit.

The primary concern of Paul, however, is the unity of the Christian community. Why is love "the more excellent way" to

98. Eph 5:2; Col 2:6; Gal 5:16; 2 Cor 12:18; cf. Rom 14:15. Cf. also Rom 5:5 with 2 Cor 1:22; Gal 4:5; Eph 3:17.

99. Rom 12:6-8, 9, 12, 18; Eph 4:2f., 7-11, 15f.; Col 3:12-15, 16.

100. 1 Cor 2:13; 14:1; cf. Rom 1:11: χάρισμα πνευματικόν; Ellis (note 16), 23-30. As is pointed out by John Koenig (*Charismata: God's Gifts for God's People* [Philadelphia, 1978], 97), χάρισμα ("gift") can be used, for example, in Rom 6:23 in a broader way than the usage examined in this chapter.

101. 1 Cor 2:13, 15; 14:37; Gal 6:1. Paul probably originated this technical use of πνευματικός.

102. 1 Cor 3:1ff., 18f.; 4:8, 18ff.; cf. Gal 5:19-23.

103. 1 Cor 12:3; 2 Cor 11:3f., 12-15; 13:5.

accomplish this? The answer is probably not, as some have thought, that Paul regards love as a substitute for the gifts of ministry. If that were the case, he would hardly have interpreted the gifts on the analogy of the unity of the human body (12:12-27). More likely, the Apostle views the gifts and love as complementary aspects of the Christian life and regards neither as dispensable. Love is the context in which the gifts have their full effectiveness.

Although Paul doubtless considered the gifts of ministry to be essential for the church, he nevertheless gives the fruit of the Spirit a certain preeminence, as 1 Cor 13 shows. Three reasons may be offered to explain the Apostle's attitude in this matter. As was mentioned above, (1) the fruit represents the character of Christ, the gifts manifest the particular ministries of Christ. That is, the fruit is substantival and the gifts adjectival to the Christian life. Furthermore (2), the fruit will abide eternally in the personality of the redeemed while the gifts are bestowed only "in part" and for the mission of the church in the present age.[104] Finally (3), the fruit of the Spirit is what all Christians have or should have in common. The gifts, on the other hand, represent a diversity in which one believer's endowment may not be fully understood or even appreciated by another. They can bring about the unity of the body of Christ only when they are used to complement one another. The fruit of the Spirit, however, is the underlying common denominator that enables the gifts to be used in this manner.

For the Apostle Paul the gifts of the Holy Spirit are the essence of Christian ministry, and apart from these gifts ministry in its essential character does not take place. While they are manifested in a considerable variety and diversity, they always have the implicit design and purpose to create an integral wholeness in the church so that the ministry of the Spirit in the body of Christ might reflect the unity of the one God, Father, Son, and Holy Spirit, to whom be glory now and forevermore. Amen.

104. 1 Cor 13:8f., 13. See above, 34.

– III –

Paul and the Eschatological Woman

It was, I believe, Professor P. A. Sorokin, the Harvard sociologist, who coined the term "sexual revolution" for the broad change in sexual behavior in Western society, the breakdown of—or some would say liberation from—traditional mores and morals. Since that introduction the term has been used both for permissive sexual practices and for the liberation of women from the exploitation of a "sexist" society, both permissive and traditionalist.[1]

Alternatively, Ms. Midge Decter, in her book *The New Chastity and Other Arguments Against Women's Liberation,* has described the women's movement itself, in its more extreme forms, as a kind of self-hatred, "a denial of oneself, one's nature and one's true possibilities."[2] The focus of the sexual question on the nature

---

1. The growing political and socioeconomic parity of women in modern society began much earlier than the present generation, of course, and has come in waves. In the United States suffrage was granted to women in 1920, in Great Britain in 1919. In his novel *Jude the Obscure* (London, 1942, [1]1895), Thomas Hardy delineated a fictional version of an earlier liberated woman and in the preface to the 1912 edition offered a striking if condescending depiction of her: . . . "the woman of the feminist movement—the slight, pale 'bachelor' girl— the intellectualized, emancipated bundle of nerves that modern conditions were producing, mainly in the cities as yet; who does not recognize the necessity for most of her sex to follow marriage as a profession, and boast themselves as superior people because they are licensed to be bred on the premises" (ix).

2. M. Decter, *The New Chastity and Other Arguments Against Women's Liberation* (New York, 1972), 180.

of *genus homo* is a true insight of her book, however one may judge Ms. Decter's other arguments.

Within the church the women's movement has come to be identified with the participation of women in ecclesiastical leadership, that is, ordination and parity in other areas of church life. In this respect it is hardly revolutionary since a number of denominations have ordained women for a very long time. But some more traditional churches still look askance at the practice, and they base their views largely on the writings of the Apostle Paul.[3]

In looking at St. Paul's teachings on the ministry of women, two prefatory comments are perhaps in order. First, the Apostle is not concerned to lay down rules for society—"those of this world," as he would put it.[4] He gives his teachings to those who recognize Jesus as Messiah and himself as the faithful transmitter of the mind of Jesus. In designating himself an "apostle of Jesus Christ," he implicitly makes the claim, which he is at pains to defend,[5] that he is a commissioned representative and bearer of Jesus' message.[6] He also claims for himself the exalted status of a "man of the Spirit," that is, a prophet through whom the resurrected and exalted Lord speaks.[7] While he calls all people to faith in Christ, he directs his apostolic teaching only to the Christian community.[8] On the topic before us, then, Paul speaks to Christians. Others will find him interesting only in the effect that his views may have on a society influenced by Christianity.

Second, the present chapter is limited to certain general prin-

---

3. For example, G. W. Knight, *The New Testament Teaching . . . on Men and Women* (Grand Rapids, 1977), 47ff., 61ff. But see A. Mickelsen (ed.), *Women, Authority and the Bible* (Downers Grove, IL, 1986).

4. Cf. 1 Cor 1:20; 5:10, 12.

5. 1 Cor 9:1-3; 15:8-11; 2 Cor 11:5; 12:1-12; Gal 1:1, 11-17; Rom 1:1; 15:17ff.

6. Cf. 1 Cor 7:10; 11:23; 1 Thess 2:13; O. Cullmann, "The Tradition," *The Early Church* (Philadelphia, 1956), 59-99; B. Gerhardsson, *The Origins of the Gospel Traditions* (Philadelphia, 1979); E. E. Ellis, "Traditions in 1 Corinthians," *NTS* 32 (1986), 485-90. See above, 36, 38.

7. See above, 38ff.; below, 116f. Cf. 1 Cor 2:6-16; Hos 9:7 with 1 Cor 14:37; E. E. Ellis, *Prophecy and Hermeneutic* (Tübingen and Grand Rapids, 1978), 59-62.

8. Cf. 1 Cor 5:12.

ciples of Pauline ethics together with a more detailed examination of several passages in which Paul appears to assign a subordinate role to women in church and family life. The latter sphere is important for our subject because, as I hope to show, one's role in the family has an important bearing upon one's role in ministry.

Let us begin by reminding ourselves that in one sense Paul may be the father of some aspects of women's liberation. He made the statement that has focused the concern of much contemporary Christian discussion, namely, that in Christ there is "no male and female."[9] At the same time he says, "Wives, subject yourselves to your husbands" and "Let women be silent in church."[10] How are these apparently contradictory views to be reconciled? Is Paul really for sexual equality or is he, as some have argued, a male chauvinist after all?[11] To answer these questions we shall first consider a number of principles on which Paul's ethics, particularly his sexual ethics, are based. Then we shall examine in more detail several Pauline passages that have been at the center of discussion about the role of women in the church.

FOUR THEOLOGICAL PRINCIPLES

Man: Corporate and Individual

The theological principles that provide the framework for Paul's teaching on the present theme include (1) corporeity and individuality, (2) equality and subordination, (3) mutuality of obligation, and (4) unity and diversity. The first and foremost principle is Paul's understanding of *man as a corporate* as well as an

9. Gal 3:28.
10. Eph 5:22; 1 Cor 14:34.
11. So P. K. Jewett, *Man as Male and Female* (Grand Rapids, 1975), 112, 119, who apparently supposes that Paul was misled by a rabbinic interpretation of Gen 2. E. S. Fiorenza (*In Memory of Her* [New York, 1984], 230-36) concludes that in 1 Cor 14:34-36 and other passages Paul modifies his egalitarian principles of Gal 3:28 and "opens the door" for "the gradual patriarchalization of the whole church" (233, 235).

individual *being*.[12] As was argued above,[13] the two headmen, Adam and Christ, the old man and the new man, express in its broadest dimension humanity's corporate nature. They set the pattern of nature and therefore the pattern of relationships, respectively, for the present age and for the age to come.

As the following diagram illustrates, in Paul's thought the present age extends from the creation and fall of Adam (C) to the parousia of Christ (P). Thus, it overlaps the initial phase of the age to come that extends from the resurrection of Christ in A.D. 33 (R) to his parousia (P):

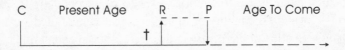

Corporately, Christian believers have been transferred from the society of Adam to the new age, the community of the resurrection where there is "no male and female,"[14] and individually they already receive indiscriminately certain benefits of the new age—the Spirit and the gifts—from the ascended Christ. But "the age to come"[15] is not yet consummated by the parousia, the glorious appearing of Jesus. Those in Christ, although not of the world, nevertheless live in the world.[16] That is, they still live as individuals in the society of Adam, the present order of nature in which the wife's "desire shall be for [her] husband," and he shall rule (*mashal* = κυριεύειν) over [her]."[17] How does Paul reconcile

12. The term "man" is sometimes used here, as it is in common English, in Greek (cf. Mt 4:4 with 19:3), and in Hebrew (Gen 5:2f.), in a corporate and generic rather than in a masculine sense. It is true, of course, that in Paul's teaching the two most decisive corporate figures, Adam and Jesus, are male.

13. See above, 8-13.

14. Gal 3:28; cf. Rom 6:4, 10f.; 8:30; 2 Cor 13:4; Gal 2:19f.; Eph 2:5f.; Col 1:13.

15. Eph 1:21; 2:7.

16. Col 2:20, cf. Rom 8:9; 1 Cor 5:9f.; 7:31; Eph 2:2; Jn 17:14-18.

17. Gen 3:16. The proposition in this verse is sociologically descriptive but also theologically prescriptive of the human condition in the present age in

the dominance of the male in the present creation in Adam[18] with the new creation in Christ in which there is freedom and equality of male and female or, in other words, of the eschatological man and the eschatological woman? A second principle in the Apostle's theology speaks to this question.

Equality and Subordination

Paul affirms both *equality and subordination* as proper and complementary roles in several kinds of relationships, roles that vary in expression according to the particular context. He expresses this principle explicitly in his teachings on diversities in ministry[19] and, as we shall see below, on social and family relationships.[20]

The mind-set that places "equality" and "subordination" in opposition[21] and that views distinctions of class and rank as evil per se is a largely modern phenomenon. It may reflect a justifiable resentment toward attitudes of disdain and elitism that often (and

---

which the marriage of male and female is the natural and normative social order. It is a punishment in that "just where the woman finds her fulfillment in life . . . , there too she finds that it is not pure bliss, but pain, burden, humiliation and subordination" (C. Westermann, *Genesis,* 3 vols. [Minneapolis, 1984-86], I, 263). The priority of the husband and subordination of the wife is also implicit at Gen 2:18 (*ibid.,* I, 262) and, according to the Jewish exegesis of the period, even in the phrase at Gen 1:27 where (as always in scripture) "male" precedes "female" (cf. Mekilta on Exod 12:1; Mishnah, Kerithoth 6:9 with 1 Cor 11:8-12; 1 Tim 2:13, 15). In Gen 3:16 it is accentuated and given the character of a judgment. But see Sharon H. M. Gritz, "A Study of I Timothy 2:9-15 in the Light of the Religious and Cultural Milieu of the First Century," Unpublished Ph.D. Dissertation, Southwestern Baptist Theological Seminary, Fort Worth, 1986, 84-87.

18. Despite wide variations in social roles male dominance is apparently a sociological fact of all human societies, apart from certain mythological races like the Amazons, if one can accept the argument of, for example, Steven Goldberg, *Male Dominance: The Inevitability of Patriarchy* (London, [2]1979). The feminist Rosemary R. Ruether (*Liberation Theology* [New York, 1972], 166f.) has also recognized the utopian, unhistorical character of feminist ideology; for a critique of her views (also from a Roman Catholic perspective) cf. Joyce A. Little, "Sexual Equality in the Church," *HJ* 28 (1987), 174-77.

19. See above, 45ff.

20. See below, 55-85.

21. For example, Jewett (note 11), 134, passim.

in a sinful society always) flow from such distinctions, but it seems to be less aware of the egoistic and antisocial evils inherent in egalitarianism itself and sometimes expressed in programs for economic or social conformity, in a libertarian rejection of authority, and in a despisal of servanthood as a "demeaning" role.

In any case Paul, like the New Testament generally, holds together quite harmoniously an equality of value and diversity in rank[22] and resolves the problems of diversity in a manner entirely different from modern egalitarianism. In this issue as in others, the Apostle finds the key to the problem in his Christology. Jesus himself,

> Who, though existing in the form of God,
> Did not count equality with God as a prize,
> But emptied himself
> By taking the form of a servant. . . .   Phil 2:6

That is, Jesus the Son of God manifested his equality with God the Father precisely in fulfilling a role of subordination to him. In Eph 5 and 1 Cor 11, passages to which we shall return, Paul applies this analogy to marriage.

Eph 5:21–6:9 is Paul's elaboration of traditional regulations for family relationships — a household code, based on scripture, taken over from Judaism and common to the Pauline and Petrine missions.[23] Eph 5:22, 24 states that wives are to "subject themselves

---

22. Cf. the perceptive essay of Madeleine Boucher, "Some Unexplored Parallels to 1 Corinthians 11:11-12 and Galatians 3:28," *CBQ* 31 (1969), 50-58, 57: "[The] ideas of equality before God and inferiority in the social order are in harmony in the New Testament. . . . The tension arises from *modern man's* inability to hold these two ideas together." On the matter of masters and slaves cf. 1 Cor 7:22.

23. Col 3:18–4:1; 1 Pet 2:18–3:7. Josephus, *Against Apion* 2.201 = 2.24 (25); Pseudo-Phocylides, *Maxims* 174-227; Philo, *Hypothetica* 7.3; 7.14: "[According to Moses' law] wives are to be subjected (δουλεύειν) to their husbands. . . ; parents are to rule children. . . ." "the husband [is] to transmit knowledge of the laws to his wife, the father to children and the master to slaves." Cf. Ellis (note 6), 484f. In the household regulations "I Peter did not borrow from Paul, but [both] . . . drew on those Hebrew codes of the primitive Christian community" (D. Daube, *The New Testament and Rabbinic Judaism* [London, 1956], 103). Cf. G. E. Cannon, *The Use of Traditional Materials in Colossians* (Macon, 1983), 114-21.

to their own husbands, as to the Lord" and that "as the church is subject to Christ, so also let wives be subject to their husbands." The passage continues with a reciprocal obligation for the husband:

> Husbands, love your wives,
> As Christ also loved the church and gave himself up for her. . . .
> Husbands ought to love their wives
> As [being] their own bodies.
> He who loves his wife loves himself.
> For no one ever hated his own flesh,
> But nourishes and cherishes it,
> As Christ does the church.   Eph 5:25, 28ff.

These analogies show that in certain respects the wife is to relate to her husband as the church does to Christ and, when Phil 2 is brought into consideration, as Christ relates to God the Father. Correspondingly, the husband is to relate to his wife as Christ does to the church. These analogies may be expressed in terms of mathematical ratios as follows:

$$\frac{\text{Wife}}{\text{Husband}} = \frac{\text{Church}}{\text{Christ}}$$

$$\frac{\text{Wife}}{\text{Husband}} = \frac{\text{Christ}}{\text{God}}$$

$$\frac{\text{Husband}}{\text{Wife}} = \frac{\text{Christ}}{\text{Church}}$$

We may now turn to 1 Cor 11:3-16. This passage, which is probably a preformed tradition that Paul here summarizes, shows the way in which a principle rooted in the household codes— teachings on relationships in the family—is applied to conduct in church.[24] The teaching of the passage, which is quite complicated, involves an oscillation in the meaning of the key words "man" (husband and male) and "head" (literal and metaphorical), and it alludes to an exegesis of Gen 1–3 which in some respects is similar to that found in 1 Cor 14:34f., Eph 5:22-33, and 1 Tim 2:9–3:1a.

24. Ellis (note 6), 493f.

Within this framework and with a clear christological analogy it expresses a principle of "equality and subordination" in the relationship of man and woman.[25] The subordination motif appears most pointedly at 1 Cor 11:3, 7:

> The head (κεφαλή) of every husband (ἀνήρ) is Christ,
> The head of the wife (γυνή) is the husband, and
> The head of Christ is God. . . .
> The husband . . . [exists as] the image and glory of God,
> But the wife is the glory of the husband.

God's headship of Christ is expressed later in the letter (1 Cor 15:28) as Christ's subjection (ὑποτάσσεσθαι) to God, and the husband's headship of the wife is in the household code of Ephesians (5:22ff.) the express reason why she is to subject herself to him. In the light of these parallels headship in 1 Cor 11:3 is most likely to be understood not primarily as "origin" but as "authority" or "leadership" of the husband.[26] However, with the appeal to Gen 2 the meaning of headship appears to be grounded more broadly in the priority of the male in creation:[27]

25. Cf. J. Delobel, "1 Cor 11, 2-16: Toward a Coherent Interpretation," *L'Apôtre Paul,* ed. A. Vanhoye (Leuven, 1986), 369-89, 387ff. See below, 67-78.

26. The term κεφαλή may carry either or both connotations. Perhaps the best treatment is S. Bedale, "The Meaning of κεφαλή in the Pauline Epistles," *JTS* 5 (1954), 211-15: "In the feminine form of the [Hebrew] noun (*re'shith*) this sense of 'beginning' or 'first' is dominant" (215). [The masculine] "quite frequently has the meaning 'chief among' or 'head over' . . . , but with the idea of priority" (213). In biblical Greek, including Paul, "κεφαλή may very well approximate in meaning to ἀρχή" (213). Further, cf. H. Schlier, "κεφαλή," *TDNT* 3 (1967/1938), 679; W. Grudem, "Does κεφαλή mean 'Source' or 'Authority Over'. . . ?" *TJ* 6 (1985), 38-57. In 1 Cor 11:3 there may be an allusion to Gen 3:16: "He shall rule (κυριεύσει) over you." According to 1 Clement 1:3 the household codes were in use in the church at Corinth and may have been part of Paul's initial teachings there. See above, 41.

27. For Paul this would be equally true of Gen 1:27, where male precedes female. See above, note 17. There is no textual basis to take 1 Cor 11:3-7b as the view of certain Corinthians which Paul then refutes in 11:7c-12, as is supposed by A. Padgett, "Paul on Women in Church," *JSOT* 20 (1984), 79ff. For a similar special pleading cf. N. M. Flanagan, "Did Paul Put Down Women in 1 Cor 14:34-36?" *BTB* 11 (1981), 10-12; P. B. Payne, "Libertarian Women in Ephesus," *TJ* 2 (1981), 169-97 (on 1 Tim 2:14a).

The man is not from the woman,
But the woman from the man (Gen 2:22f.).
Also the man was not created for the woman,
But the woman for the man (Gen 2:18).   1 Cor 11:8f.

The principle of headship/subordination is immediately qualified in 1 Cor 11:11f. by one of mutuality or parity "in the Lord":

But neither is the woman independent of the man,
Nor the man independent (χωρίς) of the woman in the Lord;
For just as the woman [came] from the man,
So also the man [comes] through the woman.

In both Eph 5 and 1 Cor 11 Paul expresses another important principle of his theology: he does not void the headship/subordination principle that he finds in Gen 1–3 but, as he does elsewhere in his use of the Old Testament, reinterprets the teaching christologically. In Eph 5 particularly he implies that the Christian wife, in fulfilling a role of subordination, does not negate but rather manifests her equality with her husband and reveals thereby her own special Christ-likeness. Also, the Christian husband is given a corresponding christological role. Just as Christ manifested his Lordship over the church not by dominating but by serving, so the Christian husband will manifest his lordship in the marriage by sacrificial love for his wife. Needless to say, such lordship excludes coercion.

Mutuality of Obligation

Mutuality of obligation represents a third theological principle that is applied to various kinds of relationships. It is probably implicit in Paul's teachings on ministry (1 Cor 12:25) and on the relationship of state and subject (Rom 13:1-7; 1 Tim 2:1f.), but it is most clearly expressed in the household codes. If servants are to give honest labor, masters are to be just and equitable. If children are to obey, parents are under a reciprocal obligation to be fair and understanding in their rules. If the wife is to give reverence, the husband is to love his wife as being his own body. This reciprocity has antecedents in Jewish writings, but it is very pronounced in the household codes of the Pauline and Petrine literature[28] and distinguishes them in some measure from similar Jewish and pagan codes in antiquity.

The principle of mutuality of obligation is the cement that gives the Pauline ethic its unity and viability. In any relationship in which the desire to minister is effaced by the desire to be prime minister, the bond is fractured. The fracture is nowhere more destructive than in the context of marriage, and this Pauline principle appears to take into account that problem.

Unity in Diversity

A fourth principle in Paul's theology is unity in diversity. As we have seen above,[29] it is fundamental for his understanding of the gifts of ministry. But it is equally important for his teaching on Christian social relationships and on the place of the Jews in the history of salvation. In Christ there is "neither circumcision nor uncircumcision" and "no distinction between Jew and Greek," for both have been incorporated in and by the Spirit into the one people of God, the olive tree of Israel, the body of Messiah, the temple of God.[30] At the same time Paul affirms that the gospel is proclaimed "to the Jew first,"[31] and he gives Jews special preroga-

---

28. Cf. Eph 5:21–6:9; Col 3:18–4:1; 1 Pet 2:18–3:7. The principle is followed, of course, when certain patristic writers cite or allude to Paul, for example, Ignatius, *Letter to Polycarp* 5:1; Clement of Alexandria, *The Instructor* 3.95.1 = 3.12; Tertullian, *Against Marcion* 5.18.8-11. For a similar usage in Judaism cf. Philo, *On the Decalogue* 165ff.: "In the fifth commandment on honoring parents [Exod 20:12] we have a suggestion of many necessary laws. . . . Many . . . other instructions are given: to the young on courtesy to the old and to the old on taking care of the young; to subjects on obeying their rulers and to rulers on promoting the welfare of their subjects; . . . to servants on rendering affectionate loyalty to their masters and to masters on showing the gentleness and kindness by which inequality is equalized." See above, note 23; cf. J. E. Crouch, *The Origin and Intention of the Colossian Haustafeln* (Göttingen, 1972), 78f., 81ff., 88-101.

29. See above, 36f., 47, 51f.

30. Gal 6:15; Rom 10:12; Gal 3:3, 27f.; 1 Cor 6:17; 12:13; Rom 11:17-24; Eph 2:11-22; 2 Cor 6:16; cf. Rom 2:28f.

31. Rom 1:16; cf. Acts 13:46; 18:5f.; 28:23-28.

tives in past and future salvation history.[32] He never forbids Jewish Christians to circumcise their children, as he does Gentile Christians,[33] or to follow a kosher life-style or to practice Jewish customs, and on occasion he does so himself.[34] But he looks askance on the attraction of Gentile Christians to traditional Jewish observances.[35]

Unity in diversity appears also in the Apostle's teaching on the relationship of believers from different social and economic strata. It underlies his teaching, for example, on the relation of masters and slaves, both in the household codes and in the particular case of Philemon's slave Onesimus. Paul sees the unity of masters and slaves in their common relation and subjection to Christ, "the Master in heaven," who will judge both in their respective roles without partiality.[36] In a similar vein he urges Philemon to receive back his slave Onesimus for what he truly is, "a beloved brother," whether or not Philemon frees him or retains him as his slave.[37] The unity "in the Lord" affects the way in which the diversity "in the flesh" is expressed but does not exclude it.[38] For Paul unity in Christ is a unity that transcends social differences and works within them but never ignores or denies them or necessarily seeks to erase them.

This principle is particularly significant when the difference is not merely social but is fixed in creation, as is the sexual differentiation between male and female (Gen 1:27). In Christ the wife and the husband and, we may add, the single woman and the single man find their fulfillment as persons within their distinctive roles. On the one hand, the single and the married states are prophetic signs of the new age, the single celibate person signifying, accord-

32. Rom 9:4f.; 11:25-29; Gal 4:4f.
33. Gal 5:2-14.
34. 1 Cor 9:19-22; Acts 16:3; 18:18; 18:21 D; 20:16; 21:23-26.
35. Gal 3:2f.; 4:8-11; Col 2:16f. (20-23); but see Rom 14; Gal 6:15.
36. Eph 6:9; 1 Cor 7:22. For Philo's view see above, note 28.
37. Phlm 16; cf. the discussion in P. T. O'Brien, *Colossians, Philemon* (Waco, 1982), 296ff.; E. Lohse, *Colossians and Philemon* (Philadelphia, 1971), 203 (GT: 282f.); P. Stuhlmacher, *Der Brief an Philemon* (Neukirchen, 1975), 42-49.
38. Phlm 17.

ing to Christ, the sexual role that all will have in the resurrection life[39] and the married couple signifying, according to Christ's Apostle, the union that exists between Christ and his church.[40] On the other hand, the male and the female are distinct categories of being within the order of creation. Differences between them may be variously expressed from time to time and place to place, and frictional differences may be transcended through love. But the distinctions themselves are, on Paul's christological model, not to be eliminated. Here one may note with approval the observation of Ben Witherington that "Paul and other New Testament authors sought to redefine, not reject, concepts of male headship and leadership in the light of Christian or biblical ideas."[41]

In conclusion, the Apostle addresses the principle of unity in diversity in at least four areas: ethnic, socioeconomic, ministerial, and sexual. He affirms that all are one in Christ and yet refuses to make Greeks into Jews, servants into masters, apostles into deacons, or, we may now add, females into males. He seeks the unity that does not sacrifice the diversity within the body of Christ. For Paul unity and equality do not exclude difference, diversity, or rank but incorporate them and express them as a many-splendored mosaic. Whenever unity or equality is interpreted as sameness we are, in Paul's eyes, on the road of illusion and frustration. This applies particularly to a current mythology that the only difference between male and female is genital.

The statements and implications of the four theological principles above, most of them scattered throughout the Pauline letters, are fundamental elements in his theology, and it is specious to nitpick through the letters seeking to trace a "development," for example, from a principle of unity to one of diversity or from a principle of equality to one of subordination, or to excise one aspect as "un-Pauline." Such a dialectical approach is destructive of any ade-

---

39. In Lk 20:34ff. Jesus teaches that the marriage relationship (not one's sexual identity) will cease in the resurrection life.

40. Eph 5:31ff. Cf. S. F. Milelic, "One Flesh". . . (Roma, 1988), 112-17.

41. B. Witherington III, *Women in the Ministry of Jesus* (Cambridge, 1984), 129. Cf. idem, "Rite and Rights for Women—Gal 3:28," *NTS* 27 (1981), 593-604.

quate understanding of Paul's thought. It is, rather, when one perceives and holds together the multifaceted dimension of the Apostle's theology that one can best appreciate its unity and wholeness.

THREE CRUCIAL TEXTS

Introduction

The above theological principles give rise to further questions when they are applied to specific issues either in Paul's congregations or in the later church. As they relate to women, two issues prominent in the mind of the church today are the role of women in ministry and a closely related question, the role of husband and wife in Christian marriage.

With regard to the role of women in the church the Apostle considers several to be his fellow ministers, specifically, Phoebe, Prisca or Priscilla, Junia, and probably Euodia and Syntyche. He calls Phoebe a διάκονος, a word he regularly uses elsewhere of Christian workers engaged in, among other things, ministries of teaching and preaching.[42] The same implications are present when he applies the term to Phoebe as a "minister" of the church at Cenchreae and commends her as a missionary worker.[43] The somewhat broader designation "coworker" (συνεργός) that is given to Prisca and to Euodia and Syntyche[44] is used of persons exercising various kinds of unspecified ministries, including teaching, preaching, and prophecy.[45]

42. For example, Rom 15:8; 1 Cor 3:5; 2 Cor 3:6; 6:4; Eph 3:7; Col 1:7, 23; 1 Thess 3:2 A; 1 Tim 4:6.

43. Rom 16:1f. "Minister" (διάκονος) here refers to a recognized and continuing status in the congregation (and in that sense a title), as it does in Phil 1:1 and 1 Tim 3:8. So C. E. B. Cranfield, *The Epistle to the Romans*, 2 vols. (Edinburgh, 1979), II, 781; F. Godet, *Epistle to the Romans* (New York, 1883), 488; O. Michel, *Der Brief an die Römer* (Göttingen, ⁵1978), 473.

44. It is not entirely clear whether Euodia and Syntyche are included under the designation "coworkers" at Phil 4:3, but it is very probable. Cf. G. F. Hawthorne, *Philippians* (Waco, 1983), 180f.

45. Rom 16:3; Phil 4:3. The term συνεργός is applied to such major as-

Paul's relatives, Andronicus and Junia, who were probably a husband and wife team like Prisca and Aquila, are described by Paul as his "fellow prisoners," as "outstanding among the apostles," and as having been "in Christ before me."[46] The last two characteristics show that they were not "apostles of Jesus Christ" but, like Epaphroditus and others, "apostles of the churches," that is, missionaries.[47] Junia was involved in ministries that brought about her imprisonment and therefore, in all likelihood, missionary activities of evangelism and preaching.

Paul's acceptance of the ministry of women is confirmed not only by his own mission-praxis but also by his recognition in 1 Cor 11 of Christian prophetesses, whose gifts of inspired speech explicitly included the teaching and building up of the congregation.[48] It is, therefore, rather puzzling to find Pauline texts that appear to place strictures on the public speaking of women in church. The most important of such texts are 1 Cor 14:34f. and 1 Tim 2:9–3:1a, passages that are also difficult to reconcile with Paul's assertion in Gal 3:28 that in Christ "there is no male and female." To

---

sociates of Paul as Titus (2 Cor 8:23), Mark (Col 4:10f.), and Silas and Timothy (Rom 16:21; 1 Thess 3:2), who exercised various gifts of inspired speech and discernment. Cf. Ellis (note 7), 6-10. In Judaism a *baraitha* in the Talmud (*Megillah* 23a) allows a woman (and a minor) to read a Sabbath scripture lesson, although she should not read the Pentateuchal lesson "out of respect for the congregation." Whether this also involved an interpretation of the passage, as in Lk 4:20f., is not stated. Cf. Tosefta, Megilla 3:11.

46. Rom 16:7. Junia is almost certainly a woman's name. Cf. Cranfield (note 43), 788. P. M. Fraser, *Lexicon of Greek Personal Names*, I (Oxford, 1987), lacks this rather rare name.

47. Rightly, Cranfield (note 43), II, 789f. Cf. 2 Cor 8:23; Phil 2:25 ("messengers" = ἀπόστολοι). If they had been "apostles of Jesus Christ," that is, had encountered and been commissioned by the risen Lord (1 Cor 9:1; 15:5-8; 1 Cor 12:12; Gal 1:15ff.), Paul could hardly have designated them "outstanding" in relation to Peter, James, and John or to the Twelve (1 Cor 15:5, 7; Gal 1:18f.; 2:9), and it would have been superfluous for him to say that they were "in Christ before me" (cf. 1 Cor 15:8). Cf. K. H. Rengstorf, "ἀπόστολος," *TDNT* 1 (1964/1933), 422f. See below, 89ff. Of course, on the Pauline criteria other women may be classed as "apostles of Jesus Christ," although with a limited commission. Cf. Mt 28:9f.; Jn 20:17f.; R. E. Brown, "Role of Women in the Fourth Gospel," *TS* 36 (1975), 691f.

48. 1 Cor 11:3-16; 14:3, 5.

attempt to resolve these questions let us look more closely at the teaching of the three passages.

1 Corinthians 14:34f.

Because of the problem it poses and because it is found after 1 Cor 14:40 in some manuscripts, 1 Cor 14:34f. is sometimes thought to be a later interpolation.[49] However, the passage is not lacking in any manuscript, is appropriate to its context, and, as we hope to show, is not inconsistent with Paul's theology. Since the Apostle's letters were in all likelihood copied and circulated among neighboring congregations from the outset,[50] to say nothing of the copy retained by Paul,[51] it is difficult if not impossible

49. For example, G. D. Fee, *The First Epistle to the Corinthians* (Grand Rapids, 1987), 699-702; H. Conzelmann, *1 Corinthians* (Philadelphia, 1975), 246. Cf. F. Lang, *Die Briefe an die Korinther* (Göttingen, 1986), 200 (probable).

50. Paul commands only that his letters be read to the congregation or Christian missioners not present in the congregation (1 Thess 5:27; cf. Ellis, note 7, 21n. = *NTS* 17 [1970-71], 451n.) or to a nearby congregation (Col 4:16; cf. 2 Thess 2:2). But in the latter instances a recopying of the letter would likely have ensued. The Corinthian letters were not sent just to one house-church congregation since 1 Corinthians presupposes more than one house-congregation (1 Cor 1:11; 16:15f.; see below, 141-45) and since 2 Corinthians (1:1) is addressed to Corinth and "the whole of Achaia." 2 Thess 2:2 (c. A.D. 51) appears to assume that copies of Paul's letters (genuine and counterfeit) might be carried to different congregations at a very early time.

51. In antiquity because, among other reasons, of the danger of damage or loss in transit an author customarily kept a copy of his correspondence, including even personal letters (cf. Cicero, *To Friends* 7.25.1), which his amanuensis made for him to retain (cf. Pliny, *Letters* 1.1; E. Randolph Richards, "The Role of the Secretary in Greco-Roman Antiquity and its Implications for the Letters of Paul," Unpublished Ph.D. dissertation, Southwestern Baptist Theological Seminary, Fort Worth, 1988, 4-10, 287). Paul's practice was probably the same since his letters were teaching-pieces to which he sometimes later referred (1 Cor 5:9; 2 Cor 7:8; 2 Thess 2:15). It is altogether possible that the later publication of Paul's collected letters was, like Cicero's (*To Atticus* 16.5, end), made from his own retained copies committed to the care of a colleague, perhaps in Ephesus or Rome (cf. 2 Tim 4:13). That partial collections, possibly with revisions by the Apostle, began during Paul's life is not unlikely (cf. 2 Pet 3:15f.), and if Papyrus 46 (c. A.D. 200) did not originally contain the Pastorals, it may represent a descendant of such a partial collection.

to suppose that a pericope found in all extant manuscripts was a later interpolation, although, given the displacement of 1 Cor 14:34f. after 14:40 and the rough seams joining it to its context, this passage may have been an inserted or marginal note in the autograph.[52] In any case it is part of the original letter and should be treated as such.[53]

The following translation offers a commonly held rendering of 1 Cor 14:34f.:

> Let the women keep silent in the churches, for it is not permitted for them to speak. But they should subordinate themselves (ὑποτασσέσθωσαν), even as the law says. If they desire to learn about something, let them ask their own husbands at home. For it is disgraceful for a woman to speak in church.

The teaching in this passage is qualified in at least four ways. First (1), the teaching is directed to married women and not to women in general. This is clearly indicated by the phrase "their own husbands" (14:35), and is supported by the fact the term γυνή may mean "wife" as well as "woman." It is also supported by the reference to "the law" (νόμος) in verse 34, which is very probably a reference to the status assigned to the wife in Gen 3:16: "Your desire shall be for your husband, and he shall rule over you."

In Paul's writings "the law," with one or two exceptions,[54] always refers to the Old Testament or teachings based on it, and elsewhere in 1 Corinthians the term uniformly has that meaning. Gen 1–3, in particular, plays an important role in the Apostle's teachings on sexual relationships and especially on the subordination of the wife to the husband.[55] Gen 3:16, which is alluded to in two Pauline passages (1 Cor 11:3-16 and 1 Tim 2:9–3:1a) that are closely related to 1 Cor 14:34f.,

---

52. See E. E. Ellis, "The Silenced Wives of Corinth (I Cor 14:34-5)," *New Testament Textual Criticism*, ed. E. J. Epp (Oxford, 1981), 213-20.

53. So E. Fascher–C. Wolff, *Der erste Brief des Paulus an die Korinther*, 2 vols. (Berlin, 1975, 1982), II, 140-43.

54. Gal 6:2; Rom 8:2; cf. 1 Cor 9:21.

55. 1 Cor 6:16 (7:10); 11:3, 7-9; Eph 5:31; 1 Tim 2:12ff. Cf. Ellis (note 6), 484f., 488, 492f.; idem, "Traditions in the Pastoral Epistles," *Early Jewish and Christian Exegesis*, ed. C. A. Evans (Decatur, 1987), 239-42.

concerns the headship of the husband and by implication the subordination of the wife. The text is used in this way in contemporary Jewish writings[56] and, while other Old Testament passages have similar connotations (cf. 1 Pet 3:5f.), Gen 3:16 is probably the passage Paul has primarily in view here.[57]

Second (2), the teaching applies only to the wives of Christians since the women are instructed to ask their husbands at home. Third (3), it may apply only to wives whose husbands were present in the service since their inquiry would presumably be about matters raised there.

Finally (4), the teaching of 1 Cor 14:34f. is probably a specific instruction to the gifted wives of the prophets whose participation in the service has been the subject of Paul's teaching in the preceding verses (14:29-33). This view of the matter is supported by several considerations.

In the immediate context Paul has encouraged prophets to speak (λαλεῖν) in the Spirit, to learn (μανθάνειν), to be silent (σιγᾶν) in deference to another's prophetic word, and severally to test (διαχρίνειν) the messages that have been given (14:29-31). Then, according to some manuscripts, he continues, "Let your wives be silent (σιγᾶν), for it is not permitted for them to speak" (λαλεῖν, 14:34 D). If the reading "your wives" is the original text (probably not) or if it is a correct interpretation of it (probably so), it is the wives of the prophets who are enjoined from "speaking." The word "to speak" is used throughout the section with reference to the exercise of spiritual gifts and, unless the clause is redundant, it should have the same meaning here.

The gifted wives of the prophets not only are enjoined from making a public inquiry (ἐπερωτάν, 14:35) into their husband's

56. Cf. Josephus, *Against Apion* 2.201 = 2.24 (25): "The wife, says [the law], is less than (χείρων) the husband in all things. Therefore, let her obey (ὑπακούειν) not for her humiliation but that she may be directed. For God gave the authority (κράτος) to the husband" (Gen 3:16). For Philo's view see above, note 23.

57. *Pace* R. P. Martin, *The Spirit and the Congregation* (Grand Rapids, 1984), 87, who supposes that "the law" in 1 Cor 14:34 refers to "Paul's own 'ruling.'"

prophetic message, but, more significantly, they are enjoined not to engage in a prophetic ministry evaluating or assessing (διακρίνειν) his message or his evaluation of another prophet's message.[58]

Any satisfactory interpretation of 1 Cor 14:34f. must explain its apparent contradiction of 1 Cor 11, where Paul recognizes Christian prophetesses, that is, women who give inspired teaching in the assembly. Several interpretations have been offered to reconcile the discrepancy. (1) 1 Cor 14:34f. is regarded by some as a later interpolation into the text. But, as we have seen above, this is very unlikely. (2) Others think that 1 Cor 11 refers to private prayer sessions of pneumatics and 1 Cor 14 to public worship where visitors might be offended by what they would consider brash and indecorous conduct.[59] On this view the restriction in 1 Cor 14 would be an application of a cultural propriety to the conduct of Christian women generally. That is, it would underscore the principle that even in the freedom of the new age the Christian continues to have obligations to the present age, even to the customs of a particular time and place.

(3) Another interpretation of 1 Cor 14 is more restricted and, I think, best supported by the context. It takes 1 Cor 14:34f. to be the application, in a particular cultural context, of an order of the present creation concerning the conduct of a Christian wife vis-à-vis her husband. Her "speaking" is regarded as a presumptuous disregard of her husband, who apparently is present and is participating in ministry. As was suggested above, her coparticipation might involve her in "testing" her husband in public, a violation not only of accepted proprieties but also of her own wifely role. It is therefore forbidden. On this understanding of the matter one may paraphrase 1 Cor 14:34 as follows:

58. On the term see above, 39f.; F. Büchsel, "διακρίνω," *TDNT* 3 (1966/1938), 946f. Cf. 1 Cor 6:5; 11:29, 31.

59. Cf. J. Calvin, *The First Epistle of Paul to the Corinthians* (Grand Rapids, 1968 [1546]), 231, 306; F. L. Godet, *Commentary on First Corinthians,* 2 vols. in 1 (Grand Rapids, 1977 [1886]), 543 = II, 115.

Prophets, let your gifted wives be silent in the assemblies.
For it is not permitted for them to speak in the interchange
   between the prophets.

The interpretation of 1 Cor 14:34-35 offered above is supported by a number of other considerations. (1) Paul elsewhere
describes a married woman as a "subject-to-a-man woman"
(ὕπανδρος γυνή, Rom 7:2). (2) He characteristically uses "submission" language in the household codes with reference to the
wife's relation to her husband and in this respect agrees with accepted tradition in Judaism and in the broader Christian mission.[60]
(3) 1 Cor 14:34f. has close linguistic affinities with 1 Tim 2:9–
3:1a, a passage also concerned with the behavior of wives, and
both pieces are probably the outworking of a common exegetical
tradition on this theme. We may now turn to that text.

1 Tim 2:9–3:1a[61]

Likewise also [I want] the women (γυναῖκας) to adorn (κοσμεῖν)
themselves in tasteful (κοσμίῳ) attire with modesty and self-
control, not with braided hair and gold jewelry or pearls or costly
dresses (ἱματισμῷ) but rather that which is proper for women pro-
fessing godliness, with good works. Let the wife (γυνή) learn in
quietness (ἡσυχίᾳ) with all submissiveness (ὑποταγῇ). I do not
permit a wife to teach (διδάσκειν) or to exercise authority over
(αὐθεντεῖν) her husband, but to be in quietness. For Adam was
first formed, then Eve.[62] And Adam was not deceived, but the
woman, having been deceived, fell into transgression.[63] But she
will be saved through childbirth if they continue in faith and love
and holiness with self-control. Faithful is the word.

This passage poses one or two preliminary problems. First,
the Pastoral epistles, and particularly 1 Timothy, have a vocabulary, idiom, and theological expression considerably different
from the other Pauline letters and for this reason have been

---

60. See above, notes 23, 55, 56.
61. For the literature and discussion cf. Gritz (note 17).
62. Gen 1:27; 2:7, 22.
63. Gen 3:6, 13; cf. 2 Cor 11:3.

ascribed by scholars in the Baur tradition to a post-Pauline period, sometimes to Pauline "disciples" teaching in his name. But as I have argued elsewhere,[64] this tradition rests on assumptions that have now been shown to be mistaken, and the letters are better understood and the differences equally well explained as letters or letter-manuals in which Paul employs a different amanuensis and uses a number of preformed traditions. Such traditions, many of them composed by Paul's associates, make up over 40 percent of 1 Timothy.

A second problem is the meaning of the term γυνή. It is not always clear whether it should be translated "wife" or "woman." In the context (2:8) the term ἀνήρ appears to mean "man" and not "husband," and on this analogy γυνή would seem to mean "woman" and not "wife." However, several considerations support the conclusion that 1 Tim 2:9–3:1a, like 1 Cor 11:3-16 and 14:34f., is the application to a church situation of a principle of the household codes and that its teaching is primarily concerned with a married woman's obligations to her husband. They are (1) the relationship of the passage to 1 Cor 14:34f. and 1 Pet 3:1-7, (2) the illustration used—Adam and Eve, and (3) the promise given to the observant woman, which is connected with childbirth.[65]

1 Tim 2:9–3:1a, 1 Cor 14:34f., and 1 Pet 3:1-7 all appear to be elaborations and/or applications of an underlying tradition, probably expositions of Genesis, on the obligations of the wife to her husband. This may best be perceived by placing portions of the three passages in parallel columns and underlining the common use of the same or cognate expressions:

64. Cf. Ellis (note 55), 237-53; idem, "Dating the New Testament," *NTS* 26 (1980), 487-502 (FT: *Communio* [Paris] 7, 1 [1982], 75-89; Revised GT: *TZ* 42 [1986], 409-30); idem, *Paul and His Recent Interpreters* (Grand Rapids, ⁵1979), 49-57 (= *EQ* 32 [1960], 151-61).

65. Cf. Euripides, *Medea* 248-51: '[Males] say that we [women] live a life free from danger. . . . I would prefer three times over to stand in the battle line [in war] than give birth [even] once" (cited in *ND* 4 [1987], 24). Gritz (note 17, 177-230) also takes 1 Tim 2:9–3:1a to refer to a married woman's obligations to her husband.

1 Cor 14:34f.	1 Tim 2:9-13	1 Pet 3:3-6
Let *the wives* be *silent* in the churches. For it is not *permitted* for them to speak, but they are to *subject themselves,* as the law says. If they wish to *learn,* let them ask *their own husbands* at home. For it is disgraceful for *a wife* to speak in church.	Likewise also [I want] *the wives* to *adorn* themselves in *tasteful* attire with modesty and self-control, not with *braided hair* and *gold jewelry* or pearls or *costly dresses, but rather . . .* with good works. Let *the wife learn* in *quietness* with all *submissiveness.* I do not *permit a wife* to teach or to exercise authority over her *husband,* but to be in *quietness.* For Adam was first formed . . .	*[Wives],* let not your *adornment* be the outward *braiding of hair,* wearing *gold jewelry,* or putting on *dresses, but rather . . . quietness* of spirit, which is *costly* in the sight of God. For thus also the holy *women* who trusted in God formerly *adorned* themselves, *subjecting themselves to their own husbands,* as Sarah obeyed Abraham . . .

A number of the italicized words above identify terms[66] and synonyms or cognate expressions[67] that are common to 1 Cor 14:34f. and 1 Tim 2:9–3:1a. Similarly, a number of italicized terms[68] and cognate expressions[69] are common to 1 Pet 3:3-6 and 1 Tim 2:9-13 and/or 1 Cor 14:34f. All three passages appeal to Genesis for scriptural support of their teaching.[70]

1 Pet 3 is part of a (partial) household code (1 Pet 2:18–3:7) stipulating the conduct of Christian servants, wives, and husbands and probably reflects the original context of a tradition underlying the three passages. The Pauline texts (as also 1 Cor 11:3-16)

66. Learn (μανθάνειν); permit (ἐπιτρέπειν); wife (γυνή); husband (ἀνήρ).

67. Quietness/silence (ἡσυχία/σιγᾶν); subjection/subject (ὑποταγή/ὑποτάσσεσθαι). Cf. 1 Tim 2:11f.; 1 Cor 14:34.

68. Gold jewelry (χρυσίον); but rather (ἀλλά); quietness (ἡσυχία); costly (πολυτελής); woman (γυνή); adorn (κοσμεῖν); husband (ἀνήρ). Cf. 1 Tim 2:9-12; 1 Pet 3:3-5.

69. Adornment/to adorn (κόσμος/κοσμεῖν); quietness/silence (ἡσυχία/σιγᾶν); dresses (ἱματισμός/ἱμάτιον); braids (ἐμπλοκή/πλέγμα). Cf. 1 Pet 3:3f.; 1 Tim 2:9, 11f.; 1 Cor 14:34.

70. Gen 1:27; 2:7, 22 (1 Tim 2:13f.); Gen 3:16 (1 Cor 14:35); Gen 18:6ff., 12 (1 Pet 3:6).

show the way in which such a household regulation has been reappropriated and *mutatis mutandis* used for the conduct of the wives in church. In particular, 1 Tim 2:9–3:1a also reveals its household-code origins in the use of a husband and wife, Adam and Eve, to ground its teaching in scripture (2:13f.). In turn, these considerations give further support to the interpretation of 1 Tim 2:15 as a reference to childbirth,[71] that is, a familial context.

In the light of these observations one may translate 1 Tim 2:12 as follows:

> I do not permit a wife
> To teach or have authority (αὐθεντεῖν)
> Over a husband.

The translation of the New Testament by Charles Williams, which pays close attention to the force of the Greek idiom and grammar, is even more pointed:

> I do not permit a married woman
> To practice teaching or domineering
> Over a husband.[72]

This understanding seems to be confirmed also in Tit 2:5, where the young wives are to be instructed to be "submissive to their own husbands." Like 1 Cor 14, 1 Tim 2 is concerned primarily with the wife's attitude toward her husband and, consequently, the way in which her marriage obligations may in turn place restrictions on the kind of ministry she may fulfill. That is, her ministry

---

71. It may be that "Paul is aiming a shaft at the false teachers" (Kelly) who forbade marriage (1 Tim 4:3). Childbearing "is not the meritorious cause of a woman's salvation; it is the sphere, being her natural duty, in which she may hope to find it." "[By it] she is trained for the kingdom of heaven" (Bernard); cf. 1 Cor 3:15 (διὰ πυρός); Gen 3:16. Cf. J. N. D. Kelly, *The Pastoral Epistles* (London, 1963), 70; J. H. Bernard, *The Pastoral Epistles* (Grand Rapids, 1980 [1899]), 49. See note 65.

72. C. B. Williams, *The New Testament in the Language of the People* (Nashville, 1986 [1937]). But see G. W. Knight III, "AYΘΕΝΤΕΩ in Reference to Women in 1 Timothy 2.12," *NTS* 30 (1984), 143-57, who argues that αὐθεντεῖν means simply "to have authority" without "any negative or pejorative overtone . . . as is . . . in the rendering 'domineer'" (154).

should always be consistent with a proper respect for and submission to her husband. But then Paul also teaches that a husband's ministry must be consistent with his obligations of love and support for his wife and children.[73] Indeed, unrestricted freedom for ministry is one of the advantages, for both male and female, that Paul sees in the single state.[74]

If 1 Cor 14 and 1 Tim 2 have been rightly understood here, they represent no theological objection whatever to the ministry of an independent single woman and pose only certain qualifications for the ministry of a married woman. There is, however, another Pauline teaching that may bear upon the ministry of women, namely, the role of overseers in the Pastoral letters.[75]

In the Pastorals the particular ministry of "oversight" or "ruling" raises a question about the role of women for at least two reasons. First, the Apostle draws a direct analogy between it and the role of the husband and father in the family:

> The bishop (ἐπίσκοπον) must . . . be the husband
>   of one wife . . .
> [And] manage (προϊστάμενον) his own house well,
> Keeping his children submissive with unruffled dignity.
> For if he does not know how to manage his own house,
> How can he take care of (ἐπιμελήσεται) the church of God?
>
> 1 Tim 3:2, 4f.

Second, this kind of ministry has been incorporated into the traditional, ordained ministry in some sectors of the church, for example, where the bishop or president has this role. If Paul teaches that the headship of the husband in the family is an abiding order for the present creation, as he clearly seems to do, then by anal-

---

73. 1 Cor 7:33; 1 Tim 5:8.

74. Cf. 1 Cor 7:32-34.

75. 1 Tim 3:2; 5:17ff.; Tit 1:5-9. Other Pauline letters refer to the same kind of ministry but with different terminology: "piloting" (κυβέρνησις, 1 Cor 12:28); "leading" (προϊστάμενοι, Rom 12:8; 1 Thess 5:12); "teaching shepherds" (οἱ ποιμένες καὶ διδάσκαλοι, Eph 4:11). See above, 37. E. Löve-stam ("Paul's Address at Miletus," *ST* 41 [1987], 1-10) has cogently argued that the role of the overseer (ἐπίσκοπος), at least in Acts 20:18-35, is based on Ezek 34 and is not so much one of authority as of shepherding care for the weak.

ogy it may be argued that his limitation of oversight or ruling to males is likewise an abiding order for that particular ministry.

However, if the ministry of oversight is not given to any one individual but is expressed corporately in a synod or presbytery or in a board of ordained elders or ordained deacons, the analogy with the patriarchal family structure would not seem to apply. Does it apply when oversight or shepherding is vested in an individual pastor or bishop? In this case two interpretations of 1 Tim 3 may be considered.

On the one hand, (1) the same analogy with the family is used for the διάκονοι or "ministers" (3:12), a role that Paul explicitly gives to a female colleague in Romans and appears to apply to women in 1 Tim 3:11.[76] That being so, he can hardly have supposed that the analogy here would exclude women from that role. It is possible, of course, that in the Pastorals the term "ministers" differs from its meaning in Paul's earlier letters. As a matter of fact, in 1 Tim 3:1b-13 the term is probably part of a preformed church regulation, perhaps in use in the church at Rome, that the Apostle has taken over.[77] Nevertheless, it is unlikely that "bishops" and "ministers" have a significance in the Pastorals that differs materially from their meaning in Phil 1:1.[78]

(2) In 1 Tim 3 the "bishops" and "ministers" are not necessarily required to be male anymore than they are required to be married. The regulation probably means only that on the assumption that overseers and ministers are married men, which should ordinarily be the case, the specified qualities are to be expected. Traditional exegesis seems to have read 1 Tim 3 too much in terms of 1 Tim 2:11-15 and, moreover, of a misreading of that foregoing regulation to prohibit the public (teaching) ministry of women generally.

---

76. Rom 16:1; 1 Tim 3:8, 11f. Cf. Kelly (note 71), 83f., who, however, limits the duties of women διάκονοι, mistakenly I think, to a ministry to women characteristic of the later order of deaconesses. While the modern Protestant "minister" is not a precise equivalent for διάκονος, the term is reasonably close and much preferable to the term "deacon." See above, 35f., 65; below, 96.

77. Ellis (note 55), 244f., 248-53. See below, 109ff.

78. See above, 40; below, 95f.

(3) In Titus 2:3 women may possibly be given a designation as "elders" (πρεσβύτιδας) that is equivalent to "bishop" or "overseer" in Tit 1:5, 7. They are to have the role of teaching (καλοδασκάλους) and certain character-qualities required of "bishops" and "ministers" in 1 Tim 3.[79] However, their specified task is training the younger women, and it is difficult to discern how formal or official the designation is. The office of "female presbyter" appears only rarely in later Christian texts.[80]

A different reading of 1 Tim 3 arises from other considerations. (1) Paul teaches elsewhere (1 Cor 11:2-16; 14:34f.; perhaps 1 Tim 2:11) that a (married) woman's role in church is to be consistent with her submissive role in the family. (2) Similarly, in 1 Tim 3:2-5 he applies to the ministry of oversight in God's "household" (3:15) the household rule on the leadership of the husband, thereby excluding women from that ministry. (3) If this was only a qualified and paradigmatic regulation to reinforce family structures and to counter an assault by an incipient Gnosticism on traditional sexual roles, it is particularly appropriate for the late twentieth century with its breakdown of family structures and an assault on them by various unisexist ideologies.

In conclusion, with regard to the ministry of ruling or oversight in the Pastorals, two interpretations are possible. (1) The Apostle makes no abiding restriction against women in principle, or (2) he reserves this ministry permanently to males, inferring it from the analogous abiding leadership role of the husband in the family. However, even if he (inferentially) restricts to males this one gift of ministry and its ordered institution, that cannot be

---

79. That is, "gifted to teach" (διδακτικός), "not addicted to wine" (πάροινος), "not a slanderer" (διάβολος); cf. also "temperate" (νηφάλιος), honorable (σέμνος), level-headed (σώφρων). Cf. 1 Tim 3:2f., 8, 11 with Tit 2:2f.

80. Cf. Acts (Martyrdom) of Matthew 28; G. W. H. Lampe, *A Patristic Greek Lexicon* (Oxford, 1961), 1131. The same problem is present in the function of Jewish women, who on rare occasions are designated ἀρχισυναγώγισσα ("female head of synagogue") or πρεσβύτερα ("female elder"). Whether the titles refer to actual (individual or corporate) roles of ruling the whole synagogue, to the leadership of women's functions, or to honorary titles or offices remains unresolved despite the valuable study of Bernadette J. Brooten, *Women Leaders in Ancient Synagogues* (Chico, CA, 1982), esp. 30-33, 54f.

grounds to deny to women the many other types of ministry and their ordered institution and ordained status in the church. That it has had this effect only underscores the need of the church to rethink its structure of ordered ministry in the light both of Paul's mission practice and of the transcultural principles in his teachings. Of course, there may be practical reasons that restrict the public ministry of a woman in a particular time and place. But it appears to be clear that in principle and practice Paul affirms their ministry. Should the church today do less?

Gal 3:28

A third crucial text for our topic is Gal 3:6-29, a commentary (midrash) on a number of Old Testament texts, mainly from Genesis.[81] It is unusual in combining the covenant promise "to Abraham and to his seed" (16 = Gen 13:15; 22:18) with an allusion to a creation typology in which the "male and female" (28 = Gen 1:27) marriage relationship of the present creation is done away.[82] The significance of Gal 3:28 may be seen best by reading it in its immediate context:

> For you are all sons of God through faith in Christ Jesus.
> For as many of you as were baptized into Christ have
>   put on (ἐνδύσασθε) Christ.
> There is neither Jew nor Greek,
> There is neither slave nor free,
> There is no "male and female" (ἄρσεν καὶ θῆλυ, Gen 1:27);

---

81. Gal 3:6-29: Opening text (6 = Gen 15:6) + Exposition (7) + Additional text (8 = Gen 12:3; 18:18) + Exposition with additional texts (10-16: 10b = Deut 27:26; 11b = Hab 2:4; 12b = Lev 18:5; 13b = Deut 21:23; 16b = Gen 22:18) + Exposition/Application (17-29) + Concluding allusion to earlier texts (29b; cf. 6, 8, 16; Gen 15:6; 18:18; 13:15). Cf. P. Borgen, *Bread from Heaven* (Leiden, 1965), 47-51.

82. On this and on the midrashic pattern cf. Ellis (note 7), 154-58, 165-69 = idem, "How the New Testament Uses the Old," *New Testament Interpretation,* ed. I. H. Marshall (Grand Rapids, 1977), 203-205, 210-12; idem, "Biblical Interpretation in the New Testament Church," *Compendia,* II, i (1988), 706-709.

For you are all one man (εἷς) in Christ Jesus.
And if you are Christ's,
Then you are Abraham's seed, heirs according to the promise.

Gal 3:26-29

These verses contain a number of words and phrases connecting them to the broader midrash[83] and indicating that the larger context is the key to understanding Gal 3:28. Specifically, they are concerned with the corporate inclusion in Christ of all races and classes and genders without distinction and thus with their equal participation in the promise given to "the seed," that is, the descendant of Abraham who is Christ. As can be seen from other Pauline texts in which these distinctions are said to be removed, the new reality in Christ Jesus is effected by the Spirit.[84] In Gal 3:28 and 1 Cor 12:13 it is termed a baptism in or by the Spirit into Christ[85] in which one "puts on" (ἐνδύειν) Christ, that is, "the new man" (Col 3:10f.).

83. For example, "sons of Abraham from faith" (Gal 3:7, 9) and "sons of God through faith" (3:26); "that the blessing of Abraham might come upon the Gentiles in Christ Jesus" (3:14) and "there is neither Jew nor Greek . . . in Christ Jesus" (3:28); "the promise of the Spirit through faith" (3:14) and "baptized [in the Spirit] into Christ" (3:27); "to one [seed of Abraham] . . . who is Christ" (3:16) and "one man in Christ Jesus and . . . the seed of Abraham" (3:28f.).

84. Rom 10:12; 1 Cor 12:13; Col 3:10f. The repetition of this theme suggests a deep-rooted motif in Paul's theology. Whether it was a preformed tradition used in the Pauline circle is less certain. Even more problematic is the idea, apparently read back from later patristic and Gnostic usage, that Gal 3:26-29 reflects a ritual at the water baptism of converts. Cf. Hippolytus, *The Apostolic Tradition* 21; among the Gnostics, the Gospel of Philip 123.21-24 (= 75.21-24). On the possible later Jewish-Christian usage cf. J. Daniélou, *The Theology of Jewish Christianity* (London, 1964), 323-32. Hippolytus (†c. A.D. 236) makes more of taking off jewelry before baptism than of disrobing and putting their clothes back on afterward; the "white robe" given to the baptized came still later. Cf. B. S. Easton, *The Apostolic Tradition of Hippolytus* (Cambridge, 1934), 93.

85. See above, pp. 30-33. That water baptism is not in view here seems evident not only from (1) the parallel passage 1 Cor 12:13, (2) Paul's own lack of interest in doing it (1 Cor 1:17), and (3) perhaps an implicit warning against overvaluing it (1 Cor 10:2), but also from (4) the absence of any reference to baptism in Galatians and (5) the emphasis in Galatians (3:2-5; 4:6, 29; 5:5, 16ff., 22, 25; 6:8), even in this segment of the letter (3:14), on the Spirit in contradistinction to any human action, even a "sacramental" action. Cf. the criticism of H. Schlier (*Der Brief an die Galater* [Göttingen, 141971], 128-31) by H. D. Betz (*Galatians* [Philadelphia, 1979], 186-89).

In Gal 3:26-29 Paul sets forth a unity of all in Christ that in certain respects transcends but does not eliminate either the diversities in clan and class or the sexual relationship of husband and wife that is constituent of the present world.[86] Supporting this understanding of the passage are three major considerations. First, Paul uses the verb "to put on" elsewhere of a corporate sphere of existence, that is, the individual's incorporation into or corporate status in Christ.[87] Second, he clarifies the thought of Gal 3:28, with respect to the Jew/Greek clause, at Eph 2:13-18, which is apparently an implicit commentary (midrash) on Isa 57:19:[88]

[Christ,] who made the two [groups] one
And broke down the dividing barrier wall . . .
That he might create (κτίσῃ) the two
Into one new man in himself,
Thus making peace.   Eph 2:14f.

It is clear that Paul is speaking here of a corporate unity "in Christ" that removes hostility between two existing groups, Jews and Gentiles (Eph 2:11f.), not the eradication of the groups nor of their distinctives. He makes this even clearer in Rom 9–11, where, in the midst of biblical expositions on past and future privileges peculiar to the Jewish nation in salvation history, he declares that on the question of salvation through faith in Messiah "there is no distinction between Jew and Greek."[89]

---

86. Cf. H. W. Beyer–P. Althaus, "Der Brief an die Galater," *Die kleinere Briefe des Apostels Paulus* (Göttingen, 1970), 31.

87. 2 Cor 5:3 B; Col 3:10. More often ἐνδύειν refers to a present process, the individual's progressive ethical actualization of the new corporate sphere of reality (Rom 13:12-14; Eph 4:24; 6:10f., 14; Col 3:12; cf. 1 Thess 5:8). For the individual's ontological actualization of "the new man" at the resurrection both ἐνδύειν and ἐπενδύειν are used (1 Cor 15:53f.; 2 Cor 5:2, 4). Cf. E. E. Ellis, "II Corinthians V.1-10 in Pauline Eschatology," *NTS* 6 (1959-60), 218f. = idem, *Interpreters* (note 64), 42f. See above, pp. 10-14.

88. In Eph 2:13-18 no commentary pattern is visible, but allusions to Isa 57:19 are fairly clear at the beginning (2:13) and close (2:17) of the section. Cf. N. A. Dahl, "Christ, Creation and the Church," *The Background of the New Testament and its Eschatology,* ed. W. D. Davies (Cambridge, 1964), 436f.

89. Rom 10:12.

A third consideration for the interpretation of Gal 3:26-29, and for the purpose of our topic the principal one, is the phrase "male and female" (ἄρσεν καὶ θῆλυ, Gal 3:28). It appears in the New Testament only here and in Jesus' biblical exposition against divorce from Gen 1:27 and Gen 2:24.[90] Since Paul knew this dominical teaching and used it to instruct his churches,[91] he probably has in mind Jesus' use of Genesis for understanding the marriage relationship. This view of the matter is strengthened (1) by the turn of phrase used and (2) by his use of these Genesis passages elsewhere. In the other clauses Paul writes "not Jew nor Greek, . . . not slave nor free"; in this one he alters the wording apparently to conform it to Gen 2:24: "not male and female." In Ephesians Paul uses Gen 2:24 explicitly of the marriage relationship,[92] and in 1 Cor 11:7 and 1 Tim 2:13, passages that as we have seen above refer to the marriage relationship, he appears to allude to Gen 1:27.

As with the other clauses in Gal 3:28 so with his declaration that in Christ "there is no male and female," the Apostle is not abolishing marriage, much less the male/female distinction. He is saying that in certain respects the conditions and attitudes of the marriage relationship "in Adam" are transcended in Christ. In Eph 5:22-31 he elaborates on the ways in which this should be true of Christian marriage. Perhaps in Gal 3:28 he also alludes to the resurrection actualization in the individual believer of the corporate "in Christ" creation when, also echoing Jesus' teaching,[93] the marriage relationship will no longer exist. Paul always thinks with a parousia perspective even where, as in Galatians, he is pursuing other theological questions.

---

90. Mt 19:3-9 = Mk 10:2-12. On form-critical grounds the Matthean passage best represents the more original formulation; cf. Ellis (note 7), 159. On disputed questions of the law Jesus did not make pronouncements in the air. He expounded scripture. This accords with his role both as a prophet and as a rabbi and, in a Jewish context, it was the only way in which his words would have received a hearing. On this and on prophecy as exegesis cf. Ellis (note 7), 147-253.

91. 1 Cor 7:10f.; cf. 1 Cor 11:7; 1 Tim 2:13. Cf. Ellis (note 6), 485-88.

92. Eph 5:31.

93. Lk 20:34f.

Hermaphroditism in Gal 3:28?

Ancient pagan mythology about a hermaphrodite origin of humanity was combined with biblical conceptions of Adam by (later) rabbinic Judaism[94] and has been ascribed, probably mistakenly, to Alexandrian Judaism[95] and even to the first-century writer Philo.[96] Some second- and third-century Gnostics embraced this kind of fantasy, both about the Aeons and about man,[97] and they may well be responsible for introducing it into (Jewish and) orthodox Christian circles. They also extended this type of speculation to the kingdom of God or spirit-world in which the hermaphrodite existence of man would be restored.[98] However, they seldom if ever

94. For example, Genesis Rabbah 8.1 (on Gen 1:26; c. A.D. 500): "When [God] created Adam, he created him hermaphrodite. . . ." Further, cf. (H. Strack and) P. Billerbeck, *Kommentar zum Neuen Testament*, 4 vols. (München, 1922-28), I, 801f. (on Mt 19:4); W. D. Davies, *Paul and Rabbinic Judaism* (London, ²1955), 53ff. Like allegorical exegesis, the rabbinic speculations about Adam were sometimes, in Davies' words, "grotesque" and doubtless in some measure tongue-in-cheek. But they served to make serious theological points, "the unity of all mankind and the duty of love" (53).

95. Mekilta Exod 12:40 (c. A.D. 200) reports a Septuagint translation of Gen 5:2 as reading, "a male with corresponding female parts he created him" (Lauterbach). But no such manuscript is extant, and it may have been a singular twisted translation by and for Gnostics, who were adept at rewriting sacred texts to serve their own interests. R. A. Baer argues that for Philo (*On the World's Creation* 134) the man of Gen 1:27 is asexual, not hermaphrodite (21). Also, "Philo's use of the categories male and female in reference to Arete, Sophia and Logos is purely functional, never ontological" (66). Cf. R. A. Baer, *Philo's Use of the Categories Male and Female* (Leiden, 1970), 21, 34, 65, 68; he also compares a number of Gnostic texts (66-75). W. A. Meeks ("The Image of the Androgyne," *HRel* 13 [1974], 185-97) surveys the pagan, Jewish, and Gnostic evidence.

96. It is thought to underlie *Questions on Genesis* I.25 (on Gen 2:21f.) and *On the World's Creation* 152. But see Baer (note 95), 38, 87f.

97. Cf. Clement of Alexandria, *Excerpta ex Theodota* 21.1f.: "The male remained in [Adam], but the entire female seed was taken from him and became Eve"; Poimandres 15f. (= *Corpus Hermeticum*, I, 15f.): "Man is hermaphrodite (ἀρρενοθῆλους) from a hermaphrodite Father." Cf. W. Foerster–R. M. Wilson, *Gnosis*, 2 vols. (Oxford, 1972, 1974), I, 224, 331, who have conveniently collected in English translation a number of the texts (indexed at II, 325).

98. For example, the Gospel of Thomas 22; 114. On 2 Clement 12:2-6 cf. K. P. Donfried, *The Setting of Second Clement in Early Christianity* (Leiden,

make an explicit reference to Gal 3:28 to promote these notions,[99] and on the very few occasions when they may allude to this passage, they give it a special twist.[100]

Certain Gnostics combined hermaphrodite speculations with promiscuous sexual intercourse,[101] and probably in the same context other Gnostics exalted homosexual practices.[102] Such cultic elements have resurfaced in modern Christian feminism in which stress upon a father/mother god[103] goes hand in hand with affirmative or permissive attitudes toward sexual promiscuity, sodomy, and lesbianism.[104]

1974), 73-77; J. B. Lightfoot, *The Apostolic Fathers,* 3 vols. in 5 (London, 1890), I, ii, 236-40.

99. Foerster (note 97) and B. Layton, *The Gnostic Scriptures* (Garden City, NY, 1987), give no index reference to Gal 3:28; there is one nonrelevant reference in E. Pagels, *The Gnostic Paul* (Philadelphia, 1975), 108.

100. For example, cf. Hippolytus, *The Refutation of all Heresies* 5.7.15 (= 5.2): "For, says [the Naasene], Attis has been emasculated, that is, he has passed over from the earthly parts of the nether world to the everlasting substance above where . . . there is neither female nor male (οὔτε θῆλυ οὔτε ἄρσεν [cf. Gal 3:28]) but a new creation [Gal 6:15; 2 Cor 5:17], a new man [Eph 2:15; 4:24], which is hermaphrodite" (ἀρσενοθῆλυς). For a few other instances cf. *Biblia Patristica,* 4 vols., ed. J. Allenbach (Paris, 1975-1982), II, 402.

101. For example, the Simonians. Cf. Hippolytus, *Refutation of all Heresies* 6.18-19.

102. For example, the Barbelites. Cf. Epiphanius, *Panarion* 26.11.8; 26.13.1.

103. For example, Hippolytus, *Refutation of all Heresies,* 5.6.4-7: The Naasene Gnostics reverence "beyond all others Man and the Son of Man. Now this man is hermaphrodite (ἀρσενοθῆλυς) and is called by them Adamas. Composed for him are hymns [such as]. . . . 'From (ἀπό) you Father and through (διά) you Mother, the two immortal names, parents of the Aeons. . . , Man of the mighty name. . . .' All [his elements] . . . have passed over and descended together into one man, Jesus. . . ." Cf. E. Pagels, "God the Father/God the Mother," *The Gnostic Gospels* (New York, 1979), 50-67 and the texts cited. For a critique cf. R. M. Frye, "Language for God and Feminist Language," *Int* 43 (1989), 45-57.

104. Cf. E. C. Bianchi and Rosemary R. Ruether, *From Machismo to Mutuality* (New York, 1976), 81-85: "Both the woman's movement and the gay movement are moving from the psychology of complementarity to the psychology of androgyny" (83f.; Ruether); Kathleen E. Corley and Karen J. Torjesen, "Sexuality, Hierarchy and Evangelicalism," *TSF Bulletin* 10.4 (1987), 23-27; Letha Scanzoni and Virginia R. Mollenkott, *Is the Homosexual My Neighbor?* (San Francisco, 1978), 122-32; somewhat similarly, S. Terrien, *Till the Heart*

It is a mistake, however, both in method and theologically to read hermaphrodite conceptions out of Gal 3:28.[105] Such ideas first appear in Christianity only in the second- and third-century Gnostic cults,[106] and they fly in the face of Paul's teachings in 1 Cor 11:7-9, 1 Cor 14:34f., Eph 5:22-33, and 1 Tim 2:13f. where the creation accounts in Genesis are used to teach not androgyny but rather the priority of the male.

More generally, Paul affirms a similar kind of unity in diversity with regard to other aspects of the new creation in Christ. In his theology of ministry in the body of Christ,[107] in the household codes,[108] and in other regulations about Christian ethics he makes abundantly clear that unity in Christ does not eliminate differences of rank in the church, in the world,[109] or in the world to come.[110]

Sings: A Biblical Theology of Manhood and Womanhood (Philadelphia, 1985), 166-69, who does not, however, adopt a hermaphrodite interpretation of Gen 1 or Gal 3:28 (207).

105. Otherwise: Meeks (note 95) who, however, rightly recognizes that in Rabbinic Judaism androgyny was never more than a special tool to solve exegetical problems. See the literature and discussion in Witherington ("Rite," note 41), Gritz (note 17), K. W. Hugghins, "The Jewish Theology of Sexuality [and] Homosexuality in Romans 1:18-32," Unpublished Ph.D. dissertation, Southwestern Baptist Theological Seminary, Fort Worth, TX, 1986, 139-79, and, more generally, Mary Hayter, *The New Eve in Christ* (Grand Rapids, 1987), 21-44.

106. To whatever extent these ideas were present in first-century Christianity, they would have belonged to the "false apostles," "false prophets," and "false teachers" whom Paul opposed. Cf. 2 Cor 11:13; 2 Pet 2:1; 1 Jn 4:1; Jude 7f.; Ellis (note 7), 104f., 107ff., 114, 231f. Against "reading back" the statements of second- to fourth-century Gnostic documents into the first century when clear first-century parallels cannot be adduced cf. R. M. Wilson, *Gnosis and the New Testament* (Philadelphia, 1968), 60-84; E. M. Yamauchi, *Pre-Christian Gnosticism* (Grand Rapids, 1973), 20-68, 170-86. Otherwise (for the Gospel of Thomas): J. M. Robinson, "From Q to the Gospel of Thomas," *Nag Hammadi, Gnosticism and Early Christianity,* ed. C. W. Hedrick (Peabody, MA, 1986), 142-64. But see C. Tuckett, "Thomas and the Synoptics," *NT* 30 (1988), 132-57.

107. 1 Cor 12:12-27, 28; 16:15f.; 1 Thess 5:12; 1 Tim 5:17; 2 Tim 2:20f.; cf. Mt 5:19. See above, pp. 7-17, 45ff.

108. Cf. Eph 5:21–6:9; Col 3:18–4:1; 1 Tim 6:1f. Cf. Ellis (note 6), 484f. See above, notes 23 and 28.

109. Rom 13:1-7; 1 Cor 16:2; 1 Tim 6:17ff.; Tit 3:1.

110. Cf. 1 Cor 3:12-14; 2 Cor 5:10; J. Héring, *The Second Epistle of Saint Paul to the Corinthians* (London, 1967), 39. See 1 Tim 6:18f.; S. B. Clark, *Man*

In the light of these and other considerations[111] Gal 3:28 cannot, on any critical reading, mean a removal of sexual differences either ontologically or in social function.

CONCLUSION

The various principles of the Pauline ethic bearing upon the role of women in the home and in the church are teachings directed to Christians. However, they may, inferentially, provide a word of wisdom for modern secular society, in particular for its attitude and response to unisexist, homosexist, and other perverse ideologies clamoring for legitimization in today's world.

Although these principles find their most elaborate New Testament exposition in the Pauline letters, they are not St. Paul's principles alone. They represent traditional ethical norms that had a wider currency in the Petrine and probably other apostolic missions.[112] By means of them Christ's Apostle mediated "the mind of Christ" (1 Cor 2:16) to the infant church and showed the way in which the biblical teaching on the relationship of the sexes could be understood and applied christologically within the Christian community. While Paul made applications that may differ widely from those made by the twentieth-century church, his teachings remain nonetheless an abiding word of God for Christ's people. For still today the church's judgment in these matters is to be discerned from the scriptures and from the Lord who has shined in

---

and Woman in Christ (Ann Arbor, MI, 1980), 137-63. In Jesus' teachings such distinctions are more common (cf. Mt 5:19; 20:23; 25:21-29; Lk 19:12-26).

111. A similar perspective prevailed elsewhere in Judaism. For Philo see above, note 28. The rabbis could also affirm the equality of all before God, although without the this-age/age-to-come salvation-history distinctions present in Gal 3:28. So Rabbi Judah ben Schalom (c. A.D. 370): "Before God, however, all are equal, women, slaves, poor and rich" (Midrash Rabbah on Exod 14:14 [15] = Beshallah 21:4). Cf. M. Bouttier, "Complexio Oppositorum: Sur les formules de I Cor XII.13; Gal III.26-28; Col III.10, 11," *NTS* 23 (1977), 12.

112. The household codes were also known (at least) to Clement, and probably to Ignatius and the author of the Didache. Cf. 1 Clement 1:3; Ignatius, *To Polycarp* 5; Didache 4:10f. See above, note 23.

our hearts to give the light of the knowledge of the glory of God in the face of Jesus Christ. To him be honor and majesty, blessing and praise, now and evermore. Amen.

– IV –

Ministry and Church Order

Church order in earliest Christianity concerns at least two matters, the regulation of the meetings of a local assembly and the constitutional patterns of the church in its various institutional manifestations. The first issue has to do with procedure, the conduct of the participants, and particularly of the leadership in the church's life and worship. The second concerns structure, the official status in the church accorded to some believers. These issues have given rise to a historical question: Did orderly procedure in a Christian congregation presuppose some ordered structure or did the congregations begin as spontaneous, charismatic meetings and only later, as problems arose, create structures, including official ministries, to meet the needs of the believing community?

CHARISM AND OFFICE

It has been observed above that for Paul ministry consists in the exercise of a charism, a gift of the Holy Spirit. However, in much of the church's history it has been identified with an office to which one is appointed or "ordained." What is the relationship between these two perceptions of ministry in the teaching of Paul? Does the Apostle even have a conception of ministry as office and, if so, what kind of office?

87

Certain Continental theologians[1] have argued that Paul regarded ministry only as the free exercise of the Spirit's gifts, unimpeded by any ecclesiastical organization. Some of them, influenced by a Hegelian philosophy of history, supposed that the Pauline "charismatic" ministry reacted with the "official" ministry of the Jerusalem church to form, in time, the episcopal structures of the second-century church (Campenhausen). Others posited a similar reaction within the Pauline churches, that is, between the charismatic ministries of apostle, prophet, and teacher and the purely local "official" ministries of bishop and deacon (Harnack). These writers rightly saw that in Paul's teaching ministry arose out of a free and sovereign gift of the Spirit, and they offered an important corrective for a church that had largely come to equate ministry with ecclesiastical appointment. But one may question whether the antithesis between charism and office, Spirit and form, that they postulated is a proper perspective from which to understand the Pauline conception or praxis.

Most of those who ministered in the congregational meetings of the Pauline churches apparently had no official status. They were recognized as gifted persons, and their ministries were accordingly received. These are the ministries that are prominent in the Apostle's discussion of the subject in 1 Cor 14, a passage to which we shall return. However, it goes too far to say that for Paul ministry is essentially only an event and that "any explicit appoint-

---

1. Beginning, apparently, with R. Sohm, *Kirchenrecht*, I (Leipzig, 1892); cf. idem, *Outlines of Church History* (London, 1895), 31-43. Cf. A. Harnack, *The Constitution and Law of the Church in the First Two Centuries* (London, 1910), 234-42; H. von Campenhausen, *Ecclesiastical Authority and Spiritual Power* (London, 1969), 81-86, 296f. The debate is conveniently summarized by U. Brockhaus, *Charisma und Amt* (Wuppertal, 1972), 1-89. Cf. also R. Banks (*Paul's Idea of Community* [Exeter, 1980], 102-12, 131-51, 194-98) and J. D. G. Dunn (*Jesus and the Spirit* [London, 1975]), who gave Sohm's theory English dress and were apparently influenced by the important earlier work of E. Schweizer, *Church Order in the New Testament* (London, 1979 [1959]). Modified, and with a sociological focus cf. also M. Y. McDonald, *The Pauline Churches* (Cambridge, 1988), 217f. For a critique of Sohm and Harnack see A. F. Zimmermann, *Die urchristliche Lehrer* (Tübingen, ²1988), 37-52; cf. T. Rendtorff, ed., *Charisma und Institution* (Gütersloh, 1985); Baumert (note 32).

ment on undertaking a form of service is impossible."[2] This dialectical opposition between charism and office appears to reflect a philosophical mind-set that is rather modern and that may be a hindrance to understanding Paul's thought. One must at least reckon with the possibility that, from the beginning of the church, charism was manifested not only as the free impulse of the Spirit but also within an ordered context.

General Considerations

Several general considerations suggest that such may well have been the case. (1) The Christian community was a recognizable entity, and simply as a social phenomenon it must have had some structure, however informal and tentative. (2) The appointment of apostles by Jesus actually preceded the coming and the gifting of the Holy Spirit.[3] The sole exception to this is Paul, who describes his own commissioning and empowerment as one event.[4] (3) An ordered ministry was traditional in first-century Judaism, in whose womb the church took form. It was clearly present in the synagogues from which the majority of the Pauline converts separated to form their Christian assemblies (ἐκκλησίαι). Moreover, (4) at Qumran a ministry of the prophetic spirit, not unlike that of the pneumatics in the Pauline community, existed within a highly structured religious community.[5]

2. Schweizer (note 1), 101 = 7k.
3. On the appointment of twelve apostles during Jesus' earthly ministry cf. 1 Cor 15:5; Mk 6:7, 30; Lk 9:1f.; E. E. Ellis, *The Gospel of Luke. Revised Edition* (Grand Rapids, [5]1987), 135ff. The Fourth Gospel, which appears either to give a proleptic word of Jesus or to have telescoped the church's Pentecost (Acts 2) and a resurrection appearance of Jesus, represents the commissioning of apostles and the endowment of the Spirit as one event (Jn 20:21f.).
4. 1 Cor 9:1; Gal 1:1, 15ff. In Acts 9:3-9, 17ff. they may also be regarded as one event, spread over several days.
5. See M. Weinfeld, *The Organizational Pattern and the Penal Code of the Qumran Sect. A Comparison with Guilds and Religious Associations of the Hellenistic-Roman Period* (Göttingen, 1986), and the literature cited; E. E. Ellis, *Prophecy and Hermeneutic* (Tübingen and Grand Rapids, 1978), 57ff. Cf. Acts 13:43; 14:1; 16:3; 17:1-10; 18:4.

The Ministry of Jesus

The picture of an "apocalyptic" Jesus wandering about Galilee proclaiming the soon end of the world gained currency in the early years of this century.[6] It contributed to the subsequent theory that the earliest followers of Jesus were not concerned about an orderly transmission of his teachings or about ecclesiastical structures[7] and that Gospel passages suggesting otherwise were to be regarded as postresurrection developments, created only after the initial fervor of the first Christian generation had subsided.

The apocalyptic Jesus was in some respects an improvement on the earlier "liberal" Jesus who "traversed Galilee in the midst of a continual feast . . . on a mule. . . , whose large black eyes, shaded by long eye-lashes, gave it an expression of gentleness"; his "preaching was impassioned and pleasing, redolent of nature and the perfume of the fields."[8] But both the liberal Jesus and the apocalyptic Jesus were quite one-sided and seriously distorted the history of Jesus' ministry.

In the last two decades it has also become increasingly clear that the Gospel traditions of Jesus' ministry were carefully formulated and transmitted in both oral and written form by apostles appointed and trained by Jesus himself.[9] While they were collated

6. J. Weiss, *Jesus' Proclamation of the Kingdom of God* (Philadelphia, 1971 [1892]); A. Schweitzer, *The Quest of the Historical Jesus* (New York, 1968 [1906]), 352-97. Cf. J. Bowman, *Which Jesus?* (Philadelphia, 1970), 25-37; W. Willis, ed., *The Kingdom of God in Twentieth-Century Interpretation* (Peabody, MA, 1987), 1-14 (Willis).

7. Cf. R. Bultmann and K. Kundsin, *Form Criticism* (New York, [2]1962 [1934]), 25-63 (Bultmann); M. Dibelius, *From Tradition to Gospel* (New York, [2]1965 [[1]1919]), 287-95; Schweizer (note 1), 20-23. But see W. Manson, *Jesus the Messiah* (London, [6]1952), 22ff. Regarding Acts cf. G. Theissen, *The First Followers of Jesus* (London, 1978), 8: In Acts 1:24ff.; 6:3f. "Luke projects into the past his ideal of a local community with collegiate government." This is an example of tailoring the evidence to fit the theory.

8. J. Ernest Renan, *Life of Jesus* (London, 1889 [1864]), 111, 97.

9. E. E. Ellis, *The Making of the New Testament Documents,* forthcoming; idem, "Gospels Criticism: . . . The State of the Art," *Das Evangelium und die Evangelien,* ed. P. Stuhlmacher (Tübingen, 1983), 27-54; idem, "New Directions in Form Criticism," *Prophecy and Hermeneutic* (note 5), 237-53; B. Gerhardsson, *The Origins of the Gospel Traditions* (Philadelphia, 1979); idem, *The*

and reworked, in some measure elaborated, and in a few instances supplemented by prophetic oracles of the risen Jesus, they—and the Gospels resting on them—represent on the whole the acts and teachings of the earthly Jesus. These developments in the research have undermined theories of the classical form criticism that large portions of the Gospels were created *de novo* after Jesus' resurrection and read back into his earthly ministry, and they have important implications for understanding the structures of the school and community of Jesus.

Jesus gathered groups of followers in both Galilee and Judea,[10] chose some as pupils (μαθηταί) and, after training them, sent out twelve and then seventy who gained and instructed converts in house groups in various towns and villages.[11] With respect to Jesus' organization of his followers the Gospels say little, but they do indicate that during the four or five years of his earthly ministry (c. A.D. 28-33)[12] the Lord did foster at least the beginnings of a distinctive religious association *(collegium),* not as formalized but probably not unlike those of the Baptist, the Pharisees, and the Qumran sect.[13] He also introduced disciplines of initiation

---

Gospel Tradition (Lund, 1986); P. H. Davids, "The Gospels and Jewish Tradition," *Gospel Perspectives I,* ed. R. T. France (Sheffield, UK, [2]1983), 75-99; H. Schürmann, "Die vorösterliche Anfänge der Logientradition," *Der historische Jesus und der kerygmatische Christus,* ed. H. Ristow (Berlin, 1961), 342-70; R. Reisner, *Jesus als Lehrer* (Tübingen, [3]1988), 422-98.

10. They sometimes met as house groups, apparently like religious associations *(collegia)* elsewhere in the Greco-Roman world, either in houses of disciples (Mk 1:29; 2:15 parr; 14:3 par; 14:14 parr; Lk 10:38) or in Jesus' own house in Capernaum (Mk 2:1; cf. Mt 17:25). See notes 5 and 13.

11. Mk 6:7, 10, 30 (διδάσκειν) + Q; Lk 10:1f.; cf. Mt 9:36–10:1.

12. His baptism was near "the fifteenth year of Tiberius Caesar" (Lk 3:1; c. A.D. 28) and his crucifixion and resurrection at Passover A.D. 33. Cf. B. Reicke, *The New Testament Era* (Philadelphia, 1968), 176-84 (A.D. 33); H. W. Hoehner, *Chronological Aspects of the Life of Christ* (Grand Rapids, [3]1979), 95-114 (A.D. 33); J. Finegan, *Handbook of Biblical Chronology* (Princeton, NJ, 1964), 300 (A.D. 30).

13. Including, for example, the identification of his followers as a "flock" (Lk 12:32 [Q]; 15:1-10; Jn 10:14ff., 27f.; Mk 14:27; Lk 22:32; cf. Jn 21:15ff.) or a church (Mt 16:18; 18:17; cf. K. L. Schmidt, "εκκλησία," *TDNT* 3 [1965/ 1938], 518-26; R. N. Flew, *Jesus and his Church* [New York, 1938], 48-136; 1 Macc 2:42; 7:12). Jesus' meals in homes were sometimes dining invitations

and conduct among his followers.[14] Accordingly the ministry of Jesus was characterized not only by charism but also by order. That the charismatic ministry of the earliest church should also take place within an ordered context would not, then, be at all surprising. Indeed, according to Acts the church at Jerusalem had from the beginning a church order similar to that found in other Jewish groups,[15] and it cannot be ruled out of any inquiry into Paul's understanding of ministry or of church order.

ORDERED MINISTRIES IN PAUL'S CHURCHES

There is evidence that, along with an unstructured or "free" charismatic ministry, an appointed ministry was also present in the Pauline churches. It had its basis and authority in the gifts of the Holy Spirit no less than that which was exercised informally, but in several respects it was distinct. Specifically it was identified with persons who were recognized to have established and continuing responsibilities and who were entitled to esteem and/or to financial support. Most prominent among this group were, of course, the apostles of Jesus Christ.[16] But others are mentioned who also fall into this category. They come into view primarily in two areas, the local administrative leadership and the missionary

---

(Mk 2:15 parr), sometimes meetings of followers (Mk 14:3 par; Lk 10:38), and the latter could have occurred also when Jesus was not in the area. Further on the role of the "house" in the early Christian mission cf. D. Lührmann, "Neutestamentliche Haustafeln und antike Ökonomie," *NTS* 27 (1981), 83-97. Its role in the mission of Jesus would not have been essentially different. See note 10.

14. That is, repentance (Mt 11:21 [Q]; 12:41 [Q]; Lk 13:3; 15:7, 10), baptism (Jn 3:22; 4:1), and instructions for prayer (Lk 11:1; Mt 6:5-13) and fasting (Mt 5:16ff.; Mk 2:18 parr).

15. Cf. Acts 6:1-6, 11, 29f. Cf. B. Reicke, "The Constitution of the Primitive Church. . . ," *The Scrolls and the New Testament,* ed. K. Stendahl (New York, 1957), 143-56; B. E. Thiering, "*Mebaqqer* and *Episkopos* in the Light of the Temple Scroll," *JBL* 100 (1981), 59-74: There are good reasons "for supposing that the earliest Christian church adopted the office of bishop [and elder] from the Essene lay communities" (74).

16. E.g., 1 Cor. 9:1-12; 2 Cor. 12:12ff. See above, 2, 38, 54; below, 116f.

enterprise. They also appear in ministries of teaching and leadership in worship.[17] Four illustrations of such ordered ministries may be offered here: (1) the collection of gifts, (2) the leadership at Philippi (3) and at Colossae, and (4) the right of some to receive pay for their ministry.

The Administration of Offerings

The collection and distribution of gifts at Philippi and at Corinth provide two examples of an ordered ministry in the Pauline churches. Collected contributions from the Philippian church were brought to Paul by "the brothers" and, on another occasion, by Epaphroditus, "the brother" and a commissioned representative (ἀπόστολος) of the church in Philippi. These contributions are called a priestly offering (λειτουργία) and a "sacrifice (θυσία) well pleasing to God."[18] That is, they are treated like the Jewish contributions, described by Philo, that were gathered in local synagogues and sent by "sacred envoys" (ἱεροπομποί) to Jerusalem to pay for sacrifices at the temple.[19] In Paul's case those who bring the gifts are termed "brothers," a title that is sometimes ascribed to coworkers of Paul who were engaged in various forms of ministry.[20] Also, persons "who distribute" and "show mercy" in this way are described in Rom 12:8 as exercising a gift of ministry. All this invites the conclusion that the appointed delegates from Philippi were engaging in an act of ministry pursuant to their charisms, charisms that were recognized and endorsed by the congregation. It is also probable that, like the synagogues, the Philippian church made the collection at their meetings.

A similar administrative function within a local church is reflected in Paul's instructions to the Corinthians about the collection for needy believers in Jerusalem, an action that he calls a min-

17. Cf. Ellis (note 5), 5-22.
18. 2 Cor 9:12; Phil 2:17, 25; 4:15-18. Apostles "of the churches" (2 Cor 8:23) are not to be identified with "apostles of Jesus Christ," who are in view in 1 Cor 9:1; 12:28; 15:5-9; Eph 4:11.
19. Philo, *Embassy to Gaius* 40 = 311ff.
20. On "the brothers" cf. Ellis (note 5), 13-22.

istry (διακονία) and a priestly service (λειτυργία).[21] In 1 Cor 16:1f. he writes as follows:

> Now concerning the collection (λογεία) for the saints. . . .
> On the first day of every week
> Let each of you in his own judgment[22] set [money] aside,
> Putting in store as he may prosper,
> That no collections be made when I come.

In this passage the term "putting in store" (θησαυρίζων) may refer either to each individual's "piggy bank" or to a deposit in a common treasury such as that which, according to Acts 5–6, existed in the Jerusalem church.[23] However, several elements in the passage show that the latter meaning is to be preferred. They are the reference to "the first day of the week," the meaning of the term "collection," and the comment on its "completion." (1) The "first day of the week" was observed by Christians from a very early time as a day of assembly,[24] and there appears to be no other reason for mentioning it here. (2) The weekly action is a "collection" equivalent to that which Paul himself would make since, if it is done, no collections (λογεῖαι) will need to be made when he arrives. This would not be the case if each individual were simply setting aside his own money at home and, indeed, (3) the word "collection" apparently never had that significance.[25] (4) The later request in 2 Cor 8 that the Corinthians "complete" the collection begun the year before would make no sense if individual believers had simply been setting aside money on their own. It assumes that

21. 2 Cor 8:4; 9:12f.; Rom 15:25f.

22. Cf. Rom 12:16; 1 Cor 3:19; 2 Cor 1:17; Gal 3:11; Eph 6:9. The phrase παρ᾽ ἑαυτῷ may also mean "at his own home" (cf. Jn 1:39) or, equivalent to a genitive case, "from his own means" (cf. Eusebius, *Demonstration of the Gospel* 9.5, middle).

23. Acts 5:1f.; 6:1f.

24. Acts 20:7. Cf. W. Rordorf, *Sunday* (London, 1968), 196-205; idem, *Liturgie, foi et vie des premiers Crétiens* (Paris, 1986), 113-22. The conjecture of A. Deissmann that the first day of the week was "pay day" in the ancient world has no evident historical basis, as he himself recognized. Cf. A. Deissmann, *Light from the Ancient East* (New York, [4]1927), 361.

25. Cf. G. Kittel, "λογεία," *TDNT* 4 (1967/1942), 282f. and the literature cited there.

certain sums had been gathered, as they had in Macedonia, and that they could be seen to fall short of the desired goal.[26] In addition to these factors, (5) the status of the local church in the Greco-Roman social order accorded a right to the group to collect money for religious purposes, and such collections are in some sources called a λογεία.[27] These aspects of the matter will be examined in the following chapter.

It is very probable, then, that the collection of gifts by Paul's churches at Philippi and at Corinth was an appointed task from the beginning. It was regarded as a ministry, and the persons involved in it were probably considered to be exercising one or another of the administrative charisms that Paul enumerates in Rom 12 and in 1 Cor 12.

Oversight and Preaching

Other instances of ordered ministries extend beyond the collection and distribution of gifts to include other forms of leadership. At least two letters of Paul, Philippians and Colossians, name specific classes of ministers as the recipients. Philippians (1:1) is addressed "to all the saints . . . with the overseers (ἐπίσκοποι) and ministers (διάκονοι)." The "overseers" or "bishops" are mentioned only here in the earlier letters of Paul, and when they appear in the later Pastoral epistles, their role appears to have been enhanced. But it is altogether probable that the term refers to persons who exercised an office, as it does in secular Greek usage, and that in the various Pauline congregations their function remained substantially the same. If so, the bishops in Philippi were not unlike those who, according to Acts 20, were present in Paul's church at Ephesus and not essentially different from those cited in the traditional regulations used in the Pastoral letters. That is, they were set apart to a continuing and recognized ministry with

26. 2 Cor 8:1-7, 10. The role of Titus in this was not to be a holder of the money, but it was surely more than urging individual believers to set aside money at home.

27. G. A. Deissmann, *Bible Studies* (Edinburgh, 1901), 142f., 219f., citing Papyrus London iii and Papyrus Paris 5. See below, 126, 129, 138.

the responsibilities of teaching and pastoral oversight.[28] They were probably equivalent to those who, in the lists of charisms, engaged in "piloting" (κυβέρνησις) and who were called "leaders" or "presiders" (οἱ προϊστάμενοι) and teaching shepherds (οἱ ποιμένες καὶ διδάσκαλοι).[29]

The second term in Phil 1:1, διάκονοι, is used frequently in the Pauline letters for those who exercise ministries of teaching and preaching.[30] The title is given to Paul and to a number of his associates who are active on a continuing basis as traveling missionaries or as coworkers in local congregations.[31] In terms of function it best corresponds to the modern designation "minister" and, in any case, it is misleading to translate it "deacon" or to equate it with that later ecclesiastical office.

In sum, at least two classes of ministers were active in the church at Philippi. They fulfilled their task in the exercise of charisms of the Holy Spirit. But they were recognized and distinguished as a group from the congregation in general and thus were set apart respectively to a continuing—though not necessarily permanent—function of oversight and of preaching. As a class they were significant enough in the life of the church to be included as addressees of Paul's letter and, as we shall see below, they were probably entitled to pay. To this extent, then, one can speak of an ordered ministry at Philippi, a ministry that was both a charism and a recognized status, that is, an office.[32] A somewhat different kind of ordered ministry in a congregation appears at Colossae.

---

28. See below, 102f. Cf. 1 Tim 3:2; Tit 1:7; Acts 20:17, 28. On the secular usage cf. H. W. Beyer, "ἐπίσκοπος," *TDNT* 2 (1964/1935), 611-14. For a possible antecedent at Qumran see above, note 15.

29. 1 Cor 12:28 (RSV: "administrators"); Rom 12:8 NAS; Eph 4:11.

30. The charism of "ministry" (διακονία) embraces these two activities. See above, 36n., on Rom 12:7-8a.

31. Rom 16:1; 1 Cor 3:5; Col 1:7; 4:7; Eph 3:7ff.

32. Cf. N. Baumert, "Charisma und Amt bei Paulus," *L'Apôtre Paul,* ed. A. Vanhoye (Leuven, 1986), 224ff.

The Role of the Brothers

The letter to the Colossians is addressed to "the holy and faithful brothers."[33] Sometimes the word "brother" may mean "fellow Christian," but in other instances it is distinguished from believers generally and has the meaning "coworker" or colleague. It is used in this way of traveling missionaries, of letter bearers, of cosenders of Paul's letters, and, as we have seen above, of those who brought gifts to Paul from the church at Philippi.[34] The same technical connotation of the term, "the brothers," in Col 1:2 is confirmed in the body of the letter.

The recipients of the letter to the Colossians are given the following instructions:

> Greet the brothers in Laodicea,
> And Nympha and the church in her house.
> When this letter is read among you,
> Have it read also in the church of the Laodiceans;
> And see that you also read the letter from Laodicea.   Col 4:15f.

The public reading of Old Testament scriptures in the synagogue service was traditional in Judaism[35] and was continued in the church.[36] The similar reading of apostolic writings in church, for which this passage provides an early illustration, not only is a striking testimony to the authority that was accorded to them but also presupposes an orderly procedure by which the reading was carried out. In the Colossian church the brothers who were the recipients of the letter performed this service. They were also to take the letter to be read at Laodicea, about ten miles to the west,

---

33. Col 1:2. Alternatively, one may translate the phrase "the saints and faithful brothers."

34. E.g., 1 Cor 16:11f.; Col 4:7ff.; Gal 1:2; 2 Cor 8:18f., 23; see above, notes 18, 20. Cf. 1 Cor 16:19f.; Phil 4:21f.

35. 2 Cor 3:14f.; Lk 4:16; Acts 13:15, 27; 15:21. In the first century a Jerusalem synagogue was dedicated "for the reading of the law and for the teaching of the commandments" (cf. E. L. Sukenik, *Ancient Synagogues in Palestine and Greece* [London, 1934], 69f.; Ellis, note 5, 245f.). Cf. Philo, *The Contemplative Life* 3; 75.

36. 1 Tim 4:13; Justin Martyr, *First Apology* 67:3. See below, 137f.

and bring back a letter Paul had sent there that it might be read in the Colossian church. In addition they are exhorted by Paul to "teach and admonish" one another, a ministry that emulates Paul's own role as a highly gifted pneumatic.[37] The brothers at Colossae were, in a word, Christian workers and, indeed more, pneumatics with gifts of teaching who had special responsibilities both as letter bearers and as appointed readers in the local worship service. Their first task agrees with the role of the brothers elsewhere in the Pauline letters;[38] the second affords a glimpse into the standing church order of an early Christian congregation.

Every letter of Paul, even those formally addressed only to "the church" or "the saints," must have been sent in the first instance to specific individuals, who then brought it before the total congregation. The letter to the Colossians sheds light on this process. That is, the letters of Paul were apparently sent to church workers with the appointed task of reading them to the congregation or congregations. If these workers themselves had gifts of teaching, as was the case at Colossae, they would doubtless exercise their charisms in the confirmation and interpretation of the Apostle's message.[39] The teaching brothers of the Colossian church show the way in which a charismatic ministry in the Pauline churches was incorporated into an organized structure of appointed tasks and ordered worship.

---

37. Col 3:16 (cf. 1:28; Rom 15:14). The parallel passage in Ephesians (5:19), which addresses the congregation as a whole rather than the leadership, significantly omits "teaching and admonishing."

38. 1 Thess 5:27; cf. Eph 3:3f.; Mk 13:14.

39. The Corinthian pneumatics apparently fulfill such a role (1 Cor 14:37), and Timothy and Titus provide examples of a similar practice at Corinth (1 Cor 4:17; 16:10f.; 2 Cor 7:13ff.; 12:18). Cf. 1 Cor 16:15-18; Col 4:7ff. The procedure follows that of the synagogue, in which the reader might also be the expositor (Lk 4:16; cf. Mk 13:14 par; but see Acts 13:15). Cf. I. Elbogen, *Der jüdische Gottesdienst in seiner geschichtlichen Entwicklung* (Hildesheim, 1967 [³1931]), 194-98; (H. L. Strack and) P. Billerbeck, *Kommentar zum Neuen Testament,* 4 vols. (München, 1922-28), IV, 171f.

Paid Ministers

A more general indication of an appointed class of ministers in Paul's churches is the right of some believers to receive remuneration for their services. It is based upon a teaching of Jesus that Paul applies, in the first instance, to himself:

> The Lord directed those who proclaim the gospel
> To get their living from the gospel.   1 Cor 9:14

In 1 Tim 5:18 the same principle appears as a citation combining an Old Testament passage with words of Jesus:[40]

> The scripture says,
> "You shall not muzzle an ox while he is threshing,"
> And "the worker (ἐργάτης) is worthy of his wages."

The "worker" embraces a large number of Paul's colleagues who are designated by several titles,[41] and their right to remuneration is alluded to in a few passages.[42] In the Galatian churches those who are taught are to "share all good things with the one who teaches." In 2 Thessalonians, which like Colossians is addressed to workers in the Christian mission, some kind of financial support, perhaps communal meals, is given to the recipients. This underlies Paul's strict rule:

> If anyone will not work, neither let him eat.   2 Thess 3:10

The rule also presupposes an administrative leadership that could enforce it.

The principle in 1 Cor 9 of the right to support is in accord with these examples. Although it is immediately concerned with the rights of apostles and other traveling missionaries, it goes beyond that to include "workers" generally. As the context shows, it

---

40. Deut 25:4; Lk 10:7.
41. Cf. Ellis (note 5), 3-17.
42. Gal 6:6; 2 Thess 3:10ff. On the addressees of 2 Thessalonians as workers in the Christian mission cf. Ellis (note 5), 19ff. If one accepts the reading "their house," found in some important manuscripts at Col 4:15, the workers in Laodicea may also follow a communal life-style.

applies to those who "sow spiritual things" (11), who "work" (13), who "proclaim the gospel" (14) and "evangelize" (16).

The most important evidence that some Christian workers received regular remuneration is Paul's own boast to the Corinthians that he has not exercised his rights in this matter. Similarly, he reminds mission workers in Thessalonica that, when he was among them, he earned his own living in order not to burden them and to give them an example to imitate.[43] His conduct is represented as exceptional, and it must have been so: it would be no grounds for boasting if his practice had been customary among the workers in the Christian mission. One does not boast that one gets out of bed in the morning.

From these observations it becomes clear that charism and office were not mutually exclusive in the churches and the mission of Paul. Office, that is, an appointed ministry for particular tasks of persons set apart and supported by the community, was a regular feature of the Pauline church.

Paul vis-à-vis the Later Church

While Paul's churches clearly had a variety of ordered ministries, in at least three important respects their church order was quite different from later forms.

(1) Charism stands out as the primary requisite for and focus of ministry in the Pauline churches, but not in the later church; the ordered forms are a vehicle to facilitate the manifestation of the gifts. The varied and rather amorphous titles given to those who function in an official or appointed capacity make this evident. The titles most often used are the brothers, coworkers (συνεργοί), those who toil, ministers (διάκονοι), and slaves (δοῦλοι). Specified titles of administrative leadership are infrequent in the burgeoning years of the Pauline mission, although they become more prominent at its close, as we shall see below.

(2) There are no priests as an appointed group in the Pauline churches. Priestly ministry (λειτυργία) is a function of all

---

43. 1 Cor 9:5f., 15; 2 Thess 3:8f.

believers, who may act corporately, as in sending "sacrificial" gifts to Paul or to Jerusalem,[44] or individually, as in "sacrificing" themselves in the service of Messiah through their varied gifts.[45] As mediators of salvation, however, certain believers do play a special role. In this sense apostles and evangelists are "priests" in that their gifts enable them to function more effectively than others as mediators of the grace of God in Christ. But unlike its function in the later church this priestly role focuses upon the word of proclamation and the hearing of faith, not upon sacramental acts.[46]

(3) Also, the Pauline letters do not refer to a ministry of "sacraments," as the Lord's Supper and water baptism later came to be called. Indeed, the Apostle mentions the administration of these ordinances only in passing. While he could baptize, he did not regard it as a significant part of his ministry and apparently did not restrict the act to any class of believers. However, since he rebukes those who gave allegiance to the one who baptized them, one may probably assume that the administration of baptism was ordinarily the function of the missionary-evangelists.[47]

Paul mentions the celebration of the Lord's Supper only in connection with the misuse of it by the Corinthians, a topic to which we shall return. In this situation he rebukes only the individuals involved and appeals to no leadership to correct the matter; so while the formula in 1 Cor 11:23ff. probably presupposes an ordered observance of the Supper, we do not know whether its administration was the specific function of an ordered ministry.[48] But the misuse of the Supper, both in Corinth and elsewhere,[49] led to a more disciplined administration of it, at least by the early years of the second century.[50] Similarly, the

44. Rom 15:16, 27.
45. Rom 12:1; 15:16; Phil 2:17.
46. See above, 32f., 79n.
47. 1 Cor 1:11-17; cf. Acts 19:4f. See below, 112f.
48. *Pace* G. Dix, "Ministry in the Early Church," *The Apostolic Ministry,* ed. K. E. Kirk (London, 1946), 247ff. Cf. 1 Cor 10:14-21; 11:20f., 27-34.
49. Cf. Jude 12.
50. Cf. Ignatius, *To the Smyrnaeans* 8:1f.; perhaps Didache 15:1 ("therefore"); 1 Clement 41:1 (if the reading "Let him give thanks" is correct).

ravages of false teachers contributed to a greater emphasis upon a more strictly prescribed administrative and teaching ministry in the Pauline churches even earlier, already in the closing years of Paul's own life. To that aspect of the matter we may now turn our attention.

CHURCH ORDER IN THE PASTORAL EPISTLES

The church order in the Pastoral epistles is in essential respects the same as that in the other Pauline letters. Ministry continues to depend upon the gifts of the Spirit and to emphasize function rather than office as such.[51] Even the "laying on of hands," employed occasionally to signify a commission to ministry or the mediation of a spiritual gift,[52] is probably not different from earlier Pauline practice. According to Acts it is employed by Paul and his circle,[53] and it may be included in the "commissioning" (χειροτονεῖν) of fellow workers in 2 Corinthians even though the express idiom does not occur there.[54] Also, appointed ministries of administration and of teaching leadership are, as we have seen,[55] a feature of Paul's mission praxis.

However, in two respects church order in the Pastorals differs considerably from that reflected in the other Pauline letters. First, the Pastorals give more attention and prominence to appointed ministries; specifically, 1 Timothy and Titus contain regulations, probably preformed pieces of tradition, that carefully detail the qualifications of the overseers and the respect due to

51. 1 Tim 4:1, 14; 2 Tim 1:6f., 14. On Tit 3:5f. see above, 31ff.

52. 1 Tim 4:14; 5:22; 2 Tim 1:6; cf. Acts 6:6; Num 27:18-23; Deut 34:9 LXX (ἐπιτίθηναι τὰς χεῖρας).

53. 2 Tim 1:6; cf. Acts 19:6.

54. 2 Cor 8:19; cf. Acts 14:23. As used for "ordination," the expression "to lay hands on" is inherited from Judaism (cf. Num 27:18-23; Tosefta, Sanhedrin 1:1; D. Daube, *The New Testament and Rabbinic Judaism* [London, 1956], 224-46). Apart from Acts, the Pastorals, and Hebrews (6:2) it is employed in this way very rarely in the Christian literature of the first and second centuries.

55. See above, 40, 95f. The teaching elders of 1 Tim 5:17 are not discernibly different from the teaching shepherds listed in Eph 4:11.

them.[56] Second and less significantly, the Pastorals introduce the term "elder" (πρεσβύτερος) as an alternative title for overseer or bishop (ἐπίσκοπος).[57] The elder represents a ministry similar to the "piloting" (1 Cor 12:28) or "presiding" (Rom 12:8) mentioned above, and he has particular affinities with the class of leadership that appears in 1 Thess 5:12f. His type of ministry is, then, observable in the other Pauline literature, but the term itself is not found there. Such differences in ecclesiastical terminology and emphasis, along with other stylistic and theological peculiarities common to the Pastorals, make it difficult to intersperse them among Paul's other epistles.[58] But do they support the nineteenth-century theory, still followed by many,[59] that assigns the letters to Paul's "disciples" writing in his name a generation or so after his death?

56. 1 Tim 3:1-13 and Tit 1:7-9. Both are relatively self-contained pieces, set off from their context. 1 Tim 3:1-13 is (1) bracketed by the "faithful saying" formula at 3:1a (whether the formula begins the section or concludes the previous one) and by the shift to the first and second persons at 3:14; (2) it may, as Harnack (note 1, 68) thought, have been inserted into a previously written section since "behave in church" (ἐν οἴκῳ θεοῦ ἀναστρέφεσθαι) at 3:15 connects better with 2:8-15; (3) "these things" (ταῦτα, 3:14) is occasionally a formula in the Pastorals introducing Paul's commentary on the preceding section, a section that sometimes is clearly a preexistent piece that is being quoted or summarized. Cf. 1 Tim 4:1-5, 6; 6:1-2b, 2c; 2 Tim 2:11-13, 14; Tit 2:11-14, 15; 1 Cor 10:6, 11. Note also 2 Tim 2:2; 3:1-5b, 5c (τούτους).

The independent character of Tit 1:7-9 is less clear; but probably a set regulation, here summarized, lies behind it. Of some two dozen substantives in the pericope, three are found only here in the New Testament and five are found in 1 Tim 3:1-13. The reference to "faithful word" (πιστοῦ λόγου) may suggest a similar background to that of the "faithful word" citations found elsewhere in the Pastorals. Cf. E. E. Ellis, "Traditions in the Pastoral Epistles," *Early Jewish and Christian Exegesis*, ed. C. A. Evans (Atlanta, 1987), 239-46.

57. 1 Tim 5:17ff. Cf. Tit 1:5 with 1:7; Acts 20:17 with 20:28. See above, 95f.

58. Otherwise: J. A. T. Robinson, *Redating the New Testament* (London, 1976), 84; B. Reicke, "Chronologie der Pastoralbriefe," *TLZ* 101 (1976), 81-94. On the differences cf. E. E. Ellis, *Paul and his Recent Interpreters* (Grand Rapids, [5]1979), 49-57.

59. For example, P. Trummer, *Die Paulustradition der Pastoralbriefe* (Frankfurt, 1978) (but see my review in *TR* 75 [1979], 459f.); L. R. Donelson, *Pseudepigraphy and Ethical Argument in the Pastoral Epistles* (Tübingen, 1986); M. Wolter, *Die Pastoralbriefe als Paulustradition* (Göttingen, 1988).

The Composition of the Pastorals

Nineteenth-century scholars, apparently rationalist and tradition-alist alike, assumed that Paul either penned his letters or dictated them word for word. On this assumption some of them, taking a few of the letters as a touchstone, rejected others—including the Pastorals — which in their view veered too far from "genuine Pauline" literary expression or theological interest and/or inter-pretation. This approach can now be seen to have been mistaken in several important respects. First, (1) Paul wrote his letters through secretaries who, in accordance with the practice of the time, exercised a variable degree of freedom in their composition. Also, (2) for a number of letters he had cosenders who exercised some influence and, in one or two instances, may have been coauthors of the letter. Consequently, vocabulary, idiom, and theo-logical expression can no longer be used in any precise way to determine the Pauline authorship of the letters ascribed to him since authorship itself is a more complex conception than scholars of the nineteenth and early twentieth century supposed. In addi-tion, (3) it has now been shown that Paul also made use of preformed literary pieces — Old Testament expositions, hymns, creedal formulas, church regulations, and oracles. The Pastorals include all of these and, indeed, have almost the appearance of a manual of such traditions with commentary on them.[60]

While much work needs to be done on the role of the secretary or amanuensis in antiquity, the basic thesis seems to have been well-

60. 1 Tim 1:9f.?; 2:11-15 (expositions); 1 Tim 3:16; 6:15f.; 2 Tim 1:9f. (hymns); 1 Tim 2:5f.; Tit 3:5ff. (creeds); 1 Tim 4:1-5; 2 Tim 3:1-5 (oracles). Such pieces are, of course, modified to fit Paul's context as they are used. Cf. Ellis (note 56), 237-53; idem, "Dating the New Testament," *NTS* 26 (1980), 497-501. Such traditions are found elsewhere, for example, in 1 Cor 2:6-16; Phil 2:6-11; 1 Cor 8:6; 11:3-12; 1 Thess 4:15ff. Cf. E. E. Ellis, "Traditions in I Corinthians," *NTS* 32 (1986), 481-502. Regarding cosenders, E. G. Selwyn (*First Epistle of St. Peter* [London, 1946], 17, 369-84) argues that Silas = Silvanus may have been the writer and joint author of 1–2 Thessalonians; E. Schweizer (*Colossians* [London, 1982], 23-26) and W. H. Ollrog (*Paulus und seine Mitarbeiter* [Neukir-chen, 1979], 214-33, 241f.) suggest that Timothy may have written Colossians on Paul's behalf.

established for the Pauline letters by Otto Roller's work, and important observations have also been made for the histories of Josephus and the letters of Pliny. The latter writings illustrate how a written source and the secretary's own contribution work together to produce a twofold effect on the vocabulary, idiom, style, and content of an author's writing. Cicero (*Letters* 295 = A, VII, 5) writes similarly of his favorite amanuensis: "[Tiro] is serviceable to me in a thousand ways . . . in every department of my business and my studies."

Although Josephus hardly mentions his literary helpers, they were, in the words of H. St.-J. Thackeray,

> no mere amanuenses, but polished his periods, occasionally took over the composition of large portions of the narrative, and hunted up, made extracts from, and translated into elegant Greek, edicts, acts, and other relevant records written in crabbed Latin characters and deposited in the imperial archives in the Roman Capitol.

These assistants, one of them something of a hack, reflect a knowledge of Greek and Latin literature scarcely attributable to Josephus and mark the narrative clearly with their distinctive phraseology and style (especially in *The Jewish War* and *Antiquities* 15-16, 17-19). Even when Josephus dictates the material, he often "dictates the general tenor of the sentence to his amanuensis who has clothed it with his own words." We should do these amanuenses justice, Thackeray concludes, "by speaking of 'Josephus and Co.' "[61]

The official correspondence between the Emperor Trajan and his governor Pliny reflects a similar situation. "It was the convention for the

---

61. H. St.-J. Thackeray, *Josephus the Man and the Historian* (New York, 1929), 100, 105, 144, cf. 100-124; idem, *Josephus* (LCL), 9 vols. (London, 1926-65), I, xv; II, xiii-xix; IV, xiv-xvii. Cf. Josephus, *Against Apion* 1.50 = 1.9. Against Thackeray it has been objected that Josephus may, with an intensive study of Greek literature, have made the literary allusions himself and may have adopted different styles in a revised edition of sections of his work (cf. R. J. H. Shutt, *Studies in Josephus* [London, 1961], 59-77, 77f.; L. H. Feldman in *Josephus* [LCL], IX, 6f.). But such objections do not really answer the many acute observations of Thackeray and are not convincing. For Cicero cf. E. S. Schuckburgh, *The Letters of Cicero,* 4 vols. (London, 1917), II, 224. For Paul cf. O. Roller, *Das Formular der paulinischen Briefe* (Stuttgart, 1933); E. Randolph Richards, "The Role of the Secretary in Greco-Roman Antiquity and its Implications for the Letters of Paul," Unpublished Ph.D. dissertation, Southwestern Baptist Theological Seminary, Fort Worth, TX, 1988.

Princeps to write to his legates as if the formulation of policy and decisions was done by himself alone" (Sherwin-White). However, Trajan did not draft the rescripts himself but assigned this to secretaries who followed a uniform chancery style while incorporating interventions and comments of the Emperor. It was the secretariat and the archives that provided both the knowledge of oriental affairs revealed in some letters and the common official vocabulary in which the letters were written. Probably Pliny's secretary (cf. *Letters* 9.36.2) is also to be credited for the same official jargon found in the governor's correspondence. Precisely what in the rescripts are the words of Trajan and what reflects the influence of his secretariat is difficult to detect and can be "determined, if at all, only by the analysis of style and content together."[62]

The works of Josephus and Pliny bear little resemblance to those of St. Paul and, as letters, the Trajan/Pliny correspondence has perhaps fewer similarities with the Pauline literature than do, say, the Senecan epistles of admonition. But Josephus and Pliny provide significant illustrations, from two quite different kinds of literature, of the influence of amanuenses and of preformed literary pieces on an author's work. It may not be too much to say that they reflect a more or less conventional role of this type of secretarial help in the latter part of the first century.

If the assistants of Josephus, Trajan, and Pliny, following the scribal practice of the day in their situations, influenced both the style and content of the writings of those authors, it is likely that Paul's amanuenses, who also incorporated preformed materials into his letters, would *mutatis mutandis* have done the same. Indeed, if Paul's helpers were—as was most likely the case—themselves persons with prophetic gifts, the Apostle would if anything have given them more freedom in shaping his compositions. However, like Josephus and Pliny, he rarely mentions their contribution (cf. Rom 16:22). Of course, Paul would have evaluated their suggestions and composition (cf. 1 Cor 14:29, 37f.) and would have been the final judge of what went out over his signature, but it is a mistake to suppose that he did not follow the secretarial usage of his day or that, like a *prima donna*, he insisted that his specific formulations be followed *verbatim et literatim*. The fact that he used preformed traditions at all shows that he did not have that kind of understanding either of writing procedures or of his apostolic inspiration and authority.

62. A. N. Sherwin-White, *The Letters of Pliny* (Oxford, 1966), 546, cf. 536-46. On the use of wax-coated writing tablets (*cerae*) cf. Pliny, *Letters* 1.6.1; Quintilian, *Instruction* 1.1.27; Juvenal, *Satires* 1.63.

When the Pauline use of cosenders, secretaries, and pre-formed material is evaluated in the light of first-century literary practice, the traditional objections to the Pauline authorship of the Pastoral epistles largely fall to the ground. Nevertheless, the Pastorals are different. They reflect the use of a different and well-trusted secretary who, on plausible grounds, has been identified with Luke.[63] They also disclose new and different theological interests and a changed working circle. They appear to use teaching pieces composed by others to a much greater degree than the earlier letters, and their creativity lies more in a bold—and eventually successful—ecclesiastical strategy than in theological interpretation. They may be properly described as a "developed Paulinism" whose splendor is "sometimes hidden" by the regulatory and mandatory motif (Barrett). Very likely they represent a later period within Paul's own mission, most appropriately located in the years following the Apostle's release from his first Roman confinement (Fee, Jeremias, Kelly).[64] What support is there for this view of the matter?

The Closing Years of Paul's Ministry

The book of Acts closes with Paul in rather mild detention with a case against him still pending. The conclusion in the middle of an episode is puzzling on any score, but it is quite intolerable if the sequel was Paul's execution. It appears to be best understood if, as Luke has already hinted, the Apostle was released, but under circumstances that were better left unadvertised.[65]

---

63. Cf. A. Strobel, "Schreiben des Lukas? Zum sprachlichen Problem der Pastoralbriefe," *NTS* 15 (1968-69), 191-210; C. F. D. Moule, "The Problem of the Pastoral Epistles: a Reappraisal," *BJRL* 47 (1965), 430-52. Somewhat differently, S. G. Wilson, *Luke and the Pastorals* (London, 1979); J. D. Quinn, "The Last Volume of Luke," *Perspectives on Luke-Acts,* ed. C. H. Talbert (Edinburgh, 1978), 62-75.

64. C. K. Barrett, *The Pastoral Epistles* (Oxford, 1963), 32ff.; J. Jeremias, *Die Pastoralbriefe* (Göttingen, [8]1963), 2f.; J. N. D. Kelly, *The Pastoral Epistles* (London, [4]1978), 33f.; G. Fee, *1-2 Timothy, Titus* (New York, 1984), xviii.

65. Acts 26:32. The completion of two years (Acts 28:30) without trial may, under later Roman law, imply a release. But see A. N. Sherwin-White,

Second-century documents state that Paul departed from Rome to Spain.[66] A more important witness, Clement of Rome,[67] a younger contemporary of Paul, wrote in a similar manner within a few years or at most three decades of the Apostle's death:

[Paul] was a herald both in the East and in the West. . . .
After he taught righteousness to all the world
And came to the extreme limits of the West
(τὸ τέρμα τῆς δύσεως)
And gave testimony before the presiding magistrates,
He thus departed the world. . . .   1 Clement 5:6f.

For a resident of Rome "the extreme limits of the West" (or "the West") could hardly designate the capital of the Empire. Since similar phrases were used of the region of Spain around Gades, the modern Cadiz,[68] Clement's comment is strong evidence, as both J. B. Lightfoot and A. von Harnack argued, that Paul fulfilled his stated goal of a mission to Spain, and it is fairly probable that Acts 1:8 also alludes to it.[69] This presupposes his release from

---

Roman Society and Roman Law in the New Testament (Oxford, 1963), 108-19. If Luke wrote before the Neronian persecution (A.D. 65), Paul's release may still have been pending or Luke may not have known of it. If during the persecution (A.D. 65-68), he would probably have wished to conceal Paul's release in order to protect the magistrate who effected it.

66. The Muratorian Canon (c. A.D. 180) and Acts of Peter (c. A.D. 185) 1-3; 6.

67. 1 Clement 5:5-7. As verse 6 shows, the list of Paul's accomplishments and sufferings is not in chronological order. So his travel to "the extreme limits of the West" is not necessarily synchronous with his "testimony before the magistrates."

68. Philostratus, *Life of Apollonius* 5.4: "the extreme limits of Europe" (τὸ τῆς Εὐρώπης τέρμα); Strabo, *Geography* 3.1.4: "the most westerly point not only of Europe but also of the whole inhabited world"; cf. 1.1.8; 3.1.8, "the ends of the earth" (ἐσχάτη ἱδρυμένη τῆς γῆς), with Acts 1:8 (ἐσχάτου τῆς γῆς), which has geographical and not merely racial connotations and may also allude to Paul's mission to Spain (notwithstanding Acts 13:47 = Isa 49:6). Cf. Diodorus Siculus, *History* 25.10.1; Pliny, *Natural History* 3.1.3.

69. Rom 15:28. On Acts 1:8 see note 68. Cf. J. B. Lightfoot, *The Apostolic Fathers*, 3 vols. in 5 (London, 1890), I, i, 30f.; A. Harnack, *Geschichte der altchristlichen Literatur*, 4 vols. (Leipzig, 1958 [1893-1904]), II *(Chronologie)*, i, 239f. In good weather Gades was a seven-day passage from Rome (cf. M. P.

Roman confinement and provides a fitting occasion for the writing of the Pastoral epistles.

During his ministry of three decades or so, Paul pursued his calling from three or four major bases of operation: Antioch, Ephesus, (Caesarea), and Rome.[70] In each place he had, in part, different coworkers and utilized, in part, their distinctive literary teaching-pieces. At Rome, and perhaps already in Caesarea, Paul apparently found traditions with an idiom and emphasis on church order akin to the formally structured ministries of the Jerusalem church.[71] In the Pastoral letters he appears to have incorporated them into his instructions to his coworkers and to the churches

---

Charlesworth, *Trade Routes and Commerce of the Roman Empire* [Chicago, 1974, [2]1926], 155). If 2 Tim 4:10 refers to Gaul, as J. B. Lightfoot thought "fairly probable," it confirms the post–Acts 28 setting of the Pastoral letters. Cf. J. B. Lightfoot, *Essays on Supernatural Religion* (London, 1893), 251; idem, *Biblical Essays* (London, 1893), 432.

70. His probable activities in Gades (1 Clement 5:7), like those in Tarsus (cf. Gal 1:21; Acts 11:25), are unknown to us. But a post–Acts 28 ministry in the East does appear in traditions used in the Acts of Paul (c. A.D. 185); cf. W. Rordorf, "Nochmals: Paulusakten und Pastoralbriefe," *Tradition and Interpretation in the New Testament,* ed. G. F. Hawthorne with Otto Betz (Grand Rapids and Tübingen, 1987), 319-27.

71. On the influence of the mission of the Jerusalem church and, specifically, of Peter and Mark upon Christianity at Rome, cf. Acts 2:10; 1 Pet 5:13; 1 Clem 5:4-7; Ignatius, *To the Romans* 4:3; Papias *apud* Eusebius, *HE* 3.39.15ff.; O. Cullmann, *Peter* (New York, 1958), 106-12 (on Rom 15:20; Gal 2:9); Lightfoot, *Fathers* (note 69), I, ii, 494 (re Papias); S. G. F. Brandon, *The Fall of Jerusalem and the Christian Church* (London, [2]1957), 145-48; Ellis (note 5), 90f., 108f. (re the presence in Rome of both Jacobean and judaizing factions of Hebraist Christians); L. W. Barnard, *Studies in Church History and Patristics* (Thessaloniki, 1978), 149-54.

On the term "elder" (1 Tim 5:17ff.) cf. Acts 11:30; 15:2ff., 6, 22f.; 16:4; 21:18; Jas 5:14. The designation "elders" in Acts 14:23 and 20:17 may well be Luke's alteration of a Pauline term, say, "overseers" (Phil 1:1; cf. Acts 20:28) to the usage of his (Roman) audience. On the formula "faithful is the word" (1 Tim 3:1) cf. Ellis (note 56), 239-42. The support of widows in 1 Tim 5:3-7 is another instance in which Paul gives more specific regulations for a group that had, on Jewish precedents, doubtless been the object of care and probably had fulfilled a corresponding role of service in Pauline congregations from the beginning. Cf. 1 Cor 7:8, 39f.; Gal 2:10; 2 Thess 3:10. Further, cf. Deut 16:10f.; 2 Macc 3:10; 8:28; Acts 6:1; 9:36-39.

under their charge. To discover why he did so we must consider, with some historical imagination, both the church problems presented in the Pastorals and the praxis of the Roman church as it is reflected in the traditions that Paul used to address those problems.

Upon his release from detention in Rome Paul completed his goal of a mission to Spain. In keeping with his earlier missionary strategy he sought to establish a church in Gades, the commercial hub of the western reaches of the Empire and a one-week voyage from Rome. While he was there or after he returned to the East, he received grave news from coworkers in his churches on the Aegean coasts and islands. Although they have grown in numbers, they have been increasingly infiltrated by false teachers.[72] They suffer from defections, even among former colleagues,[73] and some apparently are almost in a state of collapse.[74] How is Paul to respond to this crisis?

Earlier the Apostle addressed a letter to an individual congregation or city and sent a colleague to explain and apply its teachings.[75] In the Pastorals he addressed individual colleagues who would in turn impart his instructions to congregations in various places under their charge. At the same time these letters served both as personal communications with Timothy and Titus and as apostolic authorizations for the injunctions they were directed to give.[76]

The change of literary practice was anticipated previously in Paul's circular letters to the Colossians and Laodiceans, and probably to the Ephesians and Romans.[77] It was apparently dic-

---

72. 1 Tim 1:3-7; 4:1-3; 6:20; Tit 1:10-16; 3:9ff.; 2 Tim 3:1-9; 4:3f.

73. 1 Tim 1:18f.; 2 Tim 1:15-18; 2:17f.; cf. 4:10, 14f.

74. Tit 1:5: "Set right the things that remain." The task is not to evangelize but to reorganize "city by city" churches that have been ravaged by an opposing mission (1:10-16). Cf. Ellis (note 5), 113ff.

75. 1 Cor 4:17 (Timothy); 2 Cor 7:6, 12f. (Titus); Eph 6:21 (Tychicus); Col 4:7f. (Tychicus); Phil 2:25 (Epaphroditus).

76. 1 Tim 1:3; 2:1, 8; 4:6, 11; 6:2.

77. Cf. Col 4:16; T. W. Manson, "St. Paul's Letter to the Romans—and Others," *Studies in the Gospels and Epistles* (Manchester, 1962), 225-41, though one need not suppose that Rom 16 belonged in the copy sent to Ephesus.

tated by at least two factors. (1) Between the mid-fifties and the mid-sixties the rapid expansion of the Apostle's mission in the Aegean basin made it impractical for him to visit or even to write each congregation individually. Even in the mid-fifties his letters to Corinth had to suffice for numbers of congregations in the province of Achaea (1 Cor 1:1; 2 Cor 1:1). (2) During the same period his various Aegean churches were manifesting similar problems, one of which was a rather loosely structured ministry that made them an easy mark for false teachers.[78] The common need could best be met not by many separate letters but by a common response to all. For this purpose, Paul puts into the hands of his most trusted coworkers, Timothy in the regions around Ephesus and Titus in Crete, a vade mecum including special regulations on church order to use in teaching his churches. The regulations appear to be largely if not totally preformed traditions that Paul has incorporated into the letters.[79] Where did he derive these precise regulations for ministry that he has never used before?

The church at Rome was known to have a leadership richly endowed with spiritual gifts, which doubtless included inspired "prophets and teachers" able to formulate and define qualifications for administrative and teaching ministries.[80] It had recently been, for two years or more, Paul's base of operations. Probably it was the Roman colleagues who provided the Apostle with the teaching pieces on church order that he employed in the Pastoral letters to restore and strengthen his churches in the East. If so, one may discern already in the closing years of the life of Paul the incipient influence of the Roman church on the life of the church at large, an influence that in future years was to shape decisively for both good and ill the form and thought of the Christian faith.

78. Cf. Ellis (note 5), 113ff. But see G. D. Fee, "Reflections on Church Order in the Pastoral Epistles. . . ," *JETS* 28 (1985), 141-51.

79. See above, notes 56 and 60.

80. Rom 15:14; cf. 1:8 with 1:11f. where "faith" is manifested in "spiritual" charisms that "strengthen" and "encourage," characteristics of prophetic-type ministries. Cf. Ellis (note 5), 26.

THE REGULATION OF WORSHIP

The relatively lax church order at the meetings of some Pauline congregations becomes apparent rather quickly at Corinth, a church richly endowed with spiritual gifts (1 Cor 1:5ff.). The most detailed snapshot of the problem it posed and Paul's response to it is found in 1 Cor 11 and 14. The picture is one of almost carefree abandon, occasioned, it seems, by exuberant ill-mannered charismatic congregations. It reflects a spiritual animation and power that the Apostle clearly recognizes to be from the Holy Spirit. Yet he does not hesitate to criticize the Corinthian practices and to give instructions, a kind of "order of worship," to modify them. As he does later and more broadly in the Pastoral epistles, Paul here clarifies and tightens the regulation of worship in order to meet problems that have arisen in the churches.

The Apostle is particularly concerned with two glaring defects in their worship, its egocentrism and its lack of order and of social decencies. He regards these defects not as mere matters of cultural taste or custom but as the result of ethical and doctrinal error. To correct them he lays down regulations in two areas, the conduct of the Lord's Supper and the use of certain spiritual gifts.

The Lord's Supper

Apparently in accordance with the general practice of the early church, the Corinthians observed the Lord's Supper with a communal meal. In their case the meal seems to have preceded the institutional rite of bread and wine,[81] and it became the occasion for abuse:

> For in eating
> Each one goes ahead with his own supper,
> And one is hungry and another is drunk.   1 Cor 11:21

To correct this disgraceful situation, the Apostle prescribes that all

---

81. A particular liturgical act is implied in 1 Cor 10:16f. and 11:24f. ("do this"). If the meal preceded it, the Corinthians' conduct is more easily accounted for.

are to "wait for one another," that is, to make the observance a truly communal affair. He also directs that "if anyone is hungry, let him eat at home," that is, one is not to treat the Lord's Supper as an ordinary meal.[82] The regulations are imposed to correct an abuse in the practices of his congregations. But they also initiate, quite unintentionally no doubt, a process that in time will eliminate the meal altogether from the observance of the Supper. Unfortunately, this result will also minimize for the future church the joyful aspects of the service that center on the meal, that is, the believers' present communion with one another and with the risen Lord and their anticipation of the messianic banquet at the second coming of the Lord.

Ministries of inspired speech are the subject of 1 Cor 14. They arose out of "spiritual" gifts (πνευματικά) that Paul identified with the "greater" gifts[83] and that were prominent in the congregational meetings at Corinth. Because they were being misused, the Apostle set out certain principles to govern the exercise (especially) of the gifts of tongues (γλῶσσαι) and of prophecy at the worship service.

The Gift of Tongues

The gift of speaking "in strange languages (ἕτεραι γλῶσσαι) as the Spirit was giving them to utter" appears explicitly in the New Testament only in the book of Acts and in 1 Corinthians.[84] But it is probably to be inferred in one or two other New Testament passages and is witnessed in the patristic period, sporadically in later church history, and most notably in the modern charismatic movement.[85]

---

82. 1 Cor 11:20f., 33f.

83. Cf. 1 Cor 14:1 with 12:31; Ellis (note 5), 23-44.

84. Acts 2:3, 4, 7; 10:46; 19:6; 1 Cor 12:10, 28, 30; 13:1, 8; 14:2, 4ff., 13f., 18f., 22f., 39; cf. Mk 16:17.

85. Rom 8:26 (Mk 16:17); Irenaeus, *Against Heresies* 5.6.1; Tertullian, *Against Marcion* 5.8.12; Origen, *Against Celsus* 7.9, end. Cf. C. E. Hummel, *Fire in the Fireplace: Contemporary Charismatic Renewal* (Downers Grove, IL, 1978), 59f., 193; H. N. Malony and A. A. Lovekin, *Glossolalia* (New York, 1985), and the literature cited.

Acts 2 describes a phenomenon of *glossolalia* that in essential respects is no different from that in 1 Cor 12–14. We may note the following similarities: First, in Acts some think that the speakers are drunk, essentially the same reaction that Paul anticipates in Corinth. Luke apparently regarded these people as typical since Peter addresses his sermon to them.[86] Some others understand the "tongues" that are being spoken. They are foreign Jews attending the feast, or perhaps residing in Jerusalem, who are astounded to hear Galileans praising God in the foreigners' own native language. In 1 Corinthians also Paul identifies the phenomenon as "the languages of men."[87] But he ignores the possibility—a rare thing even in Acts[88]—that someone might understand a particular message in *glossolalia,* for it would in any case be exceptional and therefore irrelevant to his argument.

Second, both Acts and 1 Corinthians present *glossolalia* as a form of prophecy. Acts 2:16f. identifies it as prophecy, presumably (since Acts 19:6 distinguishes it from prophecy) on the assumption that the message is understood by the hearers. 1 Corinthians likewise attributes to it the content of prophecy, that is, divine mysteries, and equates it with prophecy when it is interpreted in understandable speech.[89] Third, the joyful and unrestrained practice in Corinth agrees with the picture in Acts except that in Acts the gift accompanies the "baptism," that is, the initial coming of the Spirit, and in Corinthians it is manifested subsequently by believers in church. It is precisely this uninhibited practice of tongues that Paul is concerned to regulate.

In 1 Cor 12–14 the nature of *glossolalia* in the early church is further clarified. It is a gift of the Holy Spirit, and as such is not

86. Acts 2:13, 15; cf. 1 Cor 14:23: "Will they not say you are mad?"; E. E. Ellis, "Gift of Tongues," *IDBS,* 908f.

87. As well as "of angels." Cf. 1 Cor 13:1; Acts 2:11.

88. It is mentioned only of the Pentecost event, where it was apparently remembered, and picked up by Luke, because of its remarkable impact on the spread of the Christian mission. In Acts 10:46 "speaking in tongues" and "extolling God" are separate phenomena; in Acts 19:6 the "prophecy" is probably the interpretation of tongues as it is in 1 Corinthians (cf. 1 Cor 13:2 with 14:2, 27).

89. Acts 2:11, 17; 1 Cor 14:5; cf. 14:2 with 13:2; Rom 16:25f.; Eph 3:3ff.

to be identified with "baptism in the Spirit." It is not given to all believers. For when Paul asks, "All do not speak in tongues, do they?" the expected answer in the Greek text is "No."[90] With this gift one mediates the message of the Spirit through one's tongue while one's mind is left in abeyance and without understanding. Therefore, the speaker in tongues must "pray to interpret,"[91] and because his mind is not ordinarily privy to the meaning of the message, the use of the gift in public worship is subjected to strict regulation.

Persons manifesting *glossolalia* in public worship, Paul directs, must be limited to two or three, speaking in order, and with a subsequent "interpretation" in the common language. Otherwise they must be silent.[92] What is the significance of this instruction? First of all, it assumes that the tongues speaker, like the prophet, can restrain the gift at will so that there is no excuse for an uncontrolled display. It also affirms the ministry of tongues even while regulating its public use. The use of tongues is not to be forbidden, and it is included among the "spiritual" gifts of inspired speech, prophetic-type gifts that are to be "earnestly desired" and that are designated as the "greater gifts."[93] Significantly, it is a gift much used by the Apostle, and he can hardly have regarded it as a "consolation prize" for immature Christians.[94]

The restrictions placed upon the manifestation of tongues reflect, then, not a depreciation of the gift but rather Paul's understanding of the purpose of the gifts and of the nature of public worship. They are justified by the importance of order in worship. Everything is to be done "decently and in order" and "for upbuilding" the hearers. This is proper because "God is not the God of confusion," and his Spirit impels no one to speak in a disruptive way.[95]

---

90. 1 Cor 12:30. See above, 36, 45ff.

91. 1 Cor 14:13f. The argument that the speaker must understand since he is edified (14:4) wrongly assumes that edification comes only through the reason.

92. 1 Cor 14:27f., 32.

93. Cf. 1 Cor 14:1 with 12:31.

94. 1 Cor 14:18.

95. 1 Cor 14:40, 26, 32f.

Indeed, as we have seen earlier,[96] Paul regards the unity and the benefit of the body, the whole community of believers, as the primary purpose of the gifts of ministry.

The Gift of Prophecy

The restrictions placed upon the exercise of prophecy in the Pauline church are similar to those placed upon the use of tongues. Prophets are also to speak in turn and to "be silent" or yield the floor when another has a revelation (ἀποκαλύπτειν) so that all those through whom God will speak will be able to participate.[97] Likewise, they are able to control the exercise of their ministry, no less than the speakers in tongues, for

> The spirits of the prophets
> Subject themselves to the prophets.   1 Cor 14:32

These prophetic spirits appear to be, in Paul's view, angels who mediate the divine messages and assist the prophets in their ministry.[98]

Moreover, the prophets are to subject their messages to the evaluation or "discernment" of other pneumatics, the community of gifted persons who are apparently to determine the extent of the "word of God" in a prophet's message.[99] The prophet, then, is not to be the final judge of his own message. Paul, as an apostle, will not let his prophetic teaching be bound by this regulation and insists that

> If anyone thinks he is a prophet or a pneumatic,
> Let him acknowledge
> That the things I am writing to you
> Are the command of the Lord.
> If anyone does not recognize this,
> He is not recognized.   1 Cor 14:37f.

---

96. See above, 45ff.
97. 1 Cor 14:29ff.
98. Cf. 1 Cor 5:4; 13:1; 14:12; Heb 1:14; Ellis (note 5), 36-44.
99. 1 Cor 14:29. See above, 39f.

With this word the Apostle draws a distinction between the authority of the ministry of the apostle and that of the prophet.[100]

Although prophecy is to be regulated in public worship, it is nevertheless given priority over speaking in tongues. It is an inspired message in the language of the hearers, and in content it is intended for their "upbuilding, exhortation, and comfort."[101] Furthermore, in a larger sense prophecy in Paul's churches also appears to encompass a divine revelation, a knowledge of the mysteries of salvation, and teaching.[102] It is therefore a much broader and more useful ministry for public worship than "prediction," the strict meaning of prophecy as it is popularly conceived today.

In 1 Cor 11 and in 1 Cor 14:34f. special regulations are also laid down for the prophetic ministry of women. But they have been considered in the preceding chapter and need not detain us here.

IMPLICATIONS FOR THE CHURCH TODAY

The remarkable impact of the charismatic movement on the contemporary church—Roman Catholic and Protestant—requires the modern Christian to relate the New Testament gifts of prophecy and tongues, no less than the gifts of evangelism or teaching or preaching, to the current ministry and order of the church. The Christian theologian does his work under the third article of the Apostles' Creed: "I believe in the Holy Spirit." He presumes, therefore, not only the divine origin of the gifts of ministry but also a continuity between that activity of the Holy Spirit in the New Testament church and his work in the church today.

But how is one to tell whether a charism is not just a natural talent or, particularly with a gift as strange and nonrational as speaking in tongues, a psychological or even a demonic aberration? The problem is real, but it applies equally to other gifts of ministry. In evangelism one must distinguish the pseudoministers, the Elmer Gantrys, from the Billy Grahams, and in ordination (or

100. Cf. 1 Cor 14:29 (διακρίνειν) with 9:1-3 (ἀνακρίνειν).
101. 1 Cor 14:3.
102. Cf. 1 Cor 14:6 with 14:25f., 30f.

117

in choosing a pastor) a church may have to discern the endowed candidate from the merely professional. In evaluating the gifts of prophecy and of tongues the same task of discrimination is required. In the view of Paul, it involves "spiritual discernment,"[103] itself a gift of the Spirit, but other more objective criteria may also be applied. The Christian character and ethics of the charismatic are tests that are as significant today as they were for the church at Corinth. Also essential is a christocentric message that agrees with the fundamentals of apostolic teaching.

On the other hand, the emotionally exalted or ecstatic state that is often associated with prophecy and tongues is a less reliable guide. In a sermon on *glossolalia* C. S. Lewis[104] cited the following passage from *Samuel Pepys' Diary* to illustrate how quite different stimuli might produce similar symptoms:

> With my wife to the King's House to see the Virgin Martyr and it is mighty pleasant. . . . But that which did please me beyond anything in the whole world was the wind musick when the angel comes down, which is so sweet that it ravaged me and, indeed, in a word, did wrap up my soul so that it made me really sick, just as I have formerly been when in love with my wife . . . and makes me resolve to practice wind musick and make my wife do the like. (February 27, 1668).[105]

Pepys records here an "internal sensation accompanying intense aesthetic delight [that] was indistinguishable from the sensation accompanying two other experiences, that of being in love and that of being, say, in a rough channel crossing." In applying this to *glossolalia* Lewis makes the point that, to the observer, the holy phenomenon may be indistinguishable from hysteria. And they may be "in a sense exactly the same phenomenon, just as the very

103. See above, 39f.
104. C. S. Lewis, "Transposition," *The Weight of Glory and other Addresses* (New York, 1949), 19f., 25f. In England the book was published under the title *Transposition.* Cf. the discussion in Malony and Lovekin (note 85), 249-53, 261f.
105. Cf. *The Diary of Samuel Pepys,* ed. R. C. Latham, 9 vols. (London, 1970-76), IX, 93f. I have followed Lewis's rendering.

same sensation came to Pepys in love, in the enjoyment of music, and in sickness."

The immediate physical and emotional "symptoms" of prophecy or tongues do not disclose to the onlooker whether the underlying stimulus is psychological or divine. If this is so, hasty or blanket judgments are hardly appropriate, particularly in the case of speaking in tongues where such judgments have often been made. Participants in the charismatic movement may tend to assume, uncritically, that all tongues-speaking is from the Holy Spirit. Christians outside the movement may be inclined to ascribe the total phenomenon to psychological causes. Some of the latter, depending on linguistic analysis that shows a lack of "language structure" in certain tongues-speaking, have concluded that such "gibberish" could not be a divine message. But then one must ask whether the "tongues of angels" would be subject to such analysis or whether repetitive vocables are to be excluded from meaningful speech.[106] If so, one wonders how such an analysis would evaluate some of the language in Handel's "Hallelujah Chorus." Or to use another analogy, an individual speaker in tongues may be like an individual instrument in a symphony. The trombone section may be horribly repetitious but nonetheless a meaningful part of a greater whole. Linguistic analysis of tongues is perhaps not unlike a photograph of a vision. The results are limited to the capacities of the instruments that are used.

The Apostle offers better criteria for distinguishing divine from emotional, pathological, or demonic phenomena. As we have seen above, he judges the charisms in terms of the effects that accompany them and in terms of the spiritual power and the character and ethics of those who manifest the charisms.[107] Can the church find a better yardstick to judge the charismatic phenomena in its midst today and to regulate its church order accordingly?

---

106. 1 Cor 13:1. Cf. Malony and Lovekin (note 85), 26-38, 254f. and the literature cited. Cf. also Hummel (note 85); Ellis (note 86), 909.
107. Cf. 1 Cor 3:1-3; 4:18ff.; 5:1f.; 12:3; 13:1. See above, 51f.

CONCLUSION

The Pauline churches, as they are observed through the letters of Paul, recognized the essence of ministry to be in the ever-renewed gifting of the Spirit, and in their worship services they were led primarily by charismatics who had no official status. However, they also set aside—apparently from the beginning—certain of the gifted believers to appointed tasks of evangelism, teaching, and administration. In the final years of Paul's life they gave more prominence to such ordered ministries, a prominence that is reflected in the Pastoral epistles.[108]

The difference between ministry in the Pauline churches and that in the later church was not that the latter was ordered and the former was charismatic. The primary difference appears to have been, rather, the manner in which charism and order were related to one another. It manifested itself in at least three ways.

First, the Apostle gave priority to the charismatic basis of ministry while the later church came more and more to stress the ordered appointment. For Paul, the manifestation of charisms was the prerequisite for appointment while too often in the later church the appointment, that is, ordination, was simply assumed to convey *ex opere operato* a charism of the Spirit. Charism was subordinated to ecclesiastical office and at length came to be viewed as the property of the office.

Second, the Pauline churches gave full expression to the ministry of all gifted persons in the congregation while the later church increasingly restricted the authority and exercise of ministry, at least "of Word and sacraments," to those who had an ordained, official status. Thus, the variety of ministries that one encounters in the Apostle's congregations was reduced to the three or four offices that are traditional in most of Christendom.

Third, the apostolic practice combined in the Lord's Supper both the joyful aspect of a communal meal anticipating the

108. There is an interesting parallel in the missionary-evangelist John Wesley (1703-91), who in his later years imposed an episcopal structure to meet the needs of American Methodists.

parousia of Messiah and the renewed identification of the believer and community with the crucified Lord. The later church came to focus almost exclusively on the Lord's death. And it removed the administration of the sacraments, together with the ministries of the Word, from a congregational context to the exclusive control of a clerical and priestly class.

These changes in church order were made with good intentions and no doubt served to protect the congregations from various kinds of bad influences. But they also carried their own defects into the institutional structure of the Christian faith. That this transformation of ministry represented in many ways a loss to the church is, I think, self-evident.

How the church can restructure its ordered ministries and its worship services to retrieve this loss is not the subject of this book. Paul's churches are not our churches, and his times are not our times. But orderly changes that give more recognition in the institutional structures to the variety of gifts and gifted persons, which the risen Christ imparted and continues to impart to his church, will better reflect the teaching of Christ's Apostle and can only bring the blessing of him who loved the church and gave himself up for her, that she might be holy and without blemish. To him be blessing and honor and glory and power forever and ever. Amen.

– V –

Pauline Christianity and the World Order

It has been observed earlier that, in the teaching of Paul, the kingdom of God both in its present and in its future aspects was distinguished from this age. As a public and universal manifestation the kingdom would come only in the parousia of Christ at the end of the age; in its present manifestation it occurs only in the acts of the Holy Spirit within the body of Christ, the church. In particular, it was considered by Paul to be present now as the gifts of the Spirit that constitute Christian ministry. However, as we saw in the previous chapter, some of these gifts were incorporated into ordered structures of the church's life in the world, that is, into the institutional forms of the church that exist in the present age and have daily relationships with it. The question then arises how, in Paul's view, Christian ministry is related to the role of the believer and of the Christian community in secular society, how it relates to their sociopolitical life in the world.

Our task appears to be straightforward enough, to describe and interpret the teaching of Paul on this subject. Yet it involves a number of complex problems that can be adequately addressed only by first seeking to determine by a historical analysis the social "place" of Paul, of Christian ministry, and of the church in the Greco-Roman world. It requires, further, that one continually keep in mind the distinction between (1) the way in which Paul and his community viewed themselves and (2) the way in which the society around them may have viewed them.

The activities of the Apostle raise the essential questions. (1) How could he preach in various cities of the world, form believers into local groups, and collect and send money to groups elsewhere, for the most part without interference, in an Empire that for political reasons was quite suspicious of such activities? (2) How did Paul's preaching relate to that of others, especially the philosophical preachers who, like him, suffered at the hands of the authorities? To address these questions we shall inquire first into the place of the church and its ministries in Greco-Roman society and then into the practice of Pauline ministry within that context and its implications for Paul's theology.

THE SOCIAL PLACE OF THE CHURCH IN THE ROMAN WORLD

There have been two principal lines of investigation into the constitution and structure of early Christian churches, the first finding analogies in Jewish models[1] and the second in mutual-aid associations or "clubs" that were widespread throughout the Empire.[2] As far as the Jewish models are concerned, two possibilities come into view, the (Qumran-type) Essenes and the synagogues of the diaspora.

The ritually strict "Hebraist" Christians (cf. Acts 6:1) were influenced to some degree, at least in Palestine, by an Essene background and ethos like that at Qumran, where organizational structures were similar to those of the clubs in the Greco-

1. The first study was, apparently, C. Vitringa, *De synogoga vetere libri tres* (Franeker, 1696) (abridged ET: *The Synagogue and the Church* [London, 1842]).

2. The first advocates of this viewpoint were G. B. de Rossi, *La Roma Sotteranea* (Rome, 1864-77), I, 83-108; idem, in *Bullettino di Archeologia Cristiana* 2 (1864), 57-62; and, more broadly, E. Renan, *The Apostles* (London, 1869 [1866]), 262-74, 278. They built on the work of T. Mommsen, *De collegiis et sodaliciis Romanorum* (Kiel, 1843).

Roman world.[3] The Hebraists or their successors may represent the kind of Christianity that the historian Eusebius mistakenly identified with Jewish Essenes (Therapeutae) in Egypt.[4] As the letters of James and Jude show,[5] they very probably had a mission to the diaspora parallel to Paul's[6] and directed particularly to ritually strict Jewish communities, who may be attested by inscriptions identifying the "synagogue of the Hebrews" at Rome and at Corinth.[7] Some of them, a judaizing-gnosticizing faction, were Paul's persistent opponents,[8] and both "orthodox" and "judaizing" Hebraist-Christian communities continued to exist into the second century,[9] and perhaps longer.[10] There is little evidence, however, to determine whether or to what extent they and the diaspora synagogues they evangelized were characterized by Essene traits. In any case the Pauline mission is related to a broader spectrum of diaspora Judaism whose general status in the pagan society has more attestation in ancient sources.

The Pauline churches may be compared both with the various types of private associations in the Empire and with the Jewish synagogues. According to Paul's sometime companion

3. On similarities of the Essene (Qumran) community to the Hellenistic clubs cf. M. Hengel, *Judaism and Hellenism,* 2 vols. (Philadelphia, 1974), I, 244f.; M. Weinfeld, *The Organizational Pattern and the Penal Code of the Qumran Sect: A Comparison with the Guilds and Religious Associations of the Hellenistic-Roman Period* (Göttingen, 1986). On Essene influences in the early Jerusalem church cf. R. Riesner, "Essener und Urkirche in Jerusalem," *BK* 40 (1985), 64-76.

4. Eusebius, *HE* 2.17-23, drawing on the description of the Essenes by Philo, *On the Contemplative Life* 25-37, 66-89.

5. Jas 1:1; Jude 1:1; see E. E. Ellis, *Prophecy and Hermeneutic* (Tübingen and Grand Rapids, 1978), 226-36.

6. Cf. E. E. Ellis, "The Circumcision Party and the Early Christian Mission" (note 5), 116-28.

7. *CIG* 9909 = *CIJ* I, 510 (Rome); *CIJ* I, 718 (Corinth). Cf. M. Stern, "The Jewish Diaspora," *Compendia,* I, i (1974), 167.

8. Cf. Ellis (note 5), 101-28, 230-36.

9. Justin Martyr, *Dialogue* 47.

10. Cf. Origen, *Against Celsus* 5.61.

Luke,[11] they were in their initial stage drawn largely from the synagogues. Also not unlike the synagogues, the churches are most closely analogous to one category of private association and apparently only one. It is the *collegium tenuiorum* or mutual-aid club for the poorer classes and similar societies (ἔρανοι, θίασοι) in the eastern provinces.[12] To discover whether and to what degree the church may have been understood as such a club, it is necessary to review briefly (1) the place of private associations within the Roman empire,[13] and the affinities between them and (2) the Jewish synagogues and (3) the Christian churches. With these results in hand we may be able to address with greater understanding the social place of the Pauline ministry within that society.

11. For example, Acts 13:5; 14:1; 17:1; 18:4; 19:8. On the Lukan authorship cf. E. E. Ellis, *The Gospel of Luke* (Grand Rapids, [5]1987), 40-51; J. A. Fitzmyer, *The Gospel according to Luke*, 2 vols. (Garden City, NY, 1985), I, 35-41; M. Hengel, *Acts and the History of Earliest Christianity* (London, 1979), 60-68.

12. For example, Pliny, *Letters* 10.93. J. P. Sampley ("*Societas Christi:* Roman Law and Paul's Conception of Community," *God's Christ and his People*, ed. J. Jervell [Oslo, 1977], 158-74) seeks analogies with legal, contractual-type relationships commented on by F. de Zulueta, *The Institutes of Gaius*, 2 vols. (Oxford, [2]1976), I, 201ff.; II, 174-81; cf. Gaius, *Institutes*, 148-54b). But this confuses the *collegium tenuiorum* with a quite different type of organization formed (ordinarily) for contracts of property, goods, and commercial services.

13. For studies of the associations cf., in addition to the work of Mommsen (note 2) and the articles in *OCD* ("Clubs") and *RAC* ("Genossenschaft"), F. de Robertis, *Il diritto associativo Romano* (Bari, 1938); W. Liebenam, *Zur Geschichte und Organisation des römischen Vereinswesens* (Leipzig, 1890); F. Poland, *Geschichte des griechischen Vereinswesens* (Leipzig, 1909); M. Rostovtzeff, *The Social and Economic History of the Hellenistic World*, 3 vols. (Oxford, 1941), II, 1061-66 *et passim;* J. P. Waltzing, *Corporations professionelles chez les Romains,* 4 vols. (Louvain, 1895-1900); idem, "Collegia," *DACL* III (1913-14), 2107-40. Brief but helpful: P. W. Duff, *Personality in Roman Private Law* (Cambridge, 1938), 95-158 (and the review by D. Daube in *JRS* 33 [1943], 86-93; 34 [1944], 125-35); E. G. Hardy, *Studies in Roman History* (London, 1906), 129-50.

The Status of Clubs under the Principate

Until the last century before the Christian era private clubs of various sorts thrived unregulated in the West[14] and in the East.[15] While information about them is relatively sparse and mainly confined to inscriptions, it provides a reasonably intelligible if only a general picture. The clubs were formed for various purposes and various groups—trades (bakers, shoemakers), professions (musicians, actors), civic functions (firemen, veterans, sports)—and were directed more to the social and religious than to the professional or economic interest of their members.[16] They held regular meetings, usually with religious ceremonies, elected officers and sometimes a patron, and exercised a certain discipline over their members. They could also hold property. For a monthly subscription to a common treasury they provided their membership with banquets and other festive and leisurely activities and, at the end, an honorable burial. The associations that were classified as clubs for the poor *(collegia tenuiorum)* —including males and females, slaves and freedmen — apparently emphasized dining and funeral benefits, and by underwriting the necessary burial proprieties they served a public interest as well.[17]

During the closing days of the Roman republic the clubs in Rome became a cover for political demonstrations and criminal acts

14. A number of Latin designations were used, for example, *collegium, corpus, ordo, societas, sodalitas, universitas*—some of which had special connotations. *Collegium* was the most general technical term.

15. A number of Greek designations were used, for example, ἔρανος, ἑταιρεία, θίασος, σύνοδος, σύστημα—some of which had special connotations. Ἔρανος and θίασος appear to have been the most generally used terms. Ἑταιρεία was used particularly for a political club.

16. Cf. A. Burford, *Craftsmen in Greek and Roman Society* (London, 1972), 160f.; R. MacMullen, *Roman Social Relations* (New Haven, 1974), 18ff.; W. L. Willis, *Idol Meat in Corinth* (Chico, CA, 1985), 49-61. For examples cf. W. M. Ramsay, *The Cities and Bishops of Phrygia* (New York, 1975 [1897]), 105f., 440.

17. Cf. Liebenam (note 13), 169-224; Poland (note 13), 246-70, 328f.; Duff (note 13), 102f. On how a patron (-founder) might become an elected officer cf. Poland, 365f.; Liebenam, 212-20; see *ND* I (1981), 5.

and were successively banned, restored, and banned.[18] For similar reasons they were dissolved on subsequent occasions by Julius Caesar (†44 B.C.) and the emperor Augustus (31 B.C.–A.D. 14), and recognized clubs were required to follow special licensing procedures. From time to time various clubs continued to get involved in riots and political disturbances, for which the silversmiths at Ephesus (Acts 19:23-41) and the (sports?) clubs at Pompeii[19] provide well-known examples, and sometimes they were dissolved for a season. But it probably goes too far to characterize such disturbances as "genuine attempts at social revolution."[20]

The clubs never suffered a blanket prohibition and, as the incident at Pompeii indicates, even unlicensed ones appear to have been dissolved only when they caused problems. But they then usually received only minor penalties.[21] According to the historian Suetonius certain clubs were exempt from the bans, for example, "those of ancient foundation" or "the old and legitimate ones."[22] And according to a senate resolution *(senatus consultum)*[23] and an ancient commentary on Roman law,[24] a whole class of clubs, the

---

18. Cf. Duff (note 13), 97f., 107f.; Cicero, *Letters to Quintus (brother)* 2.3.5; *Concerning Piso* 4.8f.; *For Sestius* 25.55.

19. Tacitus, *Annals* 14.17: For riot (c. A.D. 59) the Pompeians were prohibited for ten years from holding gladiatorial shows, and their unlicensed clubs were dissolved. On the use of clubs for political purposes cf. Philo, *Flaccus* 17 = 135-45. Further, cf. B. Reicke, *Diakonie, Festfreude und Zelos* (Uppsala, 1951), 320-38. See below, note 116.

20. M. Rostovtzeff, *The Social and Economic History of the Roman Empire* (Oxford, ²1957), 179, cf. 619-22. Cf. A. N. Sherwin-White, *The Letters of Pliny* (Oxford, 1966), 609f.

21. *Digest*. 47.22.3 (Marcian): When unpermitted clubs are dissolved, the common assets may be divided among the membership.

22. Suetonius, *Julius* 42.3; idem, *Augustus* 32.1.

23. *ILS* 7212 (? A.D. 54-68); *CIL* XIV, 2112 (A.D. 136), giving the text of a Senate resolution *(senatus consultum)* concerning private clubs. For an English translation of *ILS* 7212 cf. H. Lewis, *Roman Civilization* (New York, 1955), II, 272-75. Cf. also R. L. Wilkin, *The Christians as the Romans Saw Them* (New Haven, 1984), 36-40.

24. *Digest*. 47.22.1 (Marcian, c. A.D. 200): "It is decreed that no associations and clubs be tolerated. . . . It is permitted only to assist the poor with a monthly contribution; however, they shall be allowed to assemble only once a month in order that they not, under a pretense of this sort, form an unpermitted

collegia tenuiorum, apparently were not required to obtain a special license to exist. Two questions are less clearly answered by the sources: (1) What kinds of clubs received licenses and under what conditions? (2) To what geographical areas did the decrees of dissolution and licensing apply?

Cities allied to Rome *(civitates foederatae)*[25] and probably her colonies[26] regulated their own affairs in these matters and did not, at least in the first and early second centuries, come under the restrictions placed upon the clubs. Among such places of interest to the Pauline mission were the free cities of Antioch-Syria, Athens, Nicopolis, Thessalonica, and perhaps Miletus and the colonies of Antioch-by-Pisidia, Corinth, Lystra, Philippi, and Troas.[27] In the eastern provinces as a whole clubs may not have been much affected during this period. In Bithynia in Asia Minor, for example, they faced no restrictions until the ruling of Trajan banning them c. A.D. 110.[28] In the provinces as a whole they came under a general imperial prohibition-with-exceptions only at the end of the second century.[29] At the beginning they more often received the Emperor's exemption from the rule of licensing. This was certainly the case for the Jewish synagogue.

---

club *(collegium)*. . . . To hold meetings for religious purposes is not restricted so long as the Senate resolution forbidding unpermitted clubs is not thereby contravened."

25. Pliny, *Letters* 10.93: Trajan: If citizens of the free city of Amisus "are allowed by their own laws . . . to form a benefit society *(eranos),*" Rome should not interfere, "especially if the contributions are not used for riotous and unlawful assemblies but to relieve hardship among the poor *(tenuiorum).*"

26. Pliny, *Letters* 10.47: "As Apamea was a Roman colony, . . . it was their long-established custom and privilege to manage their internal affairs in their own way." The specific issue here was their finances, but their rights ran further. Pausanias *(Greece* 7.18.7) implies that colonies enjoyed the status of free cities. Cf. A. H. M. Jones, *The Greek City* (Oxford, 1979 [1940]), 133.

27. Cf. Jones (note 26), 129-33.

28. Pliny, *Letters* 10.96.7; cf. Sherwin-White (note 20, 608f.), who cites Dio Chrysostom's *(Discourses* 45.8) remarks on the influence of clubs in Bithynia on municipal elections at Prusa in A.D. 101.

29. Cf. *Digest.* 47.22.1 (Marcian), which dates the (general) application to the provinces to the reign of Septimius Severus (A.D. 193-211); cf. Sherwin-White (note 20), 779.

The Jewish Synagogues and the Clubs

According to the Jewish historian Josephus, Julius Caesar decreed the following:

> "It displeases me that such [local] statutes should be made against our [Jewish] friends and allies and that they should be forbidden to live in accordance with their customs and to contribute money to common meals and to sacred rites. For this they are not forbidden to do even in Rome." For Caesar . . . forbade clubs (θιάσους) to assemble in the city, but these people alone he did not forbid to do so or to collect contributions of money or to hold common meals: "Similarly, although I forbid other societies (ἄλλους θιάσους), I permit these alone to assemble and feast in accordance with their native customs and ordinances."

These rights, accorded to the Jews by Julius Caesar,[30] were later reaffirmed by the emperors Augustus and Claudius.[31] Of particular interest to our present inquiry, they were for the most part the same privileges that were enjoyed by the licensed clubs—periodic assembly, common meals, common property and treasury, limited disciplinary rights over their membership,[32] and, to judge from the inscriptions, obligations for the burial of members. Furthermore, the Jewish communities were identified in Caesar's decree as one of the θίασοι and elsewhere were called by other terms used for the private clubs.[33] Also like the clubs, they or-

---

30. Josephus, *Antiquities* 14.214ff. = 14.10.8. T. Rejak ("Was there a Roman Charter for the Jews?" *JRS* 74 [1984], 107-23) thinks that Josephus, using the decrees as an ongoing polemic, "exaggerates the scope of the grants" (122). But apologetic need not mean exaggeration, and the decrees constituted in any case vital precedents. Further, cf. A. M. Rabello, "The Legal Conditions of the Jews in the Roman Empire," *ANRW* II, 13 (1980), 662-762.

31. Josephus, *Antiquities* 16.166-78 = 16.6.3-8; 19.303ff. = 19.6.3; Philo, *Embassy to Gaius* 23 = 155ff.; 40 = 311-15.

32. Josephus, *Antiquities* 14.235 = 14.10.17. Cf. Acts 9:1f.; 18:15; 2 Cor 11:24.

33. E.g., Josephus, *Antiquities* 14.235 = 14.10.17 (σύνοδος). Cf. Liebenam (note 13), 164-69 with J. Juster, *Les Juifs dans l'empire romain,* 2 vols. (Paris, 1914), I, 414ff. On other affinities between the synagogue and the clubs cf. H. Mantel, "The Nature of the Great Synagogue," *HTR* 60 (1967), 75-91.

ganized under patrons and/or as slaves and freedmen of particular households.[34] Like the disorderly clubs in Pompeii, the Jews who created disturbances—for example, under the rule of Tiberius and Claudius—had their rights of assembly withdrawn[35] and were temporarily expelled from Rome.[36]

With these similarities to the private clubs it is not surprising that the Jewish synagogues of this period have been so classified by modern scholarship.[37] Of course, viewed as a body of teaching, Judaism and the sects within it could be compared—as Christianity also was[38]—to a school of philosophy, for example, by Josephus[39] and Philo.[40] But that is another matter.[41] Viewed in terms of their legal status within the Roman social order, the Jewish diaspora communities in most places took the form of religious clubs. Admittedly, they constituted a special legal entity (πολίτευμα) in Alexandria and perhaps elsewhere, particularly in Egypt,[42] and they had in the East the status and rights of a recognized nationality, at least before A.D. 70.[43] They also had characteristics, such as an ethnic membership, not found in other associations and were accorded rights that went beyond those granted to

34. *CIG* 9902, 9907. Cf. E. Schürer, *Die Gemeindeverfassung der Juden in Rom* (Leipzig, 1879), 15f. On honoring a patron cf. *CIJ* II, 738 = *ND* I (1981), 69.

35. Under Tiberius: Tacitus, *Annals* 2.85. Under Claudius: Dio Cassius, *History* 60.6.6; this occasion may be different from the expulsion of the Jews mentioned in Acts 18:2 and in Suetonius, *Claudius* 25.4. See note 48.

36. Under Tiberius: Tacitus, *Annals* 2.85; Suetonius, *Tiberius* 36; Josephus, *Antiquities* 18.81-84 = 18.3.5. Under Claudius: Acts 18:2; Suetonius, *Claudius* 25.4.

37. Cf. Schürer (note 34), 10; idem, *A History of the Jewish People*, 2 vols. in 6 (Edinburgh, 1898), II, ii, 243-91, 255; S. L. Guterman, *Religious Toleration and Persecution in Ancient Rome* (London, 1951), 150.

38. Tertullian, *Apology* 21.1 *(secta);* cf. Acts 24:14; 28:22 (αἵρεσις).

39. Josephus, *Antiquities* 13.171ff. = 13.5.9; idem, *War* 2.119-66.

40. Philo, *On the Contemplative Life* 26; idem, *On Dreams* 2.127; idem, *Embassy to Gaius* 23 = 156.

41. Cf. G. F. Moore, *Judaism*, 3 vols. (Cambridge, MA, 1927), I, 284.

42. Cf. A. Kasher, *The Jews in Hellenistic and Roman Egypt* (Tübingen, 1985), 233-357.

43. Cf. Guterman (note 37), 75-129.

others. But given the great variety and types of organization that fell under the umbrella designation of "clubs," the peculiarities of the synagogue associations are not sufficient to exclude them from this classification in most areas of the diaspora. Although they have been cited by some modern scholars (Juster) as grounds to exclude them,[44] the arguments have been answered point for point, and pose no real objection (Guterman).[45]

The Jewish "place" in the Empire has been viewed as an authorized religion *(religio licita)*,[46] but, strictly speaking, in Roman law there were no "authorized religions" but only "authorized associations" *(collegia licita)*. There is little reason to doubt that the countless synagogues throughout the Roman world were so regarded and so treated. When any authority questioned the Jewish communities' legitimacy or perhaps more often their irritating privileges, such as sending annual collections of money to Jerusalem, they could—as Josephus did—point to imperial decrees supporting their rights as a religious association. But were the Christian communities, as they were drawn from the womb of Judaism and constituted separate congregations through the mission of Paul and other apostles, regarded in the same light? Could they and their ministries be promoted under the shelter of the recognized rights of private religious clubs? To these questions we may now turn.

The Church, the Jewish Synagogue, and the Clubs

When Gallio was proconsul of Achaia, the Jews . . . brought [Paul] before the judgment-seat. Gallio said to the Jews, "If it were a matter of wrongdoing or crime, I should have reason to bear with you,

---

44. Juster (note 33), I, 412-24, followed essentially by E. M. Smallwood, *The Jews under Roman Rule* (Leiden, ²1981), 133f., who is followed in turn by W. A. Meeks, *The First Urban Christians* (New Haven, CT, 1983), 35; but see 80. Similarly, S. Applebaum, "The Organization of Jewish Communities in the Diaspora," *Compendia,* I, i (1974), 464-503, 502.

45. Guterman (note 37), 130-56; somewhat more qualified, E. Schürer, *The History of the Jewish People in the Age of Jesus Christ,* 3 vols., ed. G. Vermes (Edinburgh, ²1973-87), III (1986), 111-20. But see note 37.

46. Cf. Tertullian, *Apology* 21.1.

O Jews. But since they are questions about a doctrine and names and your own law, see to it yourselves." Acts 18:12, 14f.

Gallio views the "Christians" at Corinth as a faction *(hairesis)* within the Jewish association, a view that is typical of the Roman officialdom and of others throughout the Pauline mission recorded in Acts.[47] The Roman historian Suetonius reflects a similar attitude when he records a garbled report of an expulsion of Jews from Rome in the reign of the emperor Claudius, attributing it to disturbances made "at the instigation of Christ" *(Chrestus)*. Probably he refers to disturbances, like those that confronted Gallio in Corinth and the magistrates in Thessalonica, which arose in fact from the preaching of Christ in certain synagogues in Rome.[48] Only with the Neronian persecutions in A.D. 65-68 do the Roman authorities, perhaps informed by Jewish acquaintances of the emperor's wife Poppaea,[49] make a clear distinction between the Jewish and Christian communities,[50] and even at the end of the second century some still supposed that Christians sought a lawful status under the umbrella *(sub umbraculo)* of Judaism.[51]

The Church and Judaism

Certain features of Paul's ministry suggest that he also considered it to lie within the larger framework of the community of Judaism. Three such features may be considered here: its *customary praxis,*

47. Acts 24:5; 26:4-29; 28:17-22; cf. 16:20ff. In this, as in other respects, the book of Acts displays no knowledge of the post–A.D. 65 situation of the church.

48. Cf. Acts 17:5-9; Suetonius, *Claudius* 25.4: "Since the Jews constantly made disturbances at the instigation of Christ *(impulsore Chresto),* [Claudius] expelled them from Rome." *Chrestus* is another form of *Christus* (Tertullian, *Apology* 3.5). If it is the same expulsion cited in Acts 18:2, it occurred in A.D. 49 and included Jewish-Christians. See note 35. For a different interpretation cf. E. A. Judge in *RTR* 25 (1966), 81-93.

49. Cf. Josephus, *Antiquities* 20.194ff. = 20.8.11; J. J. Ensminger, "The Sadducean Persecution of the Christians in Rome and Jerusalem, A.D. 58 to 65," *SWJT* 30, 3 (1988), 9-13.

50. Tacitus, *Annals* 15.44; Suetonius, *Nero* 16.2.

51. Tertullian, *Apology* 21.1.

its *theological basis,* and its *ritual interests.* As to praxis, (1) Paul customarily preached in established synagogues and, as a faithful member of the Jewish nation, submitted at least five times to the synagogue punishment of thirty-nine lashes.[52]

(2) Theologically, the Apostle regards the church as the true "Israel of God," the "elect remnant" of God's ancient people, and the heir of the promises made to Abraham.[53] He does not suppose that the church, by accepting former pagans into its fold, is becoming Gentile; on the contrary, the believing pagans are in the status of proselytes, who through faith in Messiah have been engrafted into the long-standing tree of the Israelite nation[54] and have become God's own people (λαός) and his eschatological-christological temple (ναός).[55] Paul views the church, broadly speaking, as a Jewish entity even though he uses the expression "the Jews" more narrowly for the unbelieving and hostile Jewish establishment.[56] He would, therefore, have no theological difficulty in claiming for his congregations whatever rights diaspora Jews might enjoy in the Roman world either as a people (*natio,* ἔθνος, λαός) or as an association (*collegium,* θίασος).

(3) To a remarkable degree the Apostle to the Gentiles continued to respect and to observe Jewish rituals. He had his young Jewish colleague Timothy circumcised, and he carried out a religious vow;[57] he emulated the custom of diaspora synagogues by taking an offering to Jerusalem,[58] celebrated the Pentecost festival there, and participated in purification ceremonies at the

---

52. Acts 13:5; 14:1; 17:1f., 10, 17; 18:4; 19:8. On 2 Cor 11:24 cf. (H. L. Strack and) P. Billerbeck, *Kommentar zum Neuen Testament,* 4 vols. (München, 1922-28), III, 527-30.

53. Gal 3:29; 6:16; Rom 9:27; 11:5.

54. Rom 11:17-24. Cf. E. E. Ellis, *Paul's Use of the Old Testament* (Grand Rapids, [4]1985), 121-24; H. Ridderbos, *Paul* (Grand Rapids, 1975), 327-61; R. N. Flew, *Jesus and His Church* (New York, 1938), 211-21. Otherwise: P. Richardson, *Israel in the Apostolic Church* (Cambridge, 1969), 70-158.

55. 2 Cor 6:16-18; Eph 2:17-20; cf. Ellis (note 54), 90ff., 107f.

56. 2 Cor 11:24; 1 Thess 2:14. But see Rom 1:16; 2:28f.; 1 Cor 1:24; Gal 2:14f.

57. Acts 16:3; 18:18.

58. Acts 24:17; Rom 15:26; 1 Cor 16:1 (see above, 93ff.).

temple.[59] He knows that, since Christ has come, these practices are theological adiaphora (for Jewish Christians),[60] but nevertheless he apparently finds a practical value in them. In part he observes the rituals in order that he might bring to Christ fellow-Jews "who are under the law";[61] in part he does so, it seems, as a personal discipline and in part to illustrate the continuity of the church with the people of the old covenant.

The ritually observant Paul is, of course, found almost altogether in the writing of his companion Luke and represents an aspect of what has been called "the unknown Paul,"[62] unknown especially for those scholars who still follow the tradition of F. C. Baur and depreciate the historical value of the Lukan Acts. The inadequacy of that tradition has, I believe, been demonstrated,[63] but with the aid of a modern analogy we may pose a further question for it. Which would give the better historical perspective of, say, Field Marshall B. Montgomery's career in World War II, a dozen of his letters written in the heat of his campaigns in North Africa and Normandy or a considered historical survey written afterwards by a contemporary admirer, say, the historian A. J. P. Taylor?[64] While both accounts would be tendentious—I use the term nonpejoratively — in their own way, the latter would, I suspect, be generally regarded as giving a more balanced perspective. The analogy is not altogether inappropriate for the mission of Paul. Luke's representation both complements and stands in tension with that in the letters. But in a number of respects it also offers a better over-all historical perspective than do the letters taken alone since they are occasional pieces, often rather narrowly and one-sidedly focused on immediate issues and conflicts.[65]

---

59. Acts 20:16; 21:23f.

60. Gal 3:23-26; 1 Cor 7:19; Rom 14:5f. On παιδαγωγός (Gal 3:24) cf. F. F. Bruce, *The Epistle to the Galatians* (Grand Rapids, 1982), 182f., and (perhaps too negatively) H. D. Betz, *Galatians* (Philadelphia, 1979), 177f.

61. 1 Cor 9:20.

62. J. Jervell, *The Unknown Paul* (Minneapolis, 1984), 52-67.

63. For a number of criticisms of it cf. E. E. Ellis, "Dating the New Testament," *NTS* 26 (1980), 492-500; Hengel (note 11); Jervell (note 62), 68-76.

64. A. J. P. Taylor (*The Second World War* [London, 1966], 152), despite criticisms, calls Montgomery "the best British field-commander since Wellington."

65. Cf. J. C. Beker, *Paul the Apostle* (Philadelphia, 1980), 37f., 56ff., 69ff.

In the light of his theology and praxis, then, Paul would have good grounds to claim for his congregations the rights of association enjoyed by the local synagogues. If he could thereby secure in the local social structures and customs a niche for the furtherance of the gospel, for the teaching of his converts, and for their fellowship and worship, we may reasonably suppose that he did so.

The identification of the church, by the Roman authorities and by the Apostle, as a special part of the larger Jewish community makes it probable that, like the synagogue, the church regarded itself and was regarded by others as a religious association. Is there other evidence that may strengthen or perhaps cast doubt on that probability? At least three matters deserve to be considered in this respect: (1) the use of common terminology by the church and the clubs, (2) certain elements in the praxis of the Pauline church, and (3) the view of the church taken by Roman authorities and by Christian writers in the second century.

Terminology Used in the Church

In the past certain terminology common to Christian congregations and private religious clubs has been given considerable significance. For example, the names "assembly" (ἐκκλησία)[66] and "synagogue" (συναγωγή)[67] and the terms "overseer" (ἐπίσκοπος),[68] "elder" (πρεσβύτερος),[69] "leader" (ὁ προεστώς),[70] and

66. *CIG* 2271 (2nd century B.C.). Ἐκκλησία is Paul's usual term for the church.

67. *OGIS* 573. Cf. Poland (note 13), 356f. For Christian congregations cf. Jas 2:2; Ignatius, *To Polycarp* 4:2; Shepherd of Hermas, *Mandates* 11:9, 13f. Cf. also Irenaeus, *Against Heresies* 3.6.1. Συναγωγή is not used by Paul for the church, although the cognate verb is (1 Cor 5:4).

68. Cf. E. Hatch, *The Organization of the Early Christian Churches* (London, 1881), 27-39, 37n. (ἐπίσκοπος); Poland (note 13), 377. Cf. Phil 1:1; 1 Tim 3:2; Tit 1:7; Acts 20:28.

69. *CIG* 2221; cf. Poland (note 13), 98-102; G. A. Deissmann, *Bible Studies* (Edinburgh, 1923), 156f.; 1 Tim 5:17; Tit 1:5; Acts 20:17, 28. In Judaism πρεσβύτερος is used of teachers (see above, 103, 109) and of synagogue officials (*CIJ* I, 378; *CIJ* I [²1975], Prolegomena 52, 54, 89f.; perhaps Lk 7:3). In Epictetus (*Discourses* 1.9.10) it is used of a philosophical teacher.

70. *CIG* 3540; cf. Poland (note 13), 365f.; 1 Tim 5:17 (Rom 12:8; 1 Thess 5:12).

"patron" (προστάτης)[71] are occasionally used to designate, respectively, a club and officers of a club. Since the same words also occur for the church and ministries of the church, it has been suggested that they were taken over by the church from the clubs.[72] However, these words are used quite broadly in a number of similar contexts and have no necessary or special connection with clubs, where in fact they appear relatively infrequently and usually with a different connotation than they have in Christian contexts. Indeed, when the various terms employed for the clubs and their officials are collated,[73] the primary impression is how different most of them are from designations found in the church. But then at times they also differ strikingly from terms used by a different type of club.

Other similarities in terms used for the church and the clubs are sometimes quite interesting.[74] For example, in Acts 24:14 the church is spoken of by believers as "the Way" (ὁ ὁδός), a term whose cognate σύνοδος is used of clubs, and it is tagged by its detractors as "a sect" (αἵρεσις), a term employed for subgroups within a club. Such similarities are not really sufficient to show that the church viewed itself as a club or derived its vocabulary from them, but neither do differences in terminology prove that the church did not so regard itself. It goes beyond the evidence to say either that the church avoided club-terminology or that it imitated such terminology. The nineteenth-century debates about the

71. Cf. Poland (note 13), 365f.; Rom 16:1.

72. For example, Hatch (note 68); C. F. G. Heinrici, "Die Christengemeinde Korinths und die religiösen Genossenschaften der Griechen," *ZWT* 19 (1876), 465-526, 519ff. (ὁ προϊστάμενος). Further, idem, *Das zweite Sendschreiben an die Korinther* (Berlin, 1887), 556f. In criticism cf. Liebenam (note 13), 271-74.

73. Cf. Liebenam (note 13), 164-69, 199-220; Poland (note 13), 56-86, 337-423.

74. Later, in the early fourth century, there is a remarkable usage of the term θιασῶται for Christians and the term θίασος for the church by Eusebius, *HE* 1.3.19; 10.1.8; idem, *Preparation for the Gospel* 6.10 = 280d. Irenaeus (*Against Heresies* 1.13.4) identifies a Gnostic congregation as a θίασος. See note 117. On φίλος as a name for a club member and for a Christian cf. G. H. R. Horsley, "A Society of Friends," *ND* 4 (1987), 17f. Cf. Jn 11:11; 15:14f.; Acts 27:3; 3 Jn 15.

significance of terminology were something of a stand-off and were not decisive for the question of the church's own social self-perception or for the way it was perceived by others. More significant are the praxis of the Pauline churches and inferences that may be drawn from it.

Church Praxis

Certain practices of Pauline congregations favor viewing the constitution of his churches along the lines of a religious club. Essentially they are elements that reflect practices of the synagogue, which, as we have argued above, had the status of a club and from which the churches were originally drawn. They include particularly a church order that manifested activities suggestive of a synagogue-type religious club and an organization of congregations in the homes of members or patrons that corresponded to the usage of some synagogues and other clubs.

In the light of the Jewish framework within which Paul carried out his missionary activities, one might expect that his congregations would also reflect at least in some measure the praxis of the synagogue. Three instances may be mentioned where this was the case: the public reading of scripture, the discipline of members, and the organization of house churches.

The *reading of scripture in church* stands in continuity with synagogical practice. It is seen explicitly in Paul's exhortation to Timothy to "give attention to the reading."[75] More importantly, it underlies the contrast drawn between the use of "the old covenant" in the synagogue and its reading when "the veil is taken away,"[76] that is, reading not only in the light of Christ but also in the Christian assembly since few individuals would have possessed their own scrolls of scripture. Likewise, the reading in church of the Old Testament (as well as Paul's previous teach-

---

75. 1 Tim 4:13.
76. 2 Cor 3:14ff.; cf. Mk 13:14. Cf. C. W. Dugmore, *The Influence of the Synagogue on the Divine Office* (London, 1964 [1944]), 6ff.; A. Harnack, *Bible Reading in the Early Church* (London, 1912), 32-47, who is concerned more with private reading (cf. Acts 17:11).

ing) may lie behind his references to the Old Testament prefaced by the query, "Do you not know this?"[77] And it may be presupposed in the Apostle's instruction to read "new covenant" writings in church, specifically Paul's own letters[78] and other Christian prophetic writings,[79] since the prior use of the Old Testament in church would provide the logical background and setting for introducing the latter practice.

In urging his churches at Corinth and Thessalonica to exercise *discipline over the membership,* Paul implicitly claimed for them a prerogative granted to synagogues and other clubs,[80] and his warnings against an argumentative spirit and the abuse of wine at the Supper may have been occasioned in part because some were following a pattern known to characterize the clubs.[81] The apostle also presupposed that the church at Corinth exercised the privileges of a club when he directed them to collect money and to put it in a common treasury.[82] In the last two activities Paul's churches showed an affinity with the clubs that was related to and apparently mediated by their affinity with the diaspora synagogues. This is also the case in a third clublike characteristic of Paul's congregations, their organization as house churches.

---

77. Rom 11:2f. (1 Kings 19:10-14); 1 Cor 6:16 (Gen 2:24); 9:13 (Deut 18:1ff.). The references in 1 Corinthians may indeed be to Paul's previous teaching of these texts to the congregations. But such teaching would, in the light of Paul's synagogue background, have been in a context of an exposition (midrash) of public biblical readings and would have given the congregations a model for their own teachers to follow. Cf. E. E. Ellis, "Traditions in 1 Corinthians," *NTS* 32 (1986), 487-90; idem, *The Making of the New Testament Documents,* forthcoming

78. Col 4:16; 1 Thess 5:27; cf. 1 Cor 5:9; 2 Thess 2:15; 3:14.

79. Rom 16:26; cf. Eph 3:3ff.

80. 1 Cor 5:5, 9ff.; 6:1-6; 2 Thess 3:6, 10, 14. See above, 95f., 99, 103.

81. So Reicke (note 19), 337f. Cf. 1 Cor 1:10f.; 11:20ff.; 2 Cor 12:20.

82. 1 Cor 16:1f. See above, 94f.

House Churches

Professional and religious clubs often possessed their own meeting place, a *schola collegii*,[83] and one of them at Ephesus may have rented out their hall, the σχολή Τυράννου, to Paul and his converts.[84] Occasionally they became owners of private houses and either rented them out or used them for their assemblies and religious festivals.[85] They also met at the house of a member or, in a custom more frequent in the West, of a benefactor or patron of the club.[86] The same appears to be true of synagogue associations. In Rome the "synagogue of the Augustesians" and the "synagogue of the Agrippesians"[87] either were under the direct patronage of Augustus and Agrippa or, more loosely, were freedmen and slaves of those ruling families who were permitted to meet on the premises. If the latter, they had arrangements that were probably similar to that of the group of Christians "from Caesar's house" mentioned in Phil 4:22.

The clubs that met in private houses would ordinarily have used the main room (the atrium) and/or the usually somewhat more spacious colonnaded garden or courtyard (the peristyle) further back in the house.[88] In the latter they would, as one inscription indicates,[89] perform their rituals before the altar of their

83. *CIL* XI, 2702: "in schola collegii fabrum" ("in the clubhouse of the collegium of artisans"); cf. Martial, *Epigrams* 3.20.8; 4.61.3: "in the Poets' Club." Cf. Liebenam (note 13), 272n., 275-79.

84. Acts 19:9.

85. Cf. Poland (note 13), 460f.

86. *CIL* VI, 9148: "collegium quod est in domu Sergiae Paullinae" ("the collegium that is in the house of Sergia Paullina"). Cf. Poland (note 13), 365f., 275f.; F. W. Danker, *Benefactor* (St. Louis, 1982), 33ff. The names of eleven synagogues in ancient Rome have been preserved; cf. H. J. Leon, *The Jews of Ancient Rome* (Philadelphia, 1960), 135-59; P. Lampe, *Die stadrömischen Christen in den ersten beiden Jahrhunderten* (Tübingen, 1987), 26-28, 367-68.

87. See note 34. Leon (note 86, 141f.) rejects the suggestion that these synagogues originated from the slaves and freedmen of Augustus and Agrippa.

88. For general information, including a number of sketches and photographs, cf. A. G. McKay, *Houses, Villas and Palaces in the Roman World* (London, 1975), passim, and the literature cited.

89. *CIL* XIV, 2112 = *ILS* 7212 (c. A.D. 133); cf. Mommsen (note 2), 109, 113-16, 130ff.; Renan (note 2), 269f.

favored god[90] and hold their dinners, to which some items were brought individually and some provided by the host.

The excavations at Pompeii and Herculaneum, covered by volcanic ash and lava in A.D. 79, have revealed many excellent examples of upper-middle-class Roman homes. In Asia Minor archeological work at Ephesus and Priene has also been very rewarding in this regard, although, of course, the remains are not in the well-preserved state of the cities covered in the eruption of Mt. Vesuvius. To the student of the New Testament these sites cannot but bring to mind the congregations of St. Paul, who often held their meetings in similar surroundings. At Herculaneum the atria average about 25 × 30 feet in size, the less numerous peristyles about 33 × 50 feet[91] including the surrounding colonnaded porches of about 9 feet in width.[92] At Pompeii the averages are somewhat larger, the atria about 31 × 42 feet and the peristyles about 55 × 67 feet.[93] At Ephesus the excavated dwellings appear to be equally impressive, with the twenty-four-column peristyle of one patrician mansion measuring 4500 square feet.[94] Examples are fewer

90. Such a peristyle with an altar (a tetrastyle of c. 36′ × 45′) has been found in the excavation of the magnificent *Villa Oplontis* near Pompeii. Cf. B. Andreae, ed., *Neue Forschungen in Pompeji* (Rechlinghausen, 1975), 11.

91. Of the excavated portions when I was on the site (Spring 1983), I roughly measured the Houses of the Beautiful Courtyard (atrium: c. 12′ × 25′; peristyle: c. 18′ × 33′), of the Mosaic Atrium (atrium: c. 25′ × 26′; peristyle: c. 54′ × 84′), of the Wooden Partition (atrium: c. 24′ × 29′; peristyle: c. 27′ × 39′), of the Skeleton (atrium: c. 23′ × 26′) and the Samnite House (atrium: c. 24′ × 31′). The above measurements (in feet) have been conformed to those (in meters) in A. Maiuri, *Ercolano*, I (Rome, 1958), 198, 208, 266, 280, 384, 394.

92. The porches are usually on the four sides of the peristyle (tetrastyle) but sometimes only on two or three sides.

93. Based upon the dimensions of the Houses of the Silver Wedding, of Pansa, of the Surgeon, and of the Faun (with two peristyles). My rough measurements, taken on the site (Summer 1981), have been conformed to those found in McKay (note 88, passim). The most beautifully appointed peristyle, in the house of the Vettii, measures c. 57′ × 87′ (cf. H. Eschebach, *Pompeji* [Leipzig, 1978], 312), and even some middle- and lower-class houses have peristyles of c. 25′ × 35′ (cf. Andreae, note 90, 134f.).

94. I.e., c. 62′ × 73′. Cf. McKay (note 88), 214-17. When I was there in the Summer of 1988, I visited two newly excavated first-century "townhouses"

at the neighboring towns of Priene and Miletus, places that also lay within the scope of the Pauline mission,[95] but future archeological digs may yield more important and extensive remains.[96]

Such is the background from which the physical setting of the Apostle's assemblies, including their Lord's Supper, can best be visualized. Unlike the Jewish synagogue associations, the Christians posse·sed no church buildings. While it is not impossible that, like the clubs, some early Christian congregations may have been given property, they apparently did not set aside buildings exclusively for worship until the late second century.[97] Also like the clubs, the churches sometimes used a rented building such as the hall or club (σχολή) of Tyrannus[98] or, as was more usually the case, they met in the home of a more affluent convert or Christian missioner. Among such converts were Philemon and Nympha of Colossae, Jason at Thessalonica, and Titius Justus and Chloe at Corinth;[99] probably, Lydia at Philippi, Stephanus and

---

south of Curetes Street, one with a peristyle of c. 39′ × 45′. Cf. S. Erdemgil, *Ephesus* (Istanbul, [10]1988), 74-80.

95. Cf. Acts 19:10; 20:15ff.

96. For Corinth cf. J. Murphy-O'Connor, *St. Paul's Corinth* (Wilmington, DE, 1983), 153-61; when I was last there (Summer 1988), new excavations were in process. The so-called townhouses in Priene were excavated early in this century; on my visit (Spring 1983) they were covered with small trees and underbrush, and it was difficult to gain an impression of them. The site of Miletus is as vast as Ephesus but with much excavation yet to be done; concerning the dwellings, the words of G. Kleiner (*Die Ruinen von Milet* [Berlin, 1968], 122) are at the present writing still true: "This chapter cannot yet be written."

97. The earliest reference to such "church" buildings is presumably Clement of Alexandria, *Stromata* 7.5 (c. A.D. 200). The church probably followed synagogue precedents, but perhaps only sporadically for another century. Cf. Lampe (note 86), 307-10; W. Rordorf, "Was Wissen Wir über die christlichen Gottesdiensträume der vorconstantinischen Zeit?" *ZNTW* 55 (1964), 110-28; R. M. Grant, *Early Christianity and Society* (London, 1978), 149f. G. F. Snyder (*ANTE PACEM: Archeological Evidence of Church Life before Constantine* [Macon, GA, 1985], 67) dates the earliest dedicated church buildings to the time of Constantine, but that is doubtless too late.

98. Acts 19:9.

99. Phlm 2; Col 4:15; Acts 17:5ff.; 18:7-11; 1 Cor 1:11. Cf. P. Stuhlmacher, *Der Brief an Philemon* (Neukirchen, 1975), 70-75.

Gaius at Corinth, Phoebe at Cenchreae, and perhaps Onesiphorus at Ephesus.[100] Some of these people held slaves, operated commercial enterprises, or were generally well-traveled, and in all likelihood they belonged to the wealthier strata of society[101] and lived in the genteel surroundings exemplified by the homes in Pompeii and Ephesus described above. They not only provided the church with a place of meeting but also, like the patrons of the clubs, were sometimes its benefactors (προστάται) and leaders (συνεργοί, διάκονοι, οἱ ἀδελφοί) in its local ministry.[102] The couple, Priscilla and Aquila, Paul's fellow missionaries, also belonged to a prosperous merchant-class, having homes used by the church in one way or another in Corinth, Ephesus, and Rome. They were Paul's hosts in Corinth and may have employed him for a time in their business.[103]

The church at Rome also met in private residences, assuming that Rom 16 was part of the letter to that city.[104] In that chapter four or five Christian congregations may be distinguished. The assembly in the home of Priscilla and Aquila (5) and "the saints" with Philologus and Julia (15) were probably congregations meeting in those residences. The "brothers" with Hermas (14) may refer to a house used both for Christian workers and for congrega-

---

100. Cf. Acts 16:14f.; Rom 16:1f., 23; 1 Cor 16:15f.; 2 Tim 1:16ff.; 4:19. Against the view that 1 Cor 1:26 identifies Paul's converts as generally from the poorer classes cf. W. Wuellner, "The Sociological Implications of 1 Cor 1:26-29," *TU* 112 (1974), 666-72, and his further essay in *Donum Gentilicium,* ed. E. Bammel (Oxford, 1978), 164-84. For a resumé and perceptive critique of current sociological interpretations of Paul's letters cf. E. A. Judge, "The Social Identity of the First Christians," *JRH* 11 (1980), 201-17.

101. Cf. E. A. Judge, *The Social Pattern of Christian Groups in the First Century* (London, 1960), 49-61; idem, "St. Paul and Classical Society," *JAC* 15 (1972), 28; Meeks (note 44), 51-73.

102. Rom 16:1ff.; 1 Cor 16:16; Phlm 1.

103. Acts 18:2f. (ἠργάζετο P[74] A D); cf. Rom 16:3ff.; 1 Cor 16:19 (2 Tim 4:19).

104. Lampe (note 86), 124-53; K. P. Donfried, ed., *The Romans Debate* (Minneapolis, 1977), xi-xvi, passim; C. E. B. Cranfield, *Romans,* 2 vols. (Edinburgh, 1979), I, 9ff. For a less likely view see T. W. Manson, *Studies in the Gospels and Epistles* (Manchester, 1962), 225-41, who argues that Rom 16 was added to a copy of the letter that was addressed to Ephesus.

tional meetings.[105] Those "from Aristobulus" (10) and "from Narcissus" (11) were, like the believers "from Caesar's house" (Phil 4:22) and the Roman synagogues of the Augustesians and the Agrippesians,[106] probably congregations centering on the freedmen and slaves of those two households and meeting there. It is not unlikely that they belonged to Narcissus, the wealthy freedman and confidant of the emperor Claudius, and to Aristobulus, the brother of Herod Agrippa I, who had lived in Rome. Upon their deaths their households presumably became part of the imperial holdings but continued to be identified by their names.[107]

The locale of the church's meetings sheds light on the place of the ministries of Paul and of his congregations in the Greco-Roman social order and particularly on the affinity of his churches with the religious clubs. House churches were, of course, already part of the praxis of the earliest Jerusalem Christians,[108] including one pre-Pentecost assembly of 120 people,[109] and also of the earthly ministry of Jesus.[110] With such precedents they quickly became an established practice in early Christianity, and they give important insights into the ordered form and numerical impact of the ministry of Paul and of the diaspora Christian mission generally. A house

105. "The brothers" probably refers to Christian workers, that is, a team engaged in the missionary enterprise and perhaps, like a similar group in Thessalonica, living communally. Cf. 2 Thess 3:6-11; Acts 13:1-3; Ellis (note 5), 19-22.

106. See above, notes 34 and 87. On house synagogues in the diaspora and in Galilee cf. R. Riesner, *Jesus als Lehrer* (Tübingen, [3]1988), 136; in Rome cf. Lampe (note 86), 305f.

107. Suggested by J. B. Lightfoot, *The Epistle to the Philippians* (London, [4]1878), 174f. and followed by F. F. Bruce, *New Testament History* (London, [2]1977), 374 and Cranfield (note 104), II, 791ff. Regarding Aristobulus cf. Josephus, *Antiquities* 20.13 = 20.1.2. Regarding Narcissus cf. Juvenal, *Satires* 14.329; Tacitus, *Annals* 11.33-37; 13.1; Dio Cassius, *History* 60.14-19.

108. Acts 1:13ff.; 2:1f., 46; 4:23f.; 6:2-6; 12:12; cf. 21:8-12, 17; Rordorf (note 97), 113f.

109. Acts 1:15. Cf. K. H. Rengstorf, "The Election of Matthias," *Current Issues in New Testament Interpretation,* ed. W. Klassen (New York, 1962), 178-92.

110. That Jesus gathered and taught his pupils in houses is highly probable. Lk 10:38-42 and Mk 14:3-9 presuppose a larger group than the family (cf. also Mk 2:1; 3:19; 10:10; Jn 12:1f.), and Jesus' acquisition of a room for eating and conversational teaching was hardly an innovation at the Last Supper (Mk 14:12-25 par; cf. Lk 22:24-38; Jn 13–17). See above, 90ff.

church might involve a small gathering of twenty or so, but in the peristyle of a larger house it could, as the above examples indicate, easily accommodate a congregation of between one and two hundred. When particular house churches are specified in Colossae (2), Corinth (2 or 4), Ephesus (1 or 2), and Rome (4 or 5), the implication is that they were not the whole of the local church in that place. At the time of Paul's letters the Christian community in each of these cities probably numbered from a few hundred to over a thousand. It provoked a riot of the silversmiths' club of Ephesus, which was hardly caused by a ten percent decline in sales and presupposes that the initial Christian mission had a telling effect, an effect that within fifty years had emptied the pagan temples in the cities of the neighboring province of Bithynia.[111] Indeed, within a decade "a great multitude" (πολὺ πλῆθος) of Christians at Rome had suffered martyrdom under Nero's pogrom,[112] and there is no suggestion in the sources that the victims represented all or even a majority of Christians in Rome. Both in Palestine[113] and in the diaspora the first-generation Christian mission won a much greater following than is usually supposed.[114]

However, Paul's house churches must also be viewed from the socioreligious context of life in the cities. Their status as a religious association *(collegium)* probably best explains how their meetings and their common meals were understood by believers, by their pagan neighbors, and by the local authorities. While one

---

111. Cf. Acts 19:23-41; Pliny, *Letters* 10.96.9f. (A.D. 110): "Not only towns but villages and rural districts are infected. . . . [Until recently] the temples . . . had been almost entirely deserted for a long time . . . and scarcely anyone could be found to buy [the flesh of sacrificed animals]." Sherwin-White (note 20, 80f., 691, 709f.) thinks Pliny is reporting exaggerated hearsay, but I am not so sure.

112. 1 Clement 6:1; cf. Tacitus, *Annals* 15.44.

113. The numbers in Acts 2:41ff.; 4:4 are to be taken at face value although part of them were festival visitors. The purification baths *(mikvaoth)* at the synagogues and the south wall of the temple enclosure could easily have taken care of the baptisms. Cf. Riesner (note 3), 73; N. Avigad, *Discovering Jerusalem* (Nashville, 1983), 139-43.

114. W. Rordorf ("Die Hausgemeinden der vorkonstantinischen Zeit," *Kirche: Tendenzen und Ausblicke,* ed. C. W. Williams [Berlin, 1971], 191, 235) numbers the usual house church at "no more than two or three dozen" (191).

must avoid the materialist and reductionist tendency to interpret the church's experiences and practices simply as social processes, an aberration to which sociological approaches to the New Testament are sometimes prone,[115] the perceived status of the church as a club also seems to account for the relative freedom from official interference that its burgeoning diaspora mission enjoyed as well as the arbitrary sanctions, penalties, and dissolution that could be imposed at will upon it as upon other unlicensed clubs.[116] And, of course, this *ad hoc* status offered no protection against other, more serious charges being laid against Christians.

The Place of the Church in the Second Century

Second-century sources bearing upon the relationship of the church to the Empire support this view of the matter, as may be seen, for example, in the correspondence of the emperor Trajan with Pliny the Younger, governor of Bithynia (A.D. 110), and in the theologian Tertullian's description of the church along the lines of a religious club.[117] Pliny writes that after the edict of Trajan, banning all private clubs (ἑταιρίας) in the province, the Christians gave up their "Agape meal" meetings.[118] By this he indicates either that they considered the church to fall under the category of a (religious) club or that they knew it was regarded by the authorities in that light.[119]

At the end of the century when Tertullian asks why the

---

115. Cf. the criticism of Judge (note 100), 205ff.

116. For example, as Flaccus, the governor of Alexandria, did to the clubs of that city. Cf. Philo, *Against Flaccus* 1 = 4; cf. 17 = 135-45; see above, note 19. In Roman Africa the church apparently suffered no serious persecution until the late second century (cf. Tertullian, *To Scapula* 3.4).

117. Tertullian, *Apology* 38-39. Cf. also Lucian's *Death of Peregrinus* 11, where the latter, as a sometime Christian leader, is titled a θιασάρχης; Minucius Felix (*Octavius* 8.3) who, like Tertullian, calls the church a *factio*, a term used for the clubs.

118. Pliny, *Letters* 10.96.7; cf. 10.93; 10.94.

119. Cf. Hardy (note 13), 131ff.; Sherwin-White (note 20), 707, who takes the ban to cover "clubs of all types . . . only permitting *collegia tenuiorum*" in special circumstances (608f.; see above, note 25).

church "should not have been classed among lawful clubs *(licitas factiones)* when it commits no actions commonly feared from unlawful ones" *(inlicitis factionibus),* he implies that the church was regarded as the latter. He then goes on to speak of the church as a Christian club *(factio)* and society *(corpus)* and to describe its activities, including a monthly contribution and the feeding and burial of the poor, in terms similar to those used of a *collegium tenuiorum.*[120] It is true that this writer does not actually claim the church's right to exist under the Senate resolution pertaining to clubs;[121] and some scholars, for this and similar reasons, reject the thesis that the church of the second century represented itself as a *collegium tenuiorum.*[122] However, this is no real objection, and when Tertullian's comments are taken as a whole, they clearly place the church in the status of an unlicensed but ordinarily tolerated religious club.

This conclusion is valid not only for the church of Tertullian's day (c. A.D. 200) but very likely for the earlier Christian mission as well. Whether the development of the monarchical episcopate owes anything to the necessity under Roman law for a *collegium* (of certain kinds) to have a designated representative to act on its behalf[123] is a question that may be left unexplored since it takes us

120. Tertullian, *Apology* 38.1f.; 39.1-6. On affinities between the burial societies and the church cf. J. Gagé, *Les classes sociales dans l'empire romain* (Paris, 1964), 308ff.

121. Perhaps because "he knew very well that to claim this was to confess their breach of the law that protected them" (Duff, note 13, 170n), for example, that they met more often than was allowed. See notes 23 and 24.

122. For example, R. Sohm (*Kirchenrecht,* I [Leipzig, 1892], 75-77), whose own thesis, as was observed above (p. 88), opposed any ordered form for the earliest church. He was largely followed by Waltzing (*Corporations,* note 13, I, 314-20), who in a later article ("Collegia," note 13), however, recognizes that while in Tertullian's day the Christian society was not "a burial club" *(college funeraire),* it did have an external resemblance to all the Roman clubs (2124; cf. 2118). I am grateful to Mrs. L. C. A. Alexander of the University of Manchester for calling this passage to my attention. Cf. also T. M. Lindsay, *The Church and the Ministry in the Early Centuries* (Minneapolis, 1977 [1902]), 135f. and, for a criticism of Sohm, A. Harnack, *The Constitution and Law of the Church* (London, 1910), 175-258.

123. Cf. Duff (note 13), 129-58 and the critique of Daube (note 13), 128.

in any case beyond the situation of the Pauline church. In general the Pauline ecclesiastical organization and ministries arose from uniquely Christian experiences and to meet the church's own needs, but it is clear that some elements in its order, terminology, and praxis, and particularly its affinities with the synagogue, have resemblances to the clubs. All these factors taken together create a strong probability that the diaspora church as a social entity was perceived and perceived itself as a religious club and that, as such, it found from the beginning a degree of toleration and its "place" within the Greco-Roman social order.

PAUL'S MINISTRY AND GRECO-ROMAN SOCIETY

Paul's preaching and teaching also took place in a society where itinerant preachers abounded, specifically the Cynic "beggar philosophers" and their more sophisticated cousins, the Stoic rhetoricians.[124] These professional speakers, for whom rhetorical skills were often a highly developed art, vigorously promoted "religious" ideas and ideals, particularly in the realm of social ethics. In this context the question arises whether and to what extent they find a common spirit in the person and ministry of the Apostle Paul. I do not mean the older query about the connection, if any, between Paul's basic doctrines about Christ and salvation and the conceptions of contemporary pagan thought,[125] but rather a different set of questions that have received increasing attention in recent years. They include, specifically, (1) the way Paul as a preacher was perceived by his Gentile hearers and (2) the affinity of his views on social relationship and obligation with those of the philosophical

---

124. Cf. Dio Chrysostom, *Discourses* 32.10.

125. That question has by now received a negative verdict. Cf., for example, M. Hengel, *The Son of God* (London, 1976); H. Ridderbos, *Paul: An Outline of his Theology* (Grand Rapids, 1975), 22-29; G. Wagner, *Pauline Baptism and Pagan Mysteries* (Edinburgh, 1967). Earlier, cf. J. G. Machen, *The Origin of Paul's Religion* (New York, 1928); A. D. Nock, *Early Gentile Christianity and its Hellenistic Background* (New York, 1964 [1928]) = *Essays in Religion*, 2 vols. (Oxford, 1972), I, 49-133.

preachers, particularly the Stoics, who in the coming century or so were to be the chief rivals of Christianity for the heart and mind of ancient man. Both of these questions have broad and significant implications that cannot be adequately addressed in the brief comments here. Yet even a cursory glance at important matters may, it is hoped, serve a useful purpose in calling attention to the issues and to certain teachings of Paul that may shed light upon them.

Paul in the Eyes of the Greeks

If the church, considered as a social phenomenon, was viewed as a religious club, how were the Christian missionaries themselves perceived in the eyes of the Greeks? According to Acts, which is the only hard evidence we have of pagan conceptions of Paul from contemporary or near contemporary sources, there were at least two reactions to Paul *qua* missionary by Gentiles who encountered him. The first, caused by his miracle-working, was to call him a god (θεός)[126] and the second, occasioned by his preaching at Athens, was to identify him as "a preacher of strange deities" (ξένων δαιμονίων καταγγελεύς).[127] These two viewpoints, roughly speaking, have been picked up by a number of scholars who have attempted, on the one hand, to classify some Christian missionaries as "divine men" (θείοι ἄνδρες)[128] and, on the other hand, to classify Paul specifically as a professional rhetorician or "a sophist" without, of course, the pejorative connotations that this term came to have.[129] Upon investigation the term "divine man" has been found to be too vague and uncertain a category to offer any meaningful definition for the apostolic missioners.[130] Similarly, the

---

126. Acts 14:11-18; 28:6-9; cf. 19:11.

127. Acts 17:18.

128. D. Georgi, *The Opponents of Paul in Second Corinthians* (Philadelphia, 1986 [1964]), 230-38 (GT: 220-34).

129. E. A. Judge, "Early Christians as a Scholastic Community," *JRH* 1 (1960-61), 4-15, 125-37. Cf. R. Scroggs, "Paul as Rhetorician," *Jews, Greeks and Christians,* ed. R. Hamerton-Kelly (Leiden, 1976), 271-98.

130. Cf. C. H. Holladay, *"Theios Aner" in Hellenistic Judaism* (Missoula, MT, 1977), 233-42.

parallels between Paul and the sophists are so general[131] and the persons placed in this class so various that in the end the term seems to mean little more than an itinerant speaker. Even when one takes into account the more specific parallel between Paul's view of his apostleship and the Cynic-Stoic preachers' consciousness of their divine mission,[132] the similarity between the two concepts remains only formal and without substantive content.[133]

Further difficulties in supposing that Paul was generally accorded the status of a rhetorician are (1) his own poor abilities as a speaker and (2) the usual limitation of his diaspora preaching to the context of the (Jewish or Christian) synagogue. Jeered at Athens, thought to be quite crazy at Caesarea, and losing his audience in Jerusalem and on other occasions,[134] Paul is not represented by Acts as much of an orator, and he himself admits as much.[135]

However, the Apostle is presented both in Acts[136] and in his letters[137] as plying a trade while evangelizing, teaching, and healing mainly in the Jewish synagogues or Christian assemblies. As the biblical expositions in his letters show, Paul taught in form and method like a Jewish rabbi.[138] His speech on the Areopagus was

---

131. For example, persuasive speakers, dedicated to an itinerant mission and relying on hospitality from admirers (Judge, note 129, 125f.). Later, Judge (*ABR* 16 [1968], 37-50) called Paul "a reluctant . . . competitor in the field of professional 'sophistry'" who "promoted a deliberate collision with its standard of values" (47). See also P. Marshall, *Enmity in Corinth: Social Conventions in Paul's Relations with the Corinthians* (Tübingen, 1987), 327-33, 388ff.

132. For a (somewhat idealized) portrait of the calling of a true Cynic cf. Epictetus, *Discourses* 3.22.

133. K. H. Rengstorf, "ἀπόστολος," *TDNT* 1 (1964/1933), 409ff.

134. Acts 17:32; 26:24; 20:9; 22:22. G. A. Kennedy (*New Testament Interpretation through Rhetorical Criticism* [Chapel Hill, NC, 1984], 9f.) recognizes that Paul was a poor orator. But he may assume too much regarding the Apostle's knowledge of Greek literature, which never goes beyond "school boy" proverbs (Acts 17:28; 1 Cor 15:33; Tit 1:12).

135. 2 Cor 10:10f.; 11:6.

136. Acts 14:3, 9f.; 19:11-15; cf. 28:8 (miracles). Acts 18:3; 19:12; cf. F. F. Bruce, *The Book of the Acts* (Grand Rapids, [13]1977), 389 (artisan).

137. Rom 15:18f.; 2 Cor 12:12; cf. Gal 3:5 (miracles). 1 Cor 9:6, 11f., 15; 1 Thess 2:9; 2 Thess 3:8; cf. 2 Cor 12:13 (artisan).

138. Cf. E. E. Ellis, "Biblical Interpretation in the New Testament Church," *Compendia*, I, ii, 1 (1988), 703-36; idem (note 5), 154-57, passim.

apparently exceptional, but here also its substance, as B. Gärtner showed, was the exposition and application of Old Testament texts.[139] Even if, like the sophists, he gave instruction to private groups and interested parties and accepted hospitality from some of them, it is likely that the dominant image of the Apostle, at least during his Aegean mission, was for outsiders that of an itinerant Jewish artisan with remarkable powers, proselytizing on behalf of a Jewish sect. For his converts it was that of a prophet and teacher and (as he was able to get the idea across) an apostle of Jesus Christ. In Caesarea and Rome, of course, Paul's social position was simply that of a Jewish religious dissident imprisoned on demand of his nations' leaders and ecclesiastical authorities.

The Roman world was not unacquainted with Jewish religious figures and apparently entertained considerable curiosity about them. It gave heed to Jewish exorcists and prophets and received some of them in high places.[140] It was also well aware of the diaspora synagogue, which, although apparently without a professional ministry in the first century, was known for its zeal and success in gaining Gentile converts.[141] While the precise method of proselytizing is little known to us, it is presented by Josephus sometimes as rather passive[142] and once as the deliberate effort of a traveling Jewish merchant.[143] The latter instance probably illustrates an approach that was often employed, and it offers a significant analogy to the situation of Paul as well as of Priscilla and Aquila.

139. As represented by Luke (Acts 17:22-31), it has the general form of a biblical exposition (midrash); cf. B. Gärtner, *The Areopagus Address and Natural Revelation* (Uppsala, 1955), 66-72, 149-69, 251. In this respect it is not unlike expositions attributed to Paul elsewhere in Acts (13:16-41) and found frequently in his letters.

140. Acts 13:6ff.; 19:13ff.; cf. Josephus, *The Jewish War* 3.403-408 = 3.8.9.

141. Horace, *Satires* 1.4.142f.; Dio Cassius, *History* 67.14.1f.; Josephus, *Against Apion* 2.123 = 2.10; cf. Mt 23:15.

142. For example, Josephus, *Against Apion* 2.210 = 2.28. But was this passivity overemphasized to forestall criticism? Cf. Dio Cassius, *History* 67.14.2; 68.1.2.

143. Josephus, *Antiquities* 20.34f. = 20.2.3; cf. W. D. Davies, *Paul and Rabbinic Judaism* (Philadelphia, [4]1980), 133n. (on 2 Cor 2:17, καπηλεύειν).

Doubtless the place of Paul in Greco-Roman society was perceived in a variety of ways by a variety of people and, as an impression given to some of them, none of the above suggestions can be ruled out. But any general estimate of the Apostle's social position, to be persuasive, must give due weight to the fact that he was perceived by society first of all as a Jew. His encounters with the local Jewish authorities and the content of his message make that a virtual certainty. When Paul lost his profession as a rabbi, he did not take up another as a rhetorician; he became an apostolic rabbi in a different kind of synagogue. This would be no less the case if in his preaching and writing he (and his amanuenses and associates) used Greco-Roman literary forms and conventions since these forms were used in some measure by Jewish rabbis[144] and, almost of necessity, by any Jew speaking and writing in Greek and for Greeks.[145]

Ministry and Society

Religious parties in Judaism were represented to the Roman world as schools of philosophy,[146] and it is to be expected that Paul's

144. Cf. D. Daube, "Rabbinic Methods of Interpretation and Hellenistic Rhetoric," *HUCA* 22 (1949), 239-64; Ellis (note 138), 709; idem (note 5), 218f., where it is shown that the dialogic style, which has been ascribed to Paul's use of Cynic-Stoic rhetoric, has closer affinities with, and its more immediate background in, patterns of biblical exposition (midrash) employed in Judaism and witnessed later in rabbinical literature. Cf. Pesikta Rabbati 50.1 with Rom 9:13-23; Mekilta Exod 12:15; 21:26f. with Rom 10:18f. (ἀλλά). *Pace* A. J. Malherbe, "MĒ GENOITO in the Diatribe and Paul," *HTR* 73 (1980), 231-40.

145. For discussions of the subject cf. Marshall (note 131); A. D. Litfin, "St. Paul's Theology of Preaching," Unpublished dissertation (Oxford University, 1983), who argues that on principle Paul (in 1 Cor 1-4) rejects and critiques the use of rhetoric; A. J. Malherbe, *Social Aspects of Early Christianity* (Baton Rouge, LA, 1977), 49-59; Donfried (note 104), 95ff., 132-41, 157-74; Judge, "Society" (note 101), 33. It is probable that the literary form of some Pauline parainesis— the household codes, the virtues/vices lists, regulations on the ministry of women —was not his creation but was traditional and part of it common to the Petrine, Jacobean, Johannine, and Pauline missions. Cf. E. E. Ellis, "Gospels Criticism," *Das Evangelium und die Evangelien,* ed. P. Stuhlmacher (Tübingen, 1983), 50f.; idem, "Traditions" (note 77), 482-85; *Documents* (note 77).

146. Cf. Philo, *On Dreams* 2.127; idem, *On the Contemplative Life* 3 = 26; Josephus, *The Jewish War* 2.119 = 2.8.2; 2.166 = 2.8.14.

teachings, seen as the promotion of a Jewish sect, would also be understood by many Greeks in this way. When one adds to this the fact, made abundantly clear in the account of Acts,[147] that Paul was again and again accused by elements of the Jewish religious establishment of antisocial and politically subversive conduct, it is not improbable that the Apostle's ministry was associated in the minds of some Gentiles with those social and political gadflys of the first-century world, the Cynic and Stoic preacher-philosophers.[148]

The Cynics among the middle class and the Stoics among the aristocracy were vocal social critics—to say reformers goes too far—and during the latter half of the first century they were hostile to the Empire. Among their adherents were leading political dissidents who, dreaming and scheming to restore the Republic, in A.D. 65 turned words into action and hatched a conspiracy to assassinate the emperor Nero.[149] Of one conspirator the historian Tacitus writes:

> Plautus . . . had taken on himself
> The Stoic arrogance and mantle of a sect
> That inculcated sedition
> And an appetite for politics.[150]

What relationship does the Stoic critique and subversion of the social order have with the social dimension of Christian ministry and, specifically, of the ministry of Paul? Or, put another way, what justification is there for the accusations of the Jewish authorities that Paul fomented social disturbances and political insurrection? These questions can best be addressed in the light of a more radical, messianic movement within Judaism

147. Acts 17:5-8, 13; 21:38; 24:5, 12, 18; 25:7f.; cf. 13:50; 14:2, 5, 19.

148. So G. Theissen, *The Social Setting of Pauline Christianity* (Philadelphia, 1982), 39 = *NTS* 21 (1975), 204, who, however, draws the comparison from Paul's itinerant methods.

149. Cf. R. MacMullen, *Enemies of the Roman Order* (Cambridge, MA, 1967), 46-94. Of those implicated in the Pisonian conspiracy, all but one were Stoics (53).

150. Tacitus, *Annals* 14.57 (citing Tigellinus); cf. idem, *Histories* 4.40; Suetonius, *Nero* 39; Dio Cassius, *History* 65.13; Epictetus, *Discourses* 1.2.12-24.

itself since the Jewish context provides the most immediate background for the Apostle's life and teachings. According to both New Testament and Jewish sources,[151] there was a widespread expectation in first-century Judaism that the Old Testament messianic promises would be fulfilled by means of political revolution. It helped to propel the nation into two disastrous wars against Rome and reached its high point when the great rabbi Akiba identified the revolutionary Bar Kosiba (†c. A.D. 135) as the prophesied Bar Kokhba, the messianic son of the Star mentioned in Num 24:17.[152]

This nationalistic understanding of Israel's hope has also been attributed to Jesus and his earliest followers by some modern scholars. The reconstructions of R. Eisler and S. G. F. Brandon take this path, representing the teaching of Jesus as political theology.[153] But, as Martin Hengel and others have shown,[154] they are not convincing, for they not only have to dismiss the earliest and most coherent evidence, the Gospels and Acts, as a later fabrication but also must rest their own case on hypothetical arguments bolstered by historical material fitted, sometimes rather arbitrarily, into the hypothesis. However, even the reconstructions of Eisler and Brandon recognized that Paul's ministry, unlike their picture of the Jerusalem church, was of a spiritual and "quietist" nature and without political intent.[155]

---

151. jTaan 4.5. Cf. Jn 6:15; Acts 5:36f.; 21:38. The "prophets," who according to Josephus (*Antiquities* 20.97 = 20.5.1; 20.168ff. = 20.8.6; idem, *The Jewish War* 2.258-62 = 2.13.4f.) sought to emulate Moses, were making implicit messianic claims (cf. Deut 18:15 with Acts 3:22f.).

152. jTaan 5.

153. R. Eisler, *The Messiah Jesus* (London, 1931); S. G. F. Brandon, *The Fall of Jerusalem and the Christian Church* (London, [2]1957); idem, *Jesus and the Zealots* (Manchester, 1967).

154. M. Hengel, *Was Jesus a Revolutionist?* (Philadelphia, 1971); O. Cullmann, *Jesus and the Revolutionaries* (London, 1970).

155. Eisler (note 153), 364f., 528-40, 552f.; Brandon, *Jerusalem* (note 153), 71f., 204f.

The Eschatological Locus of Ministry

How far removed the Apostle is from a political interpretation of Old Testament promises may be illustrated by the way in which he applies the scriptures to a Christian context. Paul gives eschatological, totally nonpolitical applications to passages that originally had primarily sociopolitical implications. Two examples are Isa 28:11 and Ps 68:18. The first probably refers to the Assyrians' attack on Israel as God's judgment on the nation; in 1 Cor 14:21 it is applied to the spiritual gift of speaking in tongues, apparently as a sign of God's judgment on unbelievers. The second, Ps 68:18, concerns God's political deliverance of Israel and his sharing with them the booty of his military victory; in Eph 4:8 it is interpreted of the exalted Christ's deliverance of believers through his cross and resurrection and his sharing with them the booty of his victory over death. Such exegesis underscores the Apostle's eschatological understanding of Christian ministry, which, as we saw in Chapter One above, sets it apart from sociopolitical activities in society.[156]

In his activities as a minister Paul was fully consistent with this understanding of his role. Like Jesus and the New Testament writers generally,[157] he displayed no interest in using his ministry for broader humanitarian concerns. Unlike a Cynic preacher (or John the Baptist), he did not reproach the licentiousness of

156. See above, 23. Cf. Ellis (note 54), 108, 126-35, 138f.
157. For the General Epistles cf. B. Reicke, *The Epistles of James, Peter and Jude* (Garden City, NY, 1964), xvi-xxix. For Luke cf. Ellis (note 11), 18. For Jesus cf. Lk 12:14 (4:5-8); Jn 6:15; 18:36. The saying in Mt 25:34-40, concluding with the words, "Inasmuch as you did it to the least of these, my brothers, you did it to me" (40), does not refer to humanitarian benevolence but to kindly acts toward the persecuted ministers of Jesus. The word "brothers" in Matthew is at times virtually a technical term for Christ's followers or, more specifically, for those engaged in spreading his message (Mt 12:48ff.; 23:8; 28:10; cf. 18:15). It is used similarly by Paul (cf. Ellis, note 5, 21f.). Also, Christ's miracles and his proclamation of "good news to the poor," and liberty to "those who are oppressed" (Lk 4:18) refer, as the context shows, to his deliverance of people from the bondage of death. While his words and deeds have clear social and economic implications (cf. Ellis, note 11, 113, 187f., 192f.), to interpret their primary meaning as the satisfying of temporal needs is represented in the Gospels as a misunderstanding (Jn 6:26f.; cf. Lk 17:17f.; Mk 8:17-21). See above, 97f.

Berenice[158] and generally saw no obligation as Christ's minister to judge or to reform the society of Caesar:

> What have I to do with judging (κρίνειν)
> Those outside [the church]? . . .
> Those outside God will judge.   1 Cor 5:12f.

This attitude had nothing to do with the small number of Christians, who in any case were very quickly a larger group than the Cynic and Stoic philosophers, or with their relative lack of influence, a fact that applied just as much to their preaching of Jesus as savior of the world. It was, rather, rooted in the Apostle's total theological outlook, which, like early Christianity generally, had more affinities with Epicurean withdrawal from society than with Stoic engagement with it.[159] Nevertheless, if Paul did not direct his ministry toward the improvement of society, he also did not hesitate to instruct believers concerning their own conduct in the world, and he can hardly have failed to realize that through them his mission would have ensuing effects upon society.

The Societal Consequences of Ministry

Paul showed both in his conduct and in his teaching the way in which Christians were to be a preserving salt and a shining light in the world around them. He did not hesitate to make friends of

---

158. Contrast Acts 25–26 with Dio Cassius, *History* 65.15.3ff.; cf. Mk 6:18; Josephus, *Antiquities* 20.145f. = 20.7.3; Juvenal, *Satires* 6.156-60. Cf. E. A. Judge, "Gesellschaft: Neues Testament," *TRE* 12 (1984), 767f.

159. Partly because pagan religious acts were required duties in public life. Cf. 1 Pet 4:4; Tertullian, *Apology* 35; 42; Aelius Aristides, *Orations* 46.309.14f. ("On Behalf of the Four"; cf. W. Dindorf, *Aristides,* 3 vols. [Leipzig, 1829], II, 404): Christians "neither honor the gods nor sit on city councils" (πόλεις συνεβούλευσαν). Flavius Clemens (†A.D. 95), cousin of the emperor Domitian, who according to tradition was a Christian or Christian sympathizer and was executed for "falling into Jewish ways" (Dio Cassius, *History* 67.14.2), is denigrated by Suetonius (*Domitian* 15.2) for withdrawing from public and social life. Cf. G. Edmundson, *The Church in Rome in the First Century* (London, 1913), 224ff.; Malherbe (note 145), 25f. Cf. 1 Tim 2:2; Eusebius, *HE* 3.20.4. But see Rom 16:23.

unbelievers, to speak to "worldly" problems in which he found himself involved,[160] and to exercise his rights as a Roman citizen.[161] As a minister, however, he restricted himself to teaching and exhorting believers about their social responsibilities.

For Paul ministry is directed to and for the body of Christ, the church.[162] Yet, while it is sharply distinguished from secular activities, it frequently has its outworking in the world, especially that type of ministry to believers termed "parainesis" (παραίνεσις), that is, advice, counsel, and exhortation. In the Pauline letters it appears in its most comprehensive form in Paul's charge to believers to do good works[163] or, more pointedly, to love one's neighbor,[164] a precept that underlies the more specific exhortations concerning the various relationships of believers with those outside the church.

The Apostle apparently views acts of neighbor-love and of good works generally to be effects or "the fruit" of the Spirit and therefore to be expected of all believers.[165] Paradoxically he considers virtues that are an endowment from God to the believer also to be a demand made by God upon the believer: "Do good to all" and "love your neighbor as yourself."[166] Yet, Paul implies, it is precisely this paradox that reveals the gracious character of these virtues. One is exhorted to become in one's individual life and conduct in the world what one already is in the body of Christ, a child of God.

Paul's ministry of exhortation was usually addressed to specific situations occasioned by the needs of the recipients of his letter. Thus, the general admonitions to neighbor-love and to good works are sometimes found in regulations that are more or less set pieces of tradition, regulations that are sometimes used in com-

160. Acts 19:31; 27:9ff., 30f.; Phlm 10-18. Cf. Mt 5:13f.

161. Acts 16:37; 25:10ff., 25.

162. See above, 7-17.

163. Rom 12:20f.; 2 Cor 9:8f.; Gal 6:10; Eph 2:10; Col 1:10; 1 Thess 5:15; 1 Tim 2:10; cf. 2 Thess 2:17; 1 Tim 5:10; 2 Tim 3:17.

164. Rom 13:8ff.; Gal 5:14; 1 Thess 4:9.

165. Gal 5:22f.

166. For example, Gal 5:14; 6:10.

mon with other apostolic missions.[167] Among them several types of parainesis, although overlapping, can be distinguished: household codes[168] and what we may call "personal morality" codes[169] and "social ethics" codes.[170] Primarily they had to do with personal attitudes and conduct within familial, social, and political relationships and were not intended as a program for reforming society. But such good effects were inevitable whenever personal Christian ethics began to exercise an influence upon the practices and laws of the pagan world. In this way ministry that was directed toward the church nevertheless had effects that went beyond the church and benefited not only those who were being redeemed but the present, transient world-order as well.

Implications for the Church Today

Today's church also lives in a pagan world, a world that in the West has been long influenced by Christianity but for which Christ and his church have often become more a traditional concept than a living influence. It is a world in which the gracious gifts of God —freedom, self-government, material abundance, a peaceful social order — have themselves often become objects of worship (Rom 1:25), and "man is the measure of all things" (Protagoras). Today's secular society is, then, not all that different from St. Paul's even if its gods have different names. And it continually exerts its pressure to conform the church to its own interests.

Traditionally, the establishment of the church often served to tame it to perform the uncritical functions of a "civil religion." Today, other temptations have emerged to subvert the church to worldly ends. Two examples may be mentioned, the secularization of the Christian hope and of the command to love one's neigh-

167. Cf. Ellis, "Traditions" (note 77), 482-85; idem (note 145), 50ff.
168. Eph 5:21–6:9; Col 3:18–4:1; 1 Tim 6:1f.; Tit 2:2-10; cf. 1 Pet 2:18–3:7; 1 Clement 1:3. On their background cf. J. E. Crouch, *The Origin and Intention of the Colossian Haustafeln* (Göttingen, 1972).
169. Including virtues/vices lists: Rom 13:12ff.; Gal 5:19-26; Eph 4:25-32; 5:3-5; Col 3:5-10, 12ff.; Tit 3:2f.; cf. Jas 3:13–4:4, 11f.; 1 Pet 2:1f.
170. Rom 12:14-21; 13:1-7; Tit 3:1; cf. 1 Pet 2:13-17.

bor. (1) The biblical interpretation of some "liberation theology" gives to the Apostle's teaching a political orientation which, as we have seen above, is quite contrary to his nonpolitical ministry and to his view of salvation history, with its element of discontinuity between the present age and the kingdom of God.[171] It also appears to confuse Paul's doctrine of a received "righteousness" (δικαιοσύνη) imputed by God to the individual sinner in Christ with the teaching of a visionary social "justice" to be achieved by Adamic man through Marxist revolution.[172]

(2) In the teaching of Christ and of Paul the injunction to love one's neighbor is implicitly or explicitly always in the second position, a demand that presupposes and is defined by the first commandment, love for God.[173] When it is given first place, as it often is in modern secular society, it will inevitably be debased into idolatry, sentimentalism, or even a cloak for every kind of lust. Only when love for neighbor is defined in terms of love for God, and God's love for us and in us,[174] does it conform to the New Testament teaching and become a transforming power in every relationship that it touches. In this context it may be likened to the common grace of God which daily sustains the present creation.[175]

Ministers and the ministry of the church, no less than the church itself, are inevitably related to the society around them. In

---

171. See above, 18-23, 152-55. Cf. E. E. Ellis, "Foreword" to L. Goppelt, *TYPOS. The Typological Interpretation of the Old Testament in the New* (Grand Rapids, 1982), xiiff. For a biblically perceptive treatment of the discontinuity between the world and the kingdom of God the work of Martin Luther on "Temporal Authority" (1523) is still instructive (*Luther's Works,* 55 vols., ed. H. T. Lehmann [Philadelphia, 1962], 45, 81-129). Cf. H. Bornkamm, *Luther's Doctrine of the Two Kingdoms* (Philadelphia, 1966).

172. For example, the Roman Catholic writer J. P. Miranda, *Marx and the Bible* (Maryknoll, NY, 1964), 163-92, 273-85. It is not unfair, I think, to note the affinities of this approach with traditional Roman Catholic theological sympathies for a salvation by human works or by a mixture of God's action and human endeavor.

173. Mk 12:28-31; cf. 1 Cor 8:3-6, 9-13.

174. Eph 5:2, 25.

175. Mt 5:44f.; cf. Rom 12:14-21.

the apostolic church Paul and others used the societal structures that were at hand in order to facilitate their mission while at the same time resisting the pressures to conform it and to make it captive to those structures. They also faced the problem of maintaining their own identity and the integrity of their mission against the efforts of people around them, some well-meaning and some malign, to give them a *persona* more amenable and adaptable to the usages of their world.

Thus is posed the tension between Christian ministry and the social order as it is displayed in the mission of the Apostle Paul. Ministry works within the world, is assigned a social "place" by the world, and gives benefits to the world. Yet, when it is true to itself, it does not belong to this age, cannot really fit its structures and remains a stranger in the society of the world. Nevertheless, Paul had no doubt that it was within such a social context that Christ had called him to fulfill his ministry. We who are part of the distant harvest of his labors are also witnesses to its effects both in individual lives and, to some degree at least, upon the social order of the West. On his ministry we do well to ponder, and for it we may properly give thanks to the ascended Lord who revealed himself to Paul, who called him to minister in the society of the Caesars, and to whom may properly be ascribed blessing and riches, wisdom and honor and glory and power, forever and ever. Amen.

Index of References

160

Index of Modern Authors

175

Index of Subjects

Acts, Book of
  historical value of, 134f.
  picture of Paul in, 132, 135, 148ff.
Adam
  and Christ, 10-17
  man in, 12f.
administration, gift of, 40, 93-96
age
  age to come, 5ff., 56f.
  this age, 56f.
androgyny, *see* hermaphroditism
apostle, 37f., 90ff., 116f.

baptism
  in the Spirit, 30-33
  in water, 31f.
body
  corporate and individual, 8ff.
  of Christ, 7-17, 40-44
  of the husband, 41f.
brothers, 97f.

charism, charismata, *see* gifts
Christ
  body of, 10-14, 40-50
  existence in, 10-14
  submission to God the Father,
    58ff.
Christian

and social obligation, 23ff.,
    156-59
  as new creation, 8
church
  and Judaism, *see* Judaism
  and ministry, 36f.
  as body of Christ, 40-44
  as religious club, 123-47
  house churches, 139-45
  in the Roman world, 131-47
  in the second century, 145ff.
  praxis, 92-100, 132-35, 137-45
  terminology for, 135ff.
clubs, religious, 91, 126ff.
collection of money, 93ff., 133
collegia, *see* clubs
corporate personality, 9f., 43f.
Cynics and Stoics, 152f.

deacon, *see also* minister, 35f., 65,
    96
death
  individual, 16f.
  of society, 14, 24f.
discernment, gift of, 39f.

elder, 103, 109
Ephesus, *see* Pompeii

180